Frank Marshall Davis

The Fire and the Phoenix

A Critical Biography

Kathryn Waddell Takara, Ph.D.

Pacific Raven Press Publishing, Hawai`i

ISBN-13
97809841228-9-9
ISBN-10
09841228-9-3

Second Printing: March 2012

Book Cover Idea & Concept by Ayin M. Adams & Kathryn Waddell
Takara, Ph.D.
Cover Design and Typesetting by Saforabu Graphix

Published by PACIFIC RAVEN PRESS
P.O. Box 678, Ka`a`awa, HI 96730 USA
www.pacificravenpress.com
Email: pacificravenpress@gmail.com
Telephone : 1-808-276-6864 USA
Fax Number: 1-808-237-8974 USA

Published in the United States of America.

Printed in USA.

LITERARY REVIEWS

"Dr. Takara has brought forth a brilliant work. She has unearthed a gem and polished it with skill, wit and a keen insight. The luminosity of her work brings into sharp focus the life of an engaged writer, activist and a man with all the complications of a human being. By using a socio-historical approach, Dr. Takara reveals the scope of the work and time in which Frank Marshall Davis' life was lived. We are informed of the social, political and cultural events that shaped his life and inspired his creative world and writing. The role of a biographer as listener and recorder has been painstakingly rendered, a labor of love. This is a wonderful addition to the canon of African American Literature. We are all the richer for this work!"
Rashidah Ismaili, ret. Rutgers University
* * * * * * * *

"Dr. Takara has done a masterful job of telling the story of Frank Marshall Davis by encapsulating the experiences and circumstances that turned an imaginative and creative mind into a force for civil rights and justice who ultimately sacrificed power and career for a semblance of dignity and solace. Takara has shed light on Davis' near-disappearance from the literary limelight, making a convincing argument that he is deserving of a place in the pantheon of his contemporaries. *Frank Marshall Davis: The Fire and the Phoenix* is an eye-opening glimpse into the soul of a complicated figure, and few could duplicate the account of his journey as poignantly without Takara's precious firsthand experience."
Marsha McFadden, City Editor, Honolulu Star Advertiser
* * * * * * * *

"Kathryn Waddell Takara has organized this work both in a time line and commentary to guide the reader to appreciate Davis's work under difficult environments, including his last days in Hawai`i. Hawai`i challenged Davis to survive in economic terms and to describe and to analyze the effects of the similarities and differences of the Hawaiian influences in the Black experiences in and around Hawai`i."
Kiyoshi Ikeda, Professor Emeritus, University of Hawai`i
* * * * * * * *

"I have always known that Kathryn Takara was an astute intellectual. She writes prose with the precision and passion of a poet. Her biography of Frank Marshall Davis brings to life a man who lived in tumultuous times. The racism of the times can be experienced clearly through his eyes via the words of Dr. Takara. A wonderfully passionate story!"
Carol A. Dickson, Professor, University of Hawai`i at Manoa

BOOKS BY KATHRYN WADDELL TAKARA

New and Collected Poems. Berkeley, CA:
Ishmael Reed Publishing Co., 2003.

Pacific Raven: Hawaii Poems. Ka`a`awa, HI:
Pacific Raven Press, 2009.

Tourmalines: Beyond the Ebony Portal. Ka`a`awa, HI:
Pacific Raven Press, 2010.

DEDICATION

This book is dedicated to my loving, courageous, brilliant, and inspirational parents, William H. Waddell, VMD and Lottie Rochelle Younge Waddell, MA in French and an MA in German, and to the family of Frank Marshall Davis.

ACKNOWLEDGMENTS

I wish to extend hearty and warm thanks to my professors and colleagues who through the years gave me feedback on my ideas for this manuscript, various drafts, revisions and generously offered their time, comments, criticism, and suggestions including, but not limited to: Peter Manicas, Deane Neubauer, Manfred Henningsen, Farideh Fardhi, Majid Tehranian, Miles Jackson, Paul Lyons, Craig Howes, Rodney Roberts, John Edgar Tidwell, Ishmael Reed, Barbara Christian (d), Joe Balaz, Therese Mera Moore Lafferty, Elizabeth Buck, Marie Iding, Carolann Dickson, Steve Tracy, Robert Chrisman, Rashidah Ismaili, Karla Brundage, Diane Pikeborn (d), Pat Hickman, and Maya Angelou.

A huge bouquet of gratitude goes to my family, near and far. If it were not for the love and support of my parents, Bill and Lottie Waddell, my husband, Harvey Takara, daughters, Karla Brundage and Natasha Takara Harrington, and the extended Takara, Younge, Green, and Waddell clans, I might not have stuck with this large and sometimes thorny project.

The loving listening, reading, feedback, encouragement and abundant support, food, laughter, libations, music, prayers, and company of friends and artists gave me the amazing strength and fortitude to persist, to speak out for freedom, justice, and inclusion. I salute and give thanks to these inspiring friends who shared their care, attention, energy, and stories with me, including but not limited to: Richard Hamasaki, Daphne and Andre Wooten, Sandra Simms, Andrea Anixt, George and Terri Rainey, Tom Mountain, Gladys Crampton, Doug Matsuoka, Gary Pak, Marc Shlachter, Joan and Irwin Koff, Doug Lamerson, Carla Blank and Tennessee Reed, Debra Taniguchi and Mosso Uli`i, Lois Saruwatari, Ruth Rendely, Lyndon Fong, Brenda Andrieu, Carol Shepherd, Opal Palmer Adisa, Lucille Day, Amahra Hicks, Reginald Lockett, Kathy Sloane, Q R Hand, Percy and Joan Hintzon, Ibrahim Aoude, Mary Myers, bell hooks, Lucille Clifton, Margaret Burroughs, the Harrington family, the Carter family, the Malanaphy clan, Beth Davis Charlton, Allison Francis, Bill Danks, Adela Chu and Kim Duffett, Tony Edward, Corinna Fales, John and Jackie Streetz, Karyn Parham Jones, Francesca Calderone Steichen Stamer, Bambi Good, Marita

Rivero, Chuck Lawrence and Mari Matsuda, Haunani-Kay Trask, Kristen Timothy, Gail Hovey, The Hawai`i Links, Inc., and Ayin Adams.

Last, but certainly not least, I am grateful to Pacific Raven Press who believed in me, my research and writing, and convinced me that I had a great story to tell that would contribute to the history of Jim Crow in middle America, black journalism, black editors and community activists, the role of blacks in the labor movement, early Civil Rights issues and struggles, and the transcendence of Davis as a witness of his times and as a courageous warrior who wrote his life and documented the times, both on the mainland USA and in Hawai`i.

TABLE OF CONTENTS

INTRODUCTION

Frank Marshall Davis in Flight:
From Kansas, to Chicago, to Georgia, Hawai`i and Beyond

I first met Frank Marshall Davis in 1972 through a student in my Black Studies course, Black Americans, at the University of Hawaii where I was teaching. Four of his poems were included in the anthology I had assigned for the class, and one day, a student approached me after class and told me that Davis was currently a resident in Waikīkī, a good friend of hers, and asked me if I would like to meet him since she had spoken of me and my class to him earlier. When I told her of my interest in meeting the man, she arranged an appointment with him so that we could go together to his home. After the first meeting, which was fascinating, I continued to go and visit Davis and listen to his stories, his accounts of history, and occasionally he would read one or two of his poems to me. Since he had been a journalist and editor, we often discussed the news. Although we were separated by one or two generations, we shared many things in common: growing up in the Jim Crow South, exposure to the Quakers through education and their humanistic philosophy and pacifism, education in mostly white schools, writing and publishing poetry, a sense of community and social/political change, a passion for Black history, justice, multi-culturalism, an interracial marriage, bi-racial children, and residency in and love for Hawai`i. Naturally, I invited him to come to speak as a guest in our class and to participate in other black cultural events in Honolulu whenever possible. The following is my account of my friendship, research, and work with Frank Marshall Davis, through the years.

It is Spring 1987. Frank and I sit in his living room full of book shelves, records, a sagging faded green couch, a small stained kitchen table with two old wooden chairs, and a few pictures of him on the wall. He is in his comfortable overstuffed chair, and we hear the cacophony of Honolulu noises mingled with the melodies of blue jazz on his old phonograph--melancholy riffs punctuate the tropical night like bright stars. The music evokes bittersweet memories which weave jaggedly between us and around the room.

His worn dark, ashy feet and swollen ankles are resting up on a faded green hassock. He looks rugged: his six feet plus frame, long legs, and age spots on his cinnamon-brown skin contrast with his white hair which sits like a rebel on his aging head. He pauses, collects his thoughts, draws on his cigarette, and listens to Charlie Parker while the muted TV replays scenes of the Vietnam War over and over again.

Frank Marshall Davis (1905-87), retired journalist, poet, and activist, remains a keen observer of the world's politics and dramas, if only from a comfortable chair in his living room. Time seems unimportant in this Pacific Island haven, where judgments and pretense like slippers are shed local-style at the front door. His home is on Oʻahu, Hawaiʻi, not far from Waikīkī. The TV flashes images of power struggles, global and local violence, protest movements, epidemics, *ad nauseum*.

As Frank changes the record, he selects precisely the sequential sounds most appropriate for the particular moment from his extensive collection of jazz. I am impressed by his sensitivity to the subtle tones of music's moods and his conscious construction of a musical series for each time that I enter the house to weekly document his life story.

Although the local power establishment relegated Davis to an invisible place in Honolulu's political and social scene, Frank is anything but invisible, even after eight decades and endless challenges of living. His true strength, however, comes through in the articulation and clarity of his still-controversial ideas: "I am an atheist," "Prejudice is perennial," "Civil rights are cyclical," "Women are one of the rare delights of the world." The womanizer shows in his flirting.

As I sit in front of this large man with full lips, twinkling eyes and a compliment on his tongue, we begin again our weekly conversation which started fifteen years ago. The ritual of our visit has begun. I am here as an oral historian to chronicle his incredible story.

He pauses, collects his thoughts and begins to talk; he picks up a colorful thread of history. In his deep raspy voice, he speaks slowly, deliberately, trying to capture as accurately as possible the major events of his life, which began in Arkansas City, Kansas, where he was born on December 31, 1905.

Frank slowly gets up and turns up the volume on the news. African Americans are marching in Georgia for Martin Luther King Jr. Day, and the KKK and their supporters are telling the "niggers" to go home. The year is 1987. Perhaps prejudice **is** perennial. He pulls out another record album, this time Miles Davis, "Kind of Blue."

He reminisces about his youth and hometown. Frank's family home in Kansas was on the north part of Main Street. "Did I tell you about that time I had my first drink when I was four years old? It was the only way I would take my castor oil. Kansas was a dry state. Even cigarettes were against the law. I heard my first live jazz music when I was eight. My mother and dad took me to the monthly dance because they could not find a baby-sitter that night. On that one night, my entire world expanded."

Frank comments on his high school years. "Because I was black, my [white] classmates wouldn't speak to me, once we left the school yard, I was not permitted to play team sports and I became a loner. I read a lot and pondered and waited for a time to get away. I learned not to be dependent on anyone or anything. Was I bitter? No, just a realist at that age, and a survivor."

In commenting on the role of the church in his life, Frank states, "For most blacks, the church has been a sanctuary, but I left the church in 1917, even after all the lynching and rioting and people praying. Nothing had changed. Even after the Tulsa riots in 1921 and 1922. It seemed the more I prayed, the more it seemed like God was white and created the world for whites. My grandfather was agnostic. Nowadays, I see death as inevitable, nothing to fear, and I don't believe in heaven or hell . . . at least not today."

Davis recognized that there were few areas in his community where a young black man could excel, but he did join the scouts. He says, "I became a first class Eagle Scout, but never learned to swim. But if you want to know why I never learned to swim, Wilson Lake and the city pool were both segregated. They waived my swimming test to keep me out of the pool and that's how I became an Eagle Scout."

"I also was a member of the Hi Y's, and in 1923 attended a conference in Lawrence, Kansas. The keynote address was given by the President of the University of Kansas, who kept referring to Anglo-Saxons as the greatest race in the world. The racist attitude of the president decidedly influenced my decision to find another college to attend." According to Davis, approximately 30 other non-white students attending the conference responded as he did that day and chose other schools. "After I graduated from high school later that year, I returned to Kansas City to visit an uncle and work as a busboy in an exclusive club." Davis moved to Wichita in 1923 to live with his grandfather, take classes at Friends University (Quaker), and worked. He later headed off to college at Kansas State in the fall of 1924 to study journalism and he began to write poetry. After a leave of absence due to the Depression, he returned to Kansas State in 1929.

In the 1920's, Davis says he became interested in Marxism, leftist ideology, and social reform, an obvious direction given the bitter experiences of racism, segregation, and the lack of opportunities for African American men during this period. His monologue continued when he asked me, "Did I tell you about when I went to Atlanta in 1931 to 1933 to be editor for the *Atlanta World* and my experiences with Jim Crow?" Later he said, "When I left and returned to Chicago, I published my first book of poetry, *Black Man's Verse*, in 1935."

On another occasion Frank reveals that on one wintry Chicago day in 1948, he left with his white wife, Helen, to visit the sunny shores and turquoise waters of the Hawaiian Islands. With his customary acerbic tone, he describes Hawai`i as "the alleged racial paradise with a scarred memory of World War II, Jim Crow housing, and the Massie case buried like bones." Nevertheless, Hawaii was said to be a good place for interracial couples to settle and raise a family according to his friend and associate Paul Robeson, who spoke to Davis when he returned to Chicago after visiting Hawai`i and enjoying it so much. "He persuaded me to come and see for myself. In fact, once we arrived in 1948, I did not return to the continental United States for 25 years." Did he really come to Hawai`i to escape the racially fragmented United States? He said that he and Helen saw an advertisement in a travel magazine, came for a vacation, and never went back to the continent to live.

They arrived during the Longshoreman's strike and Frank predictably took the side of labor against the large landowners. He accepted a job as a columnist at the *Honolulu Record*, the labor newspaper, and wrote searing political commentaries on race relations, class struggles, exploitation and resistance. After the strike, he could not find a job with the local newspapers owned by the landowners. He told me, he soon "became invisible" to much of the journalistic, labor, intellectual and art worlds that had followed and admired him so much in Chicago and in the national Black scene.

During Frank's thirty year sojourn in Hawai`i, a multi-faceted historical, political, economic, and Cultural Revolution was occurring on the mainland. By the 1960's, Blacks, women, minorities, and physically challenged groups demanded equality and inclusion in society. Writers, African American and white, young and old, began to reexamine the poetry of Frank Marshall Davis. This new audience was captivated by his bold images and by his encouraging, politically utopian message, at once uplifting and critical. In addition, they learned about race and class from Frank's writings, historical perspective, and experiences, because much of his written work was what he himself called "social realism."

When Maya Angelou came to Honolulu, Hawai`i in the summer of 1984 as a featured speaker for African American Visions, a two week humanities festival, I was Project Director. Not only was I honored to introduce her with my original poem and interview her for KHET, but I took her to meet Frank Marshall Davis at his small apartment on Kapiolani Blvd. She cried when she sat down to talk with him, sharing that she had been teaching his work in her classes for many years, and due to his long silence, she had presumed he was dead like many other literary scholars and followers on the mainland.

As an African American writer, Frank spent almost forty years living in Hawai`i. He documented his observations and experiences from a rarely recorded black perspective. His poetry, autobiography and his journalistic writings have been collected and edited by John Edgar Tidwell and were posthumously published.

Because I spent a considerable amount of time with Davis during his final fifteen years in Hawai`i listening to his stories as a black scholar and friend, I decided to write a book based on the vitality and reach of his work and his role in literary, cultural, and journalistic history in the South, Chicago, Hawai`i and beyond.

I

Davis and Black Writing

A study of the life and writings of Frank Marshall Davis (1905-1987) offers the reader insight into a variety of pivotal historical moments; his life spans several generations and critical sites of American life. In spite of being a "college drop-out," Davis was an African American intellectual. He was an award winning poet, artist, journalist, critic, radical thinker and acerbic social realist, politician, union official, and later a bohemian. I explore the transformative processes of growth, corruption, and healing in Frank Marshall Davis as he changed from an alienated black youth into a public figure, social critic, and writer in a racially divided society. Also discussed is his subsequent fall from fame after his move to Hawai`i where he was pushed out of prominence into anonymity.

My contention is that Davis must now be reclaimed by the canon of literary Black history both as a representative African American writer of the Black Chicago Renaissance period, and as an outstanding editor, journalist, columnist, and poet. There is something singular about his life and work – he influenced others, and then was forgotten by them – but he also had a vision of his own that is distinctive, putting together the international labor angle of Richard Wright and others, with the critical insight about the "Negro" spirit like DuBois and Hughes. He was an expatriate like Wright and Baldwin, concerned with alternative social formations, ways of being independent, socially, economically, and even sexually. There is a continuity with his writing in Hawai`i, but there he refocuses into a more wide-angled vision, speaking to the local situation with a national/international range of reference.

To many African American writers of his generation and the 1960's, Frank Marshall Davis embodied the radical nature and tradition of African American literature. He was outspoken, self-reliant, and fearless, earning him membership in the categorical group called "Race Man" or "New Negro" in the 1930's and 1940's. He was inspired by the writings of such maverick sociopolitical Chicago poets as Fenton Johnson, Carl Sandburg, Carl Van Vechten, Vachel Lindsay, James T. Farrell, and Edgar Lee Masters.

Because of the volume and diverse forms of his writing (poetry, journalism, and prose) and his perceptive sociopolitical analysis, Davis's contributions to the canon of African American literature, journalism, and history place him beside more renowned black writers such as W. E. B. DuBois, Richard Wright, Langston Hughes, Margaret Walker, Gwendolyn Brooks, Alain Locke, Arna Bontemps, and James Baldwin. These writers also recorded their observations and experiences of Blacks in America, even as they were marginalized, withdrew, sought exile, or were defeated by the pain and the politics of race and class. According to Saunders Redding in *On Being Negro in America,*

> There is a deep sickness in the American mind and spirit, and it threatens to infect democracy itself and render it impotent as an ideal. But not only this; the sickness also threatens to make democracy ineffective as an instrument through which the individual can realize his highest self and in co-operation with other selves give zest, richness and meaning to human endeavor. For democracy is two things. It is a political instrument: it is an ideal. (135)

A study of Davis's work explores the development and maturation of a literary talent despite the oppressive sociopolitical and racial climate of this era. Such a study enables us to reconstruct and interpret the mystery of the choices that he made at significant crossroads in his life.

Questions are raised as well about the motivation behind his writing. Did he desire to write to defeat a feeling of solitude and alienation? Did he seek to repair a damaged group psychology? Was he motivated by a sense of social responsibility and hope to strengthen the race by urging African Americans to shed their feeling of inferiority, and thereby to encourage self-respect and dignity? Did he consider himself to be an historian, a sociopolitical analyst, and a chronicler of the times?

I will alternately use political, economic, social, and cultural perspectives to analyze some of the dilemmas of the African American intellectual, based on Davis's life and writings about race and class issues facing his community. I challenge some of the traditional western assumptions of art and culture that have devalued the African American vernacular tradition, deeming it political rhetoric and propaganda. I argue for the expansion and preservation of the canon of African American literature, one that privileges the oral tradition of poetry, music and literature and portrays African American culture as it exists and is preserved, even in the lives of ordinary people.

The recurring problem for African American intellectuals has been the historical polarity between the ideology of separatism based on an Afrocentric nationalism and the ideology of assimilation or integration. What was Davis's position in this seldom-articulated but nonetheless real theoretical debate? Did his writings contribute to the debate and the ideology of African American cultural philosophy as exemplified in the writings and thoughts of leaders like Booker T. Washington (1856-1915), W. E .B. DuBois (1868-1963), Marcus Garvey (1887-1940), and later Malcolm X (1925-1965) and Dr. Martin Luther King Jr. (1929-1968).

Such an assessment is an exciting and personal challenge for two reasons: because I knew and respected Frank Davis and because I believe that he and his work deserve widespread dissemination. Except for a few interviews by Stephen Henderson of Howard University, J. Edgar Tidwell of the University of Kansas and Maryemma Graham of Northeastern University, very little contemporary analysis has been conducted on the significance of his work, although in the 1960's and 1970's he was anthologized worldwide over 75 times and was called by some black radicals "the Grandfather" of African American radical poetry. The 1992 publication of his autobiography, *Livin' the Blues*, the 2002 publication of *Frank Marshall Davis: Black Moods Collected Poems*, and the 2007 publication of his journalistic columns, *Writings of Frank Marshall Davis: A Voice of the Black Press*, all edited by John Edgar Tidwell including impressive introductions, lengthy notes, and a glossary are now available for the scholarly attention and general enjoyment of Davis's life work. The attention Davis has again begun to receive confirms the continuing relevance and truth of his bold, courageous, and perceptive writing.

II

Davis as Resident of Honolulu

In December 1948, Frank Marshall Davis arrived in Hawai`i with his wife, Helen Peck Canfield, who was white. This decision to leave Chicago was based on a desire to take a vacation and a strong recommendation mentioned earlier from his friend and associate, Paul Robeson, who had been impressed by the ethnic diversity and the relative acculturation of the island residents and shared his observations with Davis. Due to the relatively favorable social conditions in Hawai`i for interracial couples, the Davises remained in Hawai`i for 25 years. In 1975, Davis finally returned to the continent on a speaking tour, where he gave lectures at Howard University, Fisk, Atlanta University, the DuSable Museum in Chicago, and at several campuses of the University of California system including Berkeley. However, by moving to Hawai`i, Davis left the national eye as journalist and man of letters, an illustrious career in journalism, and a reputation as a renowned and accomplished poet.

Did he stay in Honolulu specifically to escape the strife-torn continent? Did he hope to break the grip of prejudice that informed all aspects of his life in the United States, especially because of his marriage to a white woman? Or was his sojourn, as he has said in interviews, merely a vacation and a much-needed rest from the pressures and responsibilities of being an articulate "Race Man" in the 1940's, always called upon to publicly defend the cause of freedom and equality? Or did the web of neurotic racial coercion toward African Americans make him abandon the continent? Did his move reveal a feeling of irreconcilable estrangement?

Davis has said that he found self-dignity in Hawai`i, as well as the freedom to choose a creative life-style. He welcomed the relative obscurity and peace of mind found on the remote island of O'ahu. In the pluralistic society of Hawai`i, he felt and was treated like a human because of the many varieties of racial and ethnic groups and the acceptable intermarriage and assimilation. Even though there were few black residents at the time of their arrival, the tolerant attitudes displayed by the residents were especially attractive to the young interracial couple who were soon to have several children.

Whatever the motivating factors, Frank Marshall Davis spent the rest of his life in Hawai`i, raising five children. At various times, he penned editorials for the *Honolulu Record* (the labor newspaper), brokered property, and sold fine-quality paper products as a low-profile businessman. In addition, he wrote occasional poems, a pornographic novel published under a pseudonym, an autobiography and numerous poems in a manuscript about life in the Waikīkī "jungle," all published posthumously.

In 1971, Frank divorced Helen, moved to Waikīkī and virtually disappeared from public view. However, he did give occasional poetry readings at African American cultural events, a few guest lectures at the University of Hawai`i, and two speaking tours in 1973 and 1974 on the East Coast, in Chicago, and twice in California (Tidwell, *Moods* xix). In later years in Hawai`i, Frank kept a low profile, remaining practically anonymous, an unsung literary hero until the last few years of his life.

III

The Book According to Davis's Life

This book emphasizes the influence of the racial politics of place on Davis's life and work, reviews his work in both journalism and poetry, and affirms his influence on other writers and his significance in the African American literary canon. His contribution to African American consciousness is evident in the sources I reference: evocative and sometimes fiery poems from his three acclaimed books--*Black Man's Verse* (1935), *I Am The American Negro* (1937), *47th Street* (1948); his lesser-known publication *Through Sepia Eyes*; his many columns and editorials *A Voice of the Black Press*, various interviews both published and unpublished--*Ebony, Black World*, Tidwell, Henderson, Takara; his recent and posthumously published autobiography *Livin' The Blues*, a collection of all his poems, *Black Moods: Collected Poems*, including poems about prostitutes, entitled *Horizontal Cameos*; and miscellaneous works written after his arrival in Hawai`i in 1948 that he shared with me.

This book is arranged thematically and follows a linear historical, sociopolitical, and racial context with place as a signifier. Themes include race, authority relations, estrangement, Jim Crow, sexual taboos, civil rights and social movements, and African American intellectual expression through poetry and journalism.

The chapters reflect the chronological sequence of his life. **Chapter One: Black in Kansas: Davis and Authority**, examines the impact of the various authority figures and institutional relations in Davis's formative years--specifically, patriarchy, racism, whites, his elders, the black church, and southern Jim Crow (race, class, gender)--to reveal how the smoldering geo-politics of racism produced different role models of authority, some benign, some hostile, and the occasional conflicting ideologies of nationalism and assimilation. The sociopolitical significance of race and the impact of white dominance on African American culture and life possibilities are the focus of this chapter. Indeed, Jim Crow was effectively used to inform the African American socialization process and political perspective, creating and perpetuating a consciousness of powerlessness and victimization that Davis and other African American intellectuals explore in their literary work.

Chapter Two: Davis in Georgia: The Black Press and the Jim Crow South, focuses on southern "apartheid" and the role of the black press as a critical site for a healing in the black community. During Davis's two-year experience as editor of the *Atlanta Daily World* (1931-1933), he observed and wrote about the inflammatory politics of race and exploitation in the deep South. By the time Davis returned to Chicago in 1934 to assume an editorial position with the Associated Negro Press, he would be known as a "Race Man."

Chapter Three: Revolutionary Aesthetics: Davis and African American Writing, and Chapter Four: Creative Empowerment: the Black Chicago Renaissance, focus on the themes of aesthetics and empowerment through consciousness, coalition politics in the Chicago cultural renaissance, and the fervor of the written and spoken word of social activists. I examine Davis's role as an African American intellectual in Chicago during the 1930's and 1940's, a period now referred to as the Chicago Black Renaissance, as he grappled with the political and cultural climate of liberalism. How did the African American writer and "Race Man" affect the African American community and the Anglo-American cultural hegemony? Was there a definable African American aesthetic that informed Davis's work, and if so, what was it? How much did the Communist Party inspire and influence the ideas, ideology, and politics of Davis as an African American intellectual, an artist, and activist, particularly because Davis was all three?

Chapter Five, The Precarious Freedom of the Cold War African American Intellectual: Race, Poverty, and Exclusion, reflects the next stage in Davis's life: his growing estrangement and political impotence due to the multiple risks involved in resisting racism. Davis could not remain unaffected by the race and class privilege all around him: the structural inequality, the problem of insults, and the abundance of harmful stereotypes.

The consequences of Davis's multiple political involvements became apparent when he came under fire by the Committee on UnAmerican Activities of the U.S. House of Representatives due to his associates and involvement in what were considered in the 1940's radical (Communist) groups. Confronted with the contradictions and dilemmas of being accused of disloyalty, Davis, an idealist, and committed believer in democracy, experienced the tensions of racism that contradicted the ideology of democracy and equality.

Chapter Six, An Engaged "Expatriate": The Returns of Davis's Writing, examines Davis's life as an exile in Hawai`i, with special attention to his simmering editorial columns in the *Honolulu Record*, his political-economic struggle to survive, and to what some have considered his period of defeat. In some ways, the public life of Frank Marshall Davis became unconventional when he moved to Hawai`i. He left his career track and stopped publishing in the national arena and in Hawai`i due to his outspoken editorials about the AFL strike. In a few years, he was silenced by the power elite and plantation landowners and became an anonymous and invisible identity. Davis went from an exciting and at times rocketing public intellectual in Chicago to a private unknown intellectual in Honolulu. Nonetheless, he continued to record his observations and reflections, as well as creating poetry and writing at least two book-length manuscripts. Even though he never stopped writing, he did stop being a journalist and his work was no longer regularly published. Thus this chapter analyzes some of his later posthumously published poetry.

Unfortunately, Davis's dossier from the FBI arrived in Hawai`i shortly after he did in 1948, which kept him from acquiring a traditional job in journalism, the field for which he was best prepared. However, he did write a column for the *Honolulu Record* for a while which was the AFL newspaper. Later he accepted an innocuous job in sales and advertising to support himself and his family.

The final **Chapter Seven, The Rise of the Phoenix: The Afterlives of Frank Marshall Davis**, explores the transcendental qualities of Davis's thought and writing and his theology of hope. One can only speculate on the unfulfilled potential and possibilities in his long life. If he had stayed in Chicago, would the challenges have pushed him beyond to the fire of genius and the stature and fame of authors like W. E. B. Du Bois, Richard Wright, or Langston Hughes? Or, would he have remained invisible and ignored in his later years like Zora Neale Hurston? This chapter argues for his posthumous inclusion in the canon of literary black history.

I explore the reasons for and the quality of his failure, if failure means the loss of power, happiness, social status, political influence, and financial success? Did he forfeit his role as a molder of opinion and an informer of culture when he moved to Hawai`i in order to have dignity and to live as an ordinary human being? Were his principles and preferences so important to him that it meant more to live them rather than espouse them?

Frank Marshall Davis was enigmatic. The choices he made and the lifestyle he chose were neither conventional nor glorious, yet his work has contributed not only to the tenets of democracy but also to the pluralistic cultural repository of America.

Davis was a fighter for justice and a survivor despite powerful obstacles. His emancipatory struggle for personal freedom triumphed in his praxis as a free spirit. If he failed to ignite and transform society through his activism, he succeeded in effecting transformations in others through his writings and commitment to freedom and human dignity. He influenced many younger writers of the sixties and later through his satire, brusque tone, unrelenting searing critiques of society, and the incorporation of history, music, and jazz into his writing; he thereby contributed to the canon of African American writers, American literature, and journalism. He has left much work to be appreciated, studied, and interpreted. As his ex-wife Helen Canfield Davis stated in an interview with me, "He remained a warrior for justice and equality until his death" in July 1987.

CHAPTER 1
Black in Kansas: Davis and Authority

What embittered me most was flagrant white hypocrisy. Virtually all aspects of daily life were geared to maintaining white supremacy.

(Davis, *Livin'* 55)

From the day of his birth in the small town of Arkansas City, Kansas on December 31, 1905, Frank Marshall Davis, an only child, experienced an isolated and fragmented life. He was raised in his grandmother's modest home with his grandmother and his mother. For brief periods during his early years, his father, an itinerant barber and musician, lived with them. Later his mother remarried and his stepfather, Mr. James Monroe Boganey, lived with them. They were the only African American family living in the white section of town, where social mingling between Blacks and whites was taboo, writes Davis in his memoir, *Livin' the Blues* (7-8).

His stepfather, James Boganey, whom Davis greatly respected and loved as a father, worked for the railroad, while his mother took in laundry from white people. Both held service jobs, a common means of employment for most African Americans during this period of legal segregation commonly referred to as Jim Crow and *de facto* segregation. At the time, white authority circumscribed African American lives, constricting possibilities and hopes for better economic advancement. According to CNN, as recently as 1950, 90% of African American women in America were employed in some capacity as domestic laborers for white families. Davis's family was typical of a majority of African Americans at the beginning of the twentieth century. They lacked status, privilege, and light skin, the latter being a possible key to social mobility, success, and opportunity within the small African American middle class. African American people were thus held hostage to the politics of race and color which included legal and economic victimization.

Professional role models and images of black authority in most local African American communities were extremely limited or non-existent. There were a few preachers, porters, elders, and a handful of other African American professionals, such as an occasional teacher, doctor, or newspaper man for the "Black Dispatch," the name given to any of the African

American weekly newspapers published in metropolitan areas, such as Chicago, Illinois, or Gary, Indiana. However, in the community of Arkansas City, Kansas, there were no illusions about white hegemony.

Davis himself was of a rich cinnamon or ginger complexion and considered by some to be "dark skin". However, because his parents were nonprofessional (not college-educated), and because his grandmother's house was in the white section of town, he had little access to the bourgeois African American society of "colored town", except on Sundays, when his family went to church in the African American community.

Despite his large physical frame and because of his color, Davis was excluded from school sports in his all-white high school (there were two or three other African Americans) because, he writes, "The coaches romanced white boys with far less physical equipment, but looked through us. We were Black and therefore invisible" (*Livin'* 51).

> And yet, with generous physical attributes, in a day when all-American guards in college football sometimes weighed no more than 150, I took no part in high school athletics. The same fate befell another of the quartet, Courtland West, who was an inch or two shorter and at least 25 pounds heavier, most of it solid flesh obtained through hard work on his old man's farm.   (51)

Davis also was prohibited from social interaction with female students, which included holding a conversation. Generally, Kansas people and the town were unkind to Blacks who were forced to use back doors, unclean toilets and water fountains, and sit in segregated, unclean, and inferior sections of public facilities. At the movies, Blacks saw themselves portrayed as buffoons with greatly exaggerated features, "scaredy cats", ignorant and uneducated people, happy and childlike, tap dancers, servants, and always inferior to white children and adults.

As an intelligent young man with many questions, he was obliged to seek company and refuge in books, music and dreams. He states in *Livin' the Blues*:

> I read and lived with King Arthur and his Knights of the Round Table, fought beside Achilles in the Trojan War and

traveled home with Aeneas; I was a companion of Beowulf, Sir Galahad, Sohrab and Rustem, Charlemagne, Ivanhoe; I sought the Golden Fleece with Jason, and conquered the known world with Alexander. With hammer and saw and nails and paint I made a lance and shield and stood alone for hours on our tiny back porch guarding the castle from blackguard (whiteguard) and villain, or with a different shield and wooden sword I performed sentry duty in our backyard as a Spartan. (These heroes, of course, were white for I had not yet heard of any African heroes.) My imagination kept me busy; forced to play by myself, I made the most of it and was alone no more. I spent so much time at the library that the head librarian, a plump, bespectacled, friendly white woman called me her "bodyguard."   (17)

In this passage, Davis reveals his intellectual acumen and his early desire to be in the presence of great men; he finds self-empowerment through imagination, although the irony of cherishing all white heroes reflects the tragic absence of African American heroes in his early life and reveals his unconscious racial and cultural devaluation. He also exposes his inner conflict by evoking images of war, defense, adventure, and the rugged Spartans who were warlike, courageous, and full of fortitude.

Davis refers in his writing to developing an inferiority complex as a youth—to a "hellhole of inferiority" (*Livin'* 3). He attacks the American educational system for only portraying African Americans in a degrading way, thereby delimiting aspirations and destroying dreams. In *Livin' the Blues* he observes, "Our high school education has prepared us only to exist at a low level within the degrading status quo" (3). But Davis was neither satisfied with the status quo nor the politics of color.

His reference to being a "bodyguard" to his white librarian perhaps speaks of his need to feel important and empowered, which recurs under different guises throughout his life. He took pride in his physical size and the authority and fear it inspired. His comparisons of himself to Joe Louis, the archetypal prize fighter, indicate his aspirations: he seeks identification with a kindred African American man who struggled for excellence and respect while understanding the overwhelming odds against achieving either.

From an early age, Davis developed a basic understanding of the politics of power and race between African Americans and whites, and its relation to male dominance and patriarchy. African American authority—as represented by the African American family, the church, a few community organizations, and fewer professional people--could always be placed in an appropriate context, respected, and obeyed as long as it was not challenged by the more powerful, legally sanctioned white authority.

Davis reveals one of his first memorable experiences with power and authority in *Livin' the Blues*. He describes how his white schoolmates tried to practice lynching him when he was walking home from school one day in the first grade. He mentions how he was happily, if ironically, rescued by a kindly white man who was passing by at the time (13). This early initiation into an impotent role made him conscious at a tender age that his life and identity as an African American male was always at risk, and this perhaps fuelled his later desire to be proactive in the fight for equality and to gain respect from authority figures.

Like most African American youth, Davis endured a childhood of passive consent to white authority and domination and internalized his frustrations, since he lived in an all-white community with very little access to African American organizations. In Arkansas City, there was not even a readily accessible Black peer group or an African American community with whom he could discuss his feelings of rejection and suppressed rage. His own father and step-father were absent for extended periods of time from the nuclear family.

It is in this era of blatant racial inequality that the personal struggle of Frank Marshall Davis becomes significant in understanding how he used the written word to engage, transform, and transcend the violent, hostile, and destructive forces of racism to create for himself a strong sense of identity.

Through analysis and contemplation of significant phases of Davis's early life, along with his writings and conversations about this period, one can examine Davis's attitude toward himself and his place in society. Specifically, a study of the childhood and adolescence of Frank Marshall Davis during the first two decades of the twentieth century illustrates the psychodynamics of authority relations and social isolation which provides an interpretive vehicle for an examination of race and authority relations in Kansas.

Throughout his life, Davis focused on sociopolitical causes, consequences, and the significance of racial victimization of African Americans, revealing the complex struggle to resist and/or transcend racist authority in black public and private lives in the early part of the twentieth century. Through knowledge and activism, Davis represents the black intellectual as subject of this process of victimization and demonstrates his subsequent empowerment and the affirmation of his own identity as a black man.

Davis recognized that racial oppression constitutes the basis of a crippling collective inferiority complex, a cultural nihilism, a psychological alienation, and, for him, a subsequent atheism which influenced his writing career and life choices. Indeed, Davis bears witness to the conflict and misunderstanding between whites and African Americans that is manifest in the lives of both groups. These differences are evident with respect to the diverse priorities, economics, assumptions, life expectations, values, and norms in the black and white communities.

In order to better see the ways in which Davis developed as a person and intellectual, his life might be compared to Langston Hughes. Their lives were in many ways similar and in other ways very different. These two contemporary writers and early residents of Kansas shared similarities and differences in family status, skin color, community support, and success. Both Davis and Hughes lost their fathers in the home at an early age due to prejudice, discrimination, and the unavailability of gainful/meaningful employment for African American men in the state of Kansas. Both Davis and Hughes primarily depended on women (mother and grandmother) for much of their early socialization, thereby learning through the bitter absence of their fathers that racism emasculated African American men, denigrated the women, destroyed the family structure, and denied status and success in most of its victims.

However, Hughes was lighter-skinned and somewhat middle class, whereas Davis was neither, which perhaps serves as an indicator of the varying degrees of success that was finally attained by each man. A carryover from slavery, the relative success and power of light-skinned African Americans compared with those of darker hue was evident. This politics of color was directly proportional to the privileges of working in the master's house, including education and assimilation of the master's ways (mulattos were often found there), and the isolation and poverty found amongst those who worked in the fields.

Due to their early life experiences based on color, class and family, Davis and Hughes assumed different roles and gave tones to their writing. Darker skinned Davis became the angry, militant, social realist with his strident cry for racial and economic equality, whereas light skinned Hughes stayed more within the acceptable boundaries of rendering the African American experience. Hughes focused on the lives of everyday ordinary people: their music, their poverty, their failures and successes, and their struggles to survive and find happiness in Harlem. Rarely did he write with strong protestations and judgments against the system. Rather, he tended to write using a quieter, less threatening voice. Was Davis more secure in some ways, due to his stable home and family life, than Hughes, or perhaps he, like Malcolm X, felt more oppressed and frustrated by the inability to realize the American "dream" of freedom?

Davis's family situation might provide some insight into Davis's politics. His stepfather, Mr. Boganey, was fortunate to have a fairly secure job on the railroads, as did several African American men from the area. Consequently, Davis at least had a male authority figure with a job to look up to. He also had a clear sense of home and permanence, which probably inspired him to seek a more traditional job and lifestyle. This sense of family gave Davis a warm feeling of stability, security, and protection in an otherwise fairly hostile environment, unlike Hughes, whose family moved often according to Faith Berry (8). Moreover, Hughes's biological father moved to Mexico and became an expatriate, unlike many talented and/or educated African Americans, some with college degrees, who were denied a respectful means of earning their livelihood and were left in the USA largely with meager choices of service jobs. Unlike Boganey, who earned a modest wage at the railroad and lived with family and socialized with friends, Hughes's father chose to live in exile and maximize his talents, eventually becoming a wealthy man. However, he sacrificed his family, friends, and community and died lonely and miserable far away from his family and community (Berry, F. 226).

Regardless of the divergent paths that Davis and Hughes later took, both men were forced to become introspective as adolescents, due to the absence of their fathers, and their isolation in early childhood due to growing up black in predominantly white communities. Perhaps the politics of color of the period permitted lighter-skinned Hughes to be accepted and popular in high school writes F. Berry (11), whereas darker-skinned Davis was usually shunned. Nonetheless, due to varying degrees of social ostracism, both men were introduced to the library at an early age and spent much time reading, although neither read books on racial injustice, African American protest, or African American history until later in their lives when such books became more readily available. Davis recounts the sense of frustration and impotence he felt when faced with discrimination and isolation that he experienced almost daily in high school because of the authority and privilege of whites.

Davis sought to rectify his social status and get revenge for his oppression by employing unconventional means in a society fraught with prejudice and discrimination. His desire to defy the tradition of segregation was strong. For example, when he was in high school, he risked talking to white girls whenever no one was around and sometimes they would talk to him. Also, before he graduated from high school, he even rebelled against the church as an authority in his life.

Whereas most African Americans looked to the church and religion for sustenance and hope in an unequal society, Davis found spiritual estrangement, submission, and hypocrisy in the African American church. During his youth, like James Baldwin, Davis had spent many hours in church with his grandmother: "For many years I spent from seven to nine hours every Sunday in church, rain, snow or shine" (*Livin'* 22). But in high school, he realized that the church was powerless in the face of the terrible race riots and lynching which occurred in the summers of 1917 and 1919 in Kansas, Missouri, Michigan, Illinois, Tennessee, and in numerous other African American communities nationwide, even though he, like countless others, had prayed for divine intervention. This was the birth of his cynical attitude toward religion.

> From infancy I'd been taught the power of prayer. When
> blacks were massacred in the Tulsa riots, I knelt at night and
> prayed for retribution. When nothing happened, I was puzzled.
> Later following an especially horrible triple lynching in dear
> Dixie, with a young black mother bound and burned at the
> stake while the mob laughed at her cries, I prayed long and
> earnestly for punishment of the mob members. Apparently
> this message never got down to the sheriff, for nobody
> was ever arrested. I became deeply depressed, feeling that
> somehow God had let me down.   (*Livin'* 64)

For Davis, the role of religion in black lives became reversed. As in the
earlier days of slavery when the Africans had seized upon Christianity as
a tool and weapon of empowerment offering to slaves the concepts of "all
God's children," equality, and love, instead of the colonial strategy used to
oppress and teach them order, obedience, and respect of the master, Davis
exposed the irony and hypocrisy of Christianity. He turned the role of right
and wrong around to expose how it seemed that a white God was on the
side of evil and injustice. It is little wonder that Davis left the church in
frustration and despair at the incomprehensibility of the world. If God was
white and hell was black, then somehow, it seemed to Davis that heaven
had to be hell with the master as the evil, exploitative villain. The dark fiery
hell became the paradoxical riddle of the children of Africa, full of energy,
transformation, creativity, and birth, passing on and beyond in a kind of
heavenly alchemical process. Davis no longer wanted to be the object of
hostility and rejection, no longer wanted to be caught in someone else's
vision of hell. It is likely he wondered where his place was and what his role
was as a man in the community. Fanon writes in *Black Skin, White Masks*:

> While I was forgetting, forgiving, and wanting only to
> love, my message was flung back in my face like a slap.
> The white world, the only honorable one, barred me from
> all participation. A man was expected to behave like a man.
> I was expected to behave like a black man or at least like
> a nigger. I shouted a greeting to the world and the world
> slashed away my joy. I was told to stay within bounds, to go

back where I belonged.   (114-115)

The Christian principle of turn the other cheek did not seem equitable to Davis, when he felt continually hurt and excluded and witnessed other African Americans around the country being psychologically abused, physically mistreated, and sometimes murdered.

After the summer of 1919 and the bloody race riots which took place throughout the North and Midwest after World War I, until late in his life, Davis remained disillusioned with the power of God and the authority of the church, and he adopted a nihilistic attitude about the role of church and religion as agents of salvation. Of course, at this time, Davis was not yet aware of the Marxist view that religion is used to subordinate the oppressed classes.

Constant fear of rejection caused Davis to become somewhat of a recluse.

Thus, as a youth, Davis spent considerable time alone to avoid the rejection, becoming a loner with a strong self-consciousness and later wrote "my inferiority complex mushroomed daily" (*Livin'* 68-69).

Unlike Davis, who was unable to participate in school, social and sports activities, Hughes was popular in his urban high school once he moved to Cleveland with his mother, and his feelings of insecurity and loneliness were replaced by a measure of empowerment as he participated in outside school activities such as clubs, political discussions, summer drama at Karamu House (which provided an African American aesthetic and social activities), and athletics (Berry, F. 14). Hughes's immigrant classmates helped to awaken his international and political consciousness and an awareness of exploitation and economic oppression. They lent him copies of their parents' radical literature such as *The Liberator and Socialist Call*. They freely exchanged political ideas, and took Hughes to hear speeches by Eugene V. Debs, the Socialist leader opposed to war. Hughes even had the opportunity to celebrate the Russian Revolution of 1917 with classmates. Not afraid of controversy, he was eventually questioned with his classmates about their loyalty to America. The police regularly raided his friends' homes and confiscated their books.

Davis did not experience this kind of political education in small town

Arkansas City where his classmates, like their parents, were traditional and conservative. However, he had a quick mind and keen observation and quickly learned and understood about race relations and their political and economic implications in the USA. He also read the black newspapers that his stepfather brought home weekly from the various cities he visited while working on the railroad. Davis, unlike Hughes, also did not experience government intimidation or questions of loyalty until the forties, just before the McCarthy era and his flight to Hawai`i, although racial intimidation was certainly familiar and common for him. Furthermore, there was no compulsory military corps at Davis's high school nor was there an African American community theater like Karamu House with talented African American performers, playwrights, and productions to inspire creativity and provide a sense of culture, pride, dignity, and self-determination to those talented ones who participated. There was little comparable in Arkansas City in which Davis could participate.

Indeed, the development of a political consciousness in Davis seemed more experiential than that of Hughes, since Davis had few affluent white friends. In his writing, he often took the side of the blacks and poor victims, especially during and after his two year contract working as an editor and columnist in Atlanta. In contrast, the political consciousness of Hughes was of a more literary nature, perhaps because his skin color was lighter; he experienced racial oppression far more subtly than Davis, especially when he circulated in popular literary circles in more cosmopolitan New York. In contrast to Davis, Hughes experienced politics vicariously, first through the many immigrants' children at Cleveland's predominantly white Central High School. These children were descendants of Eastern European and Russian immigrants, often Jewish, and perhaps because they too had been recently oppressed, they seemed less prejudiced and more democratic than the white Americans with whom Davis went to school. Later, through observation of the people in Harlem, Hughes learned of the rampant dead-end poverty and despair of blacks and immigrants, but these were not usually subjects of his writings.

In order to escape victimization, liberate oneself from unwarranted authority, and survive as a minority individual with a sense of dignity and self-worth in a racially-determined society, one must learn one's own history, develop a sense of ethnic identity which includes racial and cultural pride, and empower oneself in order to most effectively deal with oppressive discriminatory authority. How did Davis proceed and how successful was he in achieving his goal?

Davis, like many African American intellectuals including Hughes, often wrote about being alienated and invisible, especially in his young and formative years. These writers found themselves precariously perched on a fence of duality with the green lure of integration and acceptance by society on one side and the red thistles and thorns of prejudice, discrimination, and rejection on the other. They were never fully accepted in the white world, yet never fully satisfied in a segregated world. Davis and Hughes struggled with the dialectic of alienation and belonging that was to characterize many African American intellectuals of the period in both their public and private lives. Davis and Hughes both subsequently became atheists.

Indeed, both Davis and Hughes wrote controversial poems attacking Christianity by satirizing Christ, deconstructing traditional religious symbols, discovering the power of the word, recovering a courageous voice, finding Black sources of authority and value, and through the unconventional use of language. Faith Berry writes:

> By the early thirties Hughes had become a mocking, blasphemous, anti-Christian, caricaturing God as a weakling drunk, in the poem "A Christian Country," and Christ as a nigger and a "most holy bastard," in Christ in Alabama," and as a willing tool of chauvinists and exploiters, in "Goodbye, Christ."   (10)

They used writing not only to sanctify African American culture, but also as a form of guerilla warfare, to attack the hypocrisy and expose white America. They proclaimed African American life and culture in much the way that whites had formerly used writing to create the colonial discourse. Both Davis and Hughes became anti-Christian, mocking and blasphemous, and both wrote controversial poems which spoke of Christ irreverently as a nigger, ironically paralleling His experience with that of the persecuted and misunderstood African Americans.

Davis's poem entitled "Christ Was A Dixie Nigger," was probably inspired by Hughes, although Davis's work seems more political in terms of socio-economic problems confronting the African American community. He writes:

> I've got my own ideas. . . . I've got a better Christ and a bigger Christ . . . one you can put your hands on today or tomorrow.
>
> My Christ is a Dixie nigger black as midnight, black as the roof of a cave's mouth
> My Christ is a black bastard . . . they all knew Christ's father was Mr. Jim who owns the big plantation. . . .
>
> Christ studied medicine up North in Chicago then came back to Mississippi a good physician with ideas for gettin' the races together. . . .
> then they found how Christ healed a white woman other doctors gave up for lost. . . .
> They called him a Communist and a menace to the Existing Relationship Between Black and White in the South
> Anyhow they got him
>
> Remember this, you wise guys
> Your tales about Jesus of Nazareth are no-go with me
> I've got a dozen Christs in Dixie all bloody and black. . . .
>
> *(American* 28)

Davis speaks to the irony of an African American doctor who healed a white woman, only to be accused of treason and a menace to white womanhood and to be subsequently lynched. The concept of Christ's suffering for others was a chilling metaphor for the historical victimization experience of African Americans, simultaneously and ironically empowering them with an image of martyrdom. However, martyrdom seems insignificant when the same events seem to happen repeatedly as Davis suggests.

These contradictory forces of alienation and belonging, white supremacy and democracy struggled for dominance in the heart and spirit of young Davis. He was confused as to the meaning and paradoxes of democracy. He understood what ought to be a positive thesis of the ideals of the American dream and creed, including admission and acceptance into the people's domain, freedom, justice, equality and the pursuit of truth and happiness of all citizens. He witnessed the reality of his environment: the hypocritical, unrepresentative, unjust, and unequal capitalistic system based on race and class in which most African Americans lived as victims, surviving according to the whims, generosities, and fears of a powerful and dominant Eurocentric America. In *Livin'*, Davis writes:

> What embittered me most was flagrant white hypocrisy. Virtually all aspects of daily life were geared to maintaining white supremacy. And yet, teachers, newspapers and speakers solemnly preached the doctrine that All Men Are Created Equal as they proudly pointed toward the Declaration of Independence and the Constitution. I had come to learn the hard way that they meant only white men. I, and that tenth of the nation like me, did not have equality. Obviously the Establishment intended to maintain the status quo until eternity. But why did they lie? Why did they not come out and say flatly what was in their hearts: equality was not for black people? Why did they teach about democracy, then shove me back when I sought my just share? Why is hypocrisy a strong national trait of American whites?   (55)

Davis used writing as a fiery weapon to attack the hypocrisy of white America and to expose the injustice.

> But the facing of so vast a prejudice could not but bring inevitable self-questioning, self-disparagement, and lowering of ideals which ever accompany repression and breed in an atmosphere of contempt and hate.   (*Livin'* 299)

Davis thirsted for equality, rejected the racial authority imposed by white society and, as he matured, set out to challenge the status quo and the low expectations of success by African Americans, perpetuated by American institutions, and reified by society at large.

Initially, Davis chose to implement his will to survive and succeed by his active participation in journalism at Kansas State in the years 1924-26. What forces were at work to steer Davis's career toward writing with social criticism and commentary as his focus?

Frank Marshall Davis did not set out to be a journalist or writer when he was a child, since his role models of male adults and professions were severely limited by color, class, and family influence. His career choices included service jobs, railroad work, entertainment (musician), teaching, or boxing. Most of these were low paying, low-status positions. During this time, most whites were convinced that higher education spoiled the African Americans and made them less manageable and more demanding.

> These were still days when whites were convinced that education "spoiled" a Negro (if indeed he was capable of college training), and that it was a kindness to dissuade him, for there were no suitable vocations for college-bred Negroes anyhow. Still, despite poverty and these discouragements, they broke through. (Bardolph 155)

Davis's consciousness of victimization gave birth to and fueled a simultaneous desire to transcend the obstacles of oppression, to excel, and to contribute a positive legacy to the African American community and to the world.

After graduating from high school, Davis worked for a summer on the railroads in secondary service jobs, and then matriculated in 1923 to Friends College (a Quaker school) in Wichita where his grandfather lived; however, when his grandfather died, he could not afford to return. The following fall, in 1924, he enrolled in Kansas State Industrial and Agricultural College where there were fewer than a dozen other African American students, and no African American professors. Unlike the University of Kansas, Kansas State did not have the reputation of overt bigotry. There, he studied journalism, determined to defy the tradition of African Americans as service and blue collar workers. He chose to pursue a profession which was deemed respectable and intellectual by society at large. Because of his talent and probably his imposing size, he caught the attention of one of his English teachers, and, with her encouragement, published his first poems.

When he entered college in Kansas, encouraged to write poetry by an English professor, Davis began to reveal his concerns exploring racial themes of alienation, injustice, inhumanity, contrasts between rural and urban America, and African American culture.

However, due to the economic pressures of the Great Depression, Davis felt he was no longer in total control of his life and the career direction. He was forced to interrupt his college education and major in journalism because of inadequate funds. He chose to work as a part-time reporter for several Negro presses in Chicago, Illinois, and Gary, Indiana in 1929.

Davis went to Gary, Indiana for his first job in the newspaper field. He quickly experienced another kind of alienation when he discovered the rampant corruption of big city politics including African American aldermen, the ruthless power of urban gangs and mobsters, the impersonal work place of factories, the exploitation and wealth of the bosses, and the various sins of hustlers and other pariahs struggling to survive. He writes in his poem "Gary, Indiana",

> In Gary/ the mills/ feast/ on ore and men . . . /Like potbellied hoboes/ the mills snore/ . . ./The mills are always hungry/ what a beast/ they make steel in their bellies/ it's hard to tell/ men from steel/ . . . A mayor/ yes/ and a city council/ and officials/ and graft/ sure/ and bands/ and stores/ and places/ they eat the crumbs/ the hoboes drop/ and grow
> potbellies/ . . . .   (*Black Man's* 32)

During that time, African Americans could not work for white presses, which in any case only reported negative African American coverage. According to Woodson and Wesley,

> The Negro newspaper had its opportunity in restricting itself largely to matters in which Negroes are interested, but which find no place in the white press. The Negro gets publicity among whites only for the crimes committed by the race. Seeing this opportunity, the Negro press displayed race wrongs, race protest, race progress, and race aspiration.
>
> (548)

Through his experience working with the African American press, Davis realized that he could develop his journalistic skills on the job and contribute to the intellectual and political growth of the African American community.

While growing up in Kansas, Davis learned the subtleties of racism and discrimination. He became aware of the concepts of power and powerlessness, of different treatment for African Americans compared with other minority groups by the dominant whites, be they rich, middle-class, or poor. He learned of the disparities between the treatment of southern African Americans and northern African Americans by whites. He writes in *Livin'*:

> And yet, rotten as the system was, I realized I fared better than my black brothers only a few miles south down in Oklahoma. There segregation at that time was legal. Some towns, like Blackwell, would not allow souls to remain overnight. I'd heard of hamlets with billboards just outside city limits reading, "Nigger, read and run. If you can't read, run anyway." My town, the jumping off place for statutory Jim Crow, was where placards went up on trains headed south announcing, "This coach for Colored Only."   (56)

Davis was alert to discrimination against other ethnic groups in America as well and was sympathetic to their struggles. For example, he resented his white instructor in high school who, when discussing the Oriental Exclusion Act barring most Asians from becoming American citizens, told the class and writes:

> What we should do . . . is tell them we are different and can never assimilate each other's culture. . . . I didn't say they really are as good as us, I said we ought to tell them that to make them feel good.   (*Livin'* 54)

Moreover, Davis was disturbed that the instructor had upheld the students' belief in white supremacy, and he questioned the presumption that white skin automatically meant superiority to all the darker people. Davis was becoming aware of other minorities' problems before he ever left Kansas.

Davis recalls other instances of humiliation and degradation of being black in Kansas, how even older African Americans, like the janitor Will Logan, a friend of his parents from Mississippi, were not respected and were looked down upon by young white classmates. These young and impudent white boys would kick Will Logan or rub his balding head, knowing that he was not expected to retaliate due to his southern upbringing and subservient attitude toward all whites, even though he was "a tremendous natural fighter." For Davis this was unacceptable behavior since the cultural value of respect for the elders was deeply ingrained in him (*Livin'* 75). Davis also "resented this double standard of [Will Logan] accepting Uncle Tom status around whites but demanding dignity and respect from us [black kids]" (55).

Before his departure to work in Atlanta, Davis still remembered stories about the South which he had heard while growing up, funny stories laced with fearful lessons of obedience, subservience, and violence. This was not unlike apartheid which was later to be established in South Africa, and he was hesitant to take the job. He writes:

> Dad had told me about Brazos Bottoms in Texas where blacks must have passes signed by Mr. Charley to come to town. He also spoke of a prosperous Negro farmer who bought the first automobile in his county in Texas. Envious whites immediately passed a law barring him from all public thoroughfares. The resourceful farmer, who owned several thousand acres, cleared a road just inside his fence and on Sundays took his family driving on his own land. (*Livin'* 56)

Davis used humor and irony to deal with the pain of racism. The resourcefulness of African Americans in the face of Jim Crow laws did not hide the reality of intimidation of "Mr. Charlie" (the white man), and the racial limitations in the South.

Wealth did not matter in the South if a man was black, for intimidation served to keep him in his place, since custom had it that there would be no comparison between African Americans and whites on an equal basis. Northerners often considered the South the earthly equivalent of hell or worse, a theme which appears in much literature of the period.

> All Dixie was hard on Blacks. When one boy left to spend the summer in Birmingham, several friends refused to write saying they didn't even want their mail going to Alabama. Some adults said if they owned a plantation in Georgia and one in hell, they'd sell the land in Georgia and live in hell.
> (*Livin'* 177)

But if Davis had heard many negative things about the South, he retained his customary sense of humor in recounting stories about the area, even those with exaggerated stereotypes and inferior roles.

That was where we were not allowed to enter a store and ask for John Ruskin cigars; we had to request Mr. John Ruskin. We weren't permitted to drink milk unless we first colored it with ink; it was also against the law to lay your black bodies down on white sheets. A Negro farmer with a team of one black and one white horse plowing his field could shout to the darker, "Giddap, you black son of a bitch," but woe unto him if he did not remove his hat and respectfully address the other, "Won't you please giddap, Mr. White Horse?" In Florida you dare not say Miami to a white person; it had to be Yourami. (*Livin'* 181)

When Davis was offered a job in Atlanta as editor for the *Atlanta World* in 1931, he asked his friends about living in Dixie. He was warned to remember his place, to remember where he was, and to avoid trouble. He was encouraged by those who said that in the South, at least one knew what was acceptable behavior, whereas in the North one could never be certain. (*Livin'* 181).

Before Frank Marshall Davis moved south to assume the job, he had experienced overt racism and some discrimination in Kansas, but had only heard stories about southern Jim Crow and its violence. However, witnessing the blatant discrimination and seeing the violence of racism in the South constituted a major portion of his experience as a journalist in Georgia. His southern experiences gave Davis a foundation and an understanding to his socio-political protest and many subsequent themes in his poetry and editorials. Davis used the African American press to reveal the unjust treatment of African Americans and to protest bias in the white press.

CHAPTER 2
Davis in Georgia: the Black Press and the Jim Crow South

In Chicago, segregation was enforced by custom; in Atlanta it was legalized.   (Davis, *Livin'* 282)

In 1931 Davis received an attractive and challenging job offer from W. A. Scott, owner of the *Atlanta World*, a weekly African American newspaper established in 1928 and in desperate need of an editor. His charge was to create a daily newspaper that was viable, respected, and of course profitable. Scott offered Davis $25 per week to start, with a raise to $35 if Davis was good, which even in Chicago during the Depression sounded fantastic. He found out that Claude Barnett at the Associated Negro Press had recommended him to Scott. Davis soon discovered that Scott also had a series of syndicated African American newspapers all printed in Atlanta and serving such cities as Birmingham, Memphis, and Chattanooga (Davis, *Livin'* 180).

The Scott Newspaper Syndicate was comprised of members who founded small newspapers and contracted to purchase so many copies weekly in which they inserted their own local news columns and advertisements into a general national format. Davis records in *Livin'*, "At one time membership totaled more than fifty newspapers from New Orleans to Florida and extended through the Carolinas, Tennessee, Alabama and Georgia" (186). Woodson and Wesley noted:

> A large share of the praise for developments favorable to Negroes belongs to the press. Without the aid of the Negro newspaper, this program of publishing to the world the grievances of the race could not have been carried out.   (547)

W. A. Scott and other African American owners and editors were aware of the influence of the black press on the psychology of the community and its function of healing through dignity and pride. E. Franklin Frazier writes in *The Negro*:

> The new role of the Negro newspaper was brought to the attention of the American people in the publication of Kerlin's *The Voice of the Negro*, 1919. As he stated in his introduction to this book, "The colored people of America

are going to their own papers in these days for the news and
for their guidance in thinking." The guidance which Negro
newspapers were providing was indicated by extracts from
80 selected newspapers on such subjects as Negro leaders,
the Negro's reaction to World War I, and the race riots
and lynching that followed the war. Although the editor
refrained from commenting on the contents, it was obvious
from reading them that the Negro newspaper was playing an
important role in changing the attitude of the Negro towards
his status in American life.   (511)

Information and guidance from the press was a key for people in the
community in discovering a positive self-identity and a motivation towards
changing their status.

From the beginning of his arrival in the South, Davis bristled at the
legal and customary patterns of race relations. Southern apartheid was the
policy of segregation by law of African Americans and whites in all areas:
political, economic, social, and religious, implemented by the police and
various coercive forms of tradition and terrorism.

In *Livin'*, Davis writes: "As usual, we were hardest hit by the depression.
And, as usual, Dixie administrators brazenly discriminated against starving
blacks" (251). Davis felt like he had "voluntarily gone to prison" when he
first arrived in Atlanta, and yet he kept his sense of control and said "To
me I was going to a place rigidly hemmed in by bars and restrictions; to
my people in the little hate-filled backwoods hamlets of the state, Atlanta
represented freedom, a city of refuge" (181 182). What he found in the
South was a racially discriminatory system legitimized by state laws/Black
Codes used to circumscribe the behavior of African Americans. There were
also ambiguous Supreme Court decisions on voting rights and interstate
transportation which were ignored by a strong police force that worked to
keep African Americans in their place.

The institutional racism which governed every aspect of African
American life in the Jim Crow South reinforced white supremacy through
economic control and political domination and aimed at preserving the
ethnic integrity, racial purity, and social superiority of the white race. On
December 3, 1933, in his editorial column, "Touring the World," Davis

critiqued a statement made by the Georgia Commissioner of Agriculture who said, "The yellow people, the brown people and the blacks are mentally inferior for directors in our form of government." Davis attacked the perpetuation of stereotypes about African Americans being unfit for leadership roles, calling for more African American teachers at the black colleges to assume leadership and responsibility. Unfortunately, since many of these colleges had white boards of directors, they often hired whites over African Americans.

> [i]t is my contention that too many jobs are given to whites. If these are to be colored schools, then colored teachers and officials ought to be solely in charge. . . . I do maintain that there are enough people of color with sufficient intelligence to supplant all Caucasians either at Spelman or in the University system.   (1931-1933)

In his October 9, 1932, weekly "Touring the World" column on southern politics, Davis attacked the whites' facile circumvention of African American voting rights.

> Dixie's colored folk have finally broken into the Democratic Party and are able to vote in the Democratic primaries, so all the whites are now Republicans--and the white primary lives on.   (1931-1933)

Davis exposed Georgia segregation in the movie theaters, state libraries, and the housing market. He announced whenever a church was desegregated, and he published editorials about the African American trend away from churches and toward small businesses. He insisted on the capitalization of the word "Negro" in the local white daily newspaper.

Davis attacked southern violence in his editorials and he also recounted in his autobiography a conversation he had in Chicago in 1934 with W. C. Handy, the "Father of the Blues," about the latter's musical tours of the South, reflecting the aggressive violent attitudes of southern whites. He writes in *Livin'*:

> [Handy was] a leader of a small dance band playing for rednecks. One of the favorite tunes of the day was *If the Man In The Moon Was A Coon*. He received many requests

nightly for this number . . . but as the hour grew late and the
male dancers became drunk, they would gather in front of
the band waiting. As the singers finished the line, "if the man
in the moon was a coon, what would you do," the listeners,
almost as if on signal, would draw revolvers and empty them
-- at the moon. The point was obvious.   (219)

Davis understood that Whites were often plagued by an irrational fear
of tragic social and cultural chaos if segregation broke down; they felt
it necessary to arm themselves against the enemies of white supremacy.
Segregation offered an order, a means of control, and a legally sanctioned
barrier to social equality. The day that Davis arrived in Atlanta, he made the
following observation in *Livin'*:

> I left the Jim Crow railroad coach, walked through the Jim
> Crow waiting room and took a Jim Crow taxi for the Jim
> Crow Butler St. Y.M.C.A., two blocks from the *World* office.
> I walked over to the newspaper plant on Auburn Avenue,
> the Jim Crow main street of Jim Crow Atlanta. Still, to all
> outward appearances, this was not too greatly different from
> Chicago.   (182)

Comparing the North and the South, Davis soon discovered that the
differences between *de jure* and *de facto* segregation were sometimes slight.
In Georgia, he found illegal, yet socially sanctioned, coercive forces of
terrorism and violence used in the name of preserving the old South and its
tradition of white supremacy manifested in its institutions and private social
organizations.

Davis pondered the meaning of Jim Crow, the racial creed supported
by the legal and moral authority of the entire American judicial system
including the Supreme Court. He observed the racial politics of the
"Negro Problem" which reinforced the mythology and ideology of African
Americans as irresponsible, childlike, inferior beings, unfit for the privileges
of citizenship, and thus unworthy and unqualified to vote or receive the
privileges and protection of the American creed of democracy and Bill of
Rights. Of this time, E. Frazier writes in *The Negro*,

> The period beginning in the nineties and extending through
> the first decade of the twentieth century was, as we have seen,

> a period in which the Negro was forced to accept a status
> similar to a subordinate caste in the South.   (503)

The endless migrations north reflected how African Americans tried to escape the oppressive conditions in the South. It was during this period that great numbers of African Americans turned to the printed word, especially the newspapers. Frazier continues in *The Negro,*

> The mass migrations during and after World War I were followed not only by a literary renaissance but by an expansion of the Negro newspaper. Before the development of the Negro communities in northern cities, the relatively few secular Negro newspapers did not have a very large circulation, the Negro newspaper had few readers and few advertisers. "It refused to print anything . . . that would damage the good name or morals of the race, and kept all scandal and personalities. . . in the background."   (510)

Davis's boss, Robert S. Abbott, editor of the ANP, was also a pioneer in the growth and expansion of the African American press to satisfy the need of the African American public for relevant news and to heighten the consciousness of the people.

It was his southern experience recollected which provided Davis the subject matter, emotion, and protest for some of his best poetry first published in *Black Man's Verse* in 1935 shortly after he left Atlanta. His feeling of impotence and rage in the face of such overwhelming forces of racism and poverty, led him to write some of his strongest poems: "What Do You Want America?," "I Sing No New Songs," "Lynched," "The Slave," "Georgia's Atlanta," "I Am The American Negro," "Christ Is A Dixie Nigger," "Snapshots of The Cotton South," "Coincidence," "Adam Smothers," and a series of eulogies: "George Brown," "Moses Mitchell," "Nicodemus Perry," and "Editor Ralph Williamson." In "I Sing No New Songs," he knew and wrote about the circle of poverty and despair, which repeated like a dance step. Davis writes:

> Once I cried for new songs to sing . . . a black rose . . . a brown sky . . . the moon for my buttonhole . . . pink dreams for the table/ . . . Later I learned [that] life is a servant girl . . . dusting the same pieces yesterday, today, tomorrow . . . a

never ending one two three one two three one two three. . . .

(*Black Man's* 24)

Davis believed that the role and function of the African American newspaper was essential in restoring a positive self-image to the African American public since African Americans were constantly attacked and dehumanized in the white newspapers. Davis notes,

> Blacks didn't get their names in the white press unless they committed crimes. But the *World* devoted column after column to club news, social notes and religious activities. And, of equal importance, they were Mr. and Mrs. They were hungry enough to read any publication which supplied emotional sustenance, no matter how poorly edited.
>
> (*Livin'* 184)

As editor of the *Atlanta Daily World*, Davis quickly followed the protest tradition in African American journalism and wrote searing "vitriolic editorials," columns about a racially constituted repressive system despite warnings "to take it easy editorially" from publisher Scott.

But Davis says in *Livin' the Blues* that an editor is first of all a reporter, certainly not for the money, but more like a missionary taking the word to the people.

> A reporter is an odd amalgam of opposites. He is a voyeur, peeping and prying into the naked lives of others. He is a parasite, living off the blood and meat of fellow humans. He is a great gray wolf, lurking in the shadows, always set to pounce upon those who stray too far from the pack of social acceptance. And yet, at the same time, he is a policeman armed with the authority of the printed page to protect the public. He is an overworked Saint George, slaying some new dragon in virtually every issue of his rag.   (138)

Davis enjoyed the power of being a reporter, of revealing and exposing people's weaknesses, of protecting the public. Like other African American writers, he used animals to lend power to his descriptions. As a journalist, he found a way to help the community of African Americans by discussing political and socio-economic issues, African history, and fearlessly exposing the wrongs of racism. Frazier notes similar patterns in other Black newspaper and writes in *Black Bourgeoisie*:

> In 1922, an analysis was made of the contents of 64 Negro newspapers. Out of a total of 705 news items and 174 editorials, about 21 per cent of the news items and 40 per cent of the editorials were on the subject of racial wrongs or clashes. Nearly 18 per cent of the news items and 7 per cent of the editorials were concerned with race progress and race pride. The welfare efforts, including education, and movements for the solution of the Negro problem accounted for about 22 per cent of the news items and 10 per cent of the editorials. Twelve per cent of the news items and 1 per cent of the editorials were devoted to Negro crime. The remaining 27 percent of the news items and 40 per cent of editorials were on "all other subjects."   (511)

Davis's editorials and columns followed a similar format. He reported racial injustice and progress and promoted race pride.

When Davis arrived in Atlanta, the newspaper plant was bustling with activity and the staff was hopeful and full of a sense of purpose. He was surprised that the small staff consisted mainly of Scott's family and a few reporters whom Davis said could not write. He notes Scott, the owner, was:

> a strong, positive man with imagination and a natural knack for business . . . he never went into anything unless he had prepared an escape route in advance . . . a lightening quick thinker . . . giving himself the advantage. . . . He also had his faults. Loud, ruthless, domineering, cold-blooded and a confirmed egotist, he created many enemies . . . we got along fantastically well together because he realized he knew nothing about the editorial side of newspaper work and respected my ability."   (*Livin'* 185-186)

Perhaps it was due to his dark skin that "[d]espite his power, W.A. was frowned upon by the black social register" (*Livin'* 217).

Indeed, Davis found the organization efficient in most areas except the editorial department. He was also dismayed to find there was little general news except for police reports, the sports section, the cartoons, an occasional article by J.C. Chunn who had a menial position at the *Atlanta Constitution*, a feature of earthy black philosophy and occasional verse, and the releases from the Associated Negro Press which were copied verbatim (*Livin'* 184).

Davis worked long hours teaching his reporters how to write, often rewriting their articles in order to create a newspaper he could be proud of. As the paper developed from a bi-weekly to a tri-weekly, W.A. started a rotogravure section "allowing each publication a quota of local pictures . . . popularly termed 'the brown sheet'" which quickly became "a major circulation builder as people struggled to get their pictures in this section," again working toward a positive self-image and cultural pride (187). The compensatory features of the African American press were considerable. Frazier notes:

> Moreover, the Negro newspapers must carry news concerning the people and happenings in the Negro community. Much of the news of happenings in the Negro community is concerned with Negro "society." The compensatory feature of Negro newspapers is especially prominent in the "society" news in that "society" news is an answer to the derogatory attitudes of whites concerning the activities of Negroes. The "society" news also reflects the appeal of the Negro press to the upper and middle classes in the Negro community.
>
> (*Bourgeoisie* 515)

The middle and upper classes of African Americans competed to create newsworthy activities and gain the status inherent in being featured in the press, which in turn provided role models for leadership to the community.

A year after Davis had come to Atlanta, Scott asked him to start producing a daily newspaper, and Davis accepted the challenge with the help of additional daily stories, the world wide picture service associated with the Associated Negro Press (ANP), and important national and world news with a focus on the global black community, wired regularly from the ANP in Chicago. The daily competition of the *Atlanta Daily World* with the white dailies caused many African Americans to cancel their subscriptions to the white papers and created a new climate of consideration by the editors and reporters of white publications for African Americans as they sought to improve service, and refrain from insulting articles about African Americans which heretofore had been so common (*Livin'* 208-209).

If Davis sometimes felt impotent as an African American man in the South, his editorial position at the *Atlanta World* helped him meet and exchange ideas with other African American editors, leaders, prominent intellectuals, officers in the military, and people from all strata and status in southern society which increased his sense of self-esteem. Occasionally he conferred with white journalists who applauded him on his editorials and guts (*Livin'* 274).

Indeed, as the *Atlanta World* expanded, more African American journalists went South seeking work to escape the continuing devastating effects of the Depression in the North. Many journalists later became editors of other prominent African American newspapers such as the Chicago *Defender*, the *Birmingham World*, the Baltimore *Afro-American* and the Kansas City *Call* (*Livin'* 271). Davis worked with and came to respect these people throughout his subsequent years in journalism.

Davis also had a sports column called "Speakin' 'Bout Sports" in which he used the pen name Frank Boganey, the last name honoring his stepfather. On October 9, 1932, Davis was unafraid to attack two prestigious black colleges, Tuskegee and Wilberforce, and include his voice in a critique of black coaches and "seasoned players" on college teams.

> Yes, we have a say-so about Grandpaw Stevenson--and we take the liberty to tell the cock-eyed world (all the other sport writers seem to be afraid to do it) that Tuskegee is guilty of breaking the first rule of good sportsmanship in allowing Abbott to continue playing Ben Stevenson ad infinitum!
>
> (1931-1933)

His boldness in exposing any area where he found injustice extended to the heart and soul of the African American community and institutions.

His pointed comments appeared in a weekly Sunday column entitled "Touring the World" and he also added a small front page box in which he offered rhymed summaries of the daily news in a reprised column called "Jazzin' the News" (*Livin'* 188).

In his Sunday editorial column, "Touring the World," he offered thorny analyses on a variety of subjects including segregation in the military and schools. He reported race riots and discussed issues of class, caste, disunity, unions, and Third World problems of colonization and oppression. On December 18, 1932, he critiqued the southern penal system and the chain gang, devoting a column to Robert Burns, an African American who escaped the Georgia chain gang and later wrote a book attracting nationwide attention exposing the sanctioned atrocities against African American men (1931-1933). He openly discussed the lack of unity among African American professionals, and the rivalries between the Pan Hellenic sororities and fraternities. He critiqued the Negroes' blind belief in the white interpretation of African and African American history and the imitation and blind assimilationist tendencies of African Americans. He taught African American history in his columns, recounting stories of cultured Africans such as his November 27, 1932, column on Sabala Rannavalona (1931-1933).

His irony and disgust were barely camouflaged as he critiqued the ignorance of his own people of their long and noble history. His futurist politics of color and Afrocentrism is evident in the September 10, 1933, column:

> I do not value my African ancestry because my white folks tell me black Africa has contributed nothing to civilization. My historians speak of the glories of the ancient empires of Mandingo, Benin, Yoruba; of old Timbuctoo, Kano, Zimbabwe, Gegzeg; of the great king Abuacde Izchia. But I will not believe for no white tongue has said these things and therefore they cannot be true.   (1931-1933)

Today the vanguard movement of Afrocentrism, led by scholars such as Martin Bernal, Ivan Van Sertima, and David Diop finally lend irrefutable credibility to theories of ancient illustrious African civilizations, and their universities, architecture, navigation skills, medical science, and technology.

Lack of self-determination was another theme of Davis in "Touring the World." For example, the column of December 3, 1933, on the topic of qualified African Americans' being denied responsible positions in the education system, reads:

> Negroes do not have responsible positions at schools where the student body is entirely white and the reverse should be

equally true. Dixie is the section of segregation. Very well.
Since colored cannot attend white schools, then let the race's
young sit at the feet of Negro teachers. It is unthinkable
for whites here to be taught in the classroom by colored.
When colored are taught by whites, it not only deprives
trained Aframerican teachers of jobs, but also insinuates that
Negroes are not smart enough to teach their own.

(1931-1933)

Davis discussed the issues of race and power confronting black
unions. The Brotherhood of Sleeping Car Porters and A. Philip Randolph's
struggles with the labor movement were much in the news during this time,
often meeting opposition from prominent Negroes, the African American
church, African American fraternal organizations, and even the black press
itself which was sometimes overly cautious, not wanting to awaken more
hostility, fear, hatred, and intimidation from whites.

Some members of the African American press did not want to alienate
liberal whites and their philanthropy. Indeed, this was an issue which was
nationally debated in the African American community throughout the
twenties and thirties. A contemporary of Davis and noted African American
critic and philosopher, Alain Locke, wrote about the challenges facing
the new African American intellectuals in his prescient essay, "The New
Negro," one of the definitive works of the Negro Renaissance:

The challenge of the new intellectuals among them is clear
enough - the "race radicals" and realists who have broken
with the old epoch of philanthropic guidance, sentimental
appeal and protest. . . . It is the "man farthest down" who is
most active in "gettin up" . . . In a real sense it is the rank
and file who are leading, and the leaders who are following.
A transformed and transforming psychology permeates the
masses.   (Peplow and Davis 391)

Davis came from poverty and persisted in his aim to transform the
psychology of the masses.

In his September 25, 1932, "Touring the World" column Davis critiqued,
for example, "the atrocious and hellish conditions in the government
controlled levee camps," the segregated public facilities, the terrorism

committed against African American factory workers, and the exploitation of the Negro vote by Republicans and Democrats alike who both promised better conditions yet did nothing.

> Segregation and discrimination flourish in the capital under the nose of Hoover as they have in the past before other presidents. Disfranchisement, lynching, etc., continue to exist with neither disapproval or approval by the powers that be.   (1931-1933)

Davis avoided the white part of Atlanta as much as possible, observing the rules and restrictions of Jim Crow: sitting in the back of the bus, waiting in the Jim Crow line to go to the movies, sitting in the balcony in "nigger heaven," trying on clothes in a white store in the janitor's closet (*Livin'* 190). Usually, he had little contact with whites in the South, although he often ate in a restaurant owned by a Spanish Jew. However, whenever African Americans traveled in the South, it was hard to avoid all contact with whites. Confrontation or humiliation lurked at any turn of the head. African Americans were always at risk.

In *Livin' the Blues*, Davis recounts what he calls the most humiliating experience of his life which occurred in Atlanta. It happened after he sustained a serious cut on his head while horsing around with a fellow employee at the *Atlanta Daily World* office. When he was taken to Grady Hospital which had an all-white staff, his doctor was a young intern who had been informed that Davis was the Editor of the *World*. The intern asked Davis a question and without thinking, he responded "yes" instead of "yes, sir." The intern, insulted and holding the scalpel in his hand, said:

> I expect a nigger to say "yes sir" and "no sir" when they address a white man. You know I'm in control in this room. I can fix your wound, or I can put something in it that will take care of you permanently. Your life is in my hands. Now again, what did you say?"   (*Livin'* 197-198)

Davis obligingly if reluctantly said "yes, sir," anxious to leave the hospital as soon as possible with his health and life intact. Once again, Davis was forced to recognize his powerlessness, his lack of free will, his inability to choose with dignity, for if he had refused to say "sir" he might have ended up dead or maimed. Black people survived by avoiding confrontation with whites. The culture of fear was alive and dominant from the Ku Klux Klan, the justice system, the commercial culture, the military, and the city and state governments to the hospital and health care systems.

All of his life he had recoiled from the acts and terms of servility left over from slavery. He had rebelled as a child "to Granny's insistence that all white males be addressed in this manner" (288), but at this moment, he remembered that

> . . . no matter how renowned in the rest of creation, in Dixie
> our best [blacks] were lower than the lowest white. . . . Now
> because of one mental lapse, I was cornered. There was no
> way out unless I chose to gamble with my life. . . . And the
> emotional hurt surpassed by far the ache in my split head.
>
> (Livin' 198)

The experience left Davis bitter, perhaps with the burning desire to prove his manhood, to rescue it from the passive state where he as an African American Other was expected to remain. He urgently wanted equality and the dignity to stand up for what he believed in. Life itself for an African American man or woman during this period of Jim Crow was always uncertain. Humiliation was a common occurrence in the presence of most whites. To maintain a measure of self-esteem required enormous efforts.

> Even though he knew I edited the *World* and was therefore
> somewhat intelligent, I was black; therefore, I was a nigger
> and trash. . . .   (*Livin'* 198)

Davis wrote of the "sizeable Book of Etiquette on Race Relations designed to keep the Aframerican 'in his place'" which had developed through generations, since the days of slavery and the instituting of Black Codes. He clearly understood the psychological effects and consequences of slavery, racism, patriarchy, and emasculation, as well as the countermeasures employed by the African American community, when he said with his typical ironic tone:

> A male Duskymerican may have reached the venerable age
> of a hundred but he was still a boy; this attempt to consign
> us to perpetual childhood was back of our insistence, even

among the very young, of addressing each other as "man"
and was a group way of compensating. Evidently we were
like the lower animals; we could mate but we did not marry
for no white supremacist referred to our women as Mrs. An
Afro-American could be called "Doctor" or "Professor" or
"Reverend" but the Dixiecrat mind rejected Mr. and Mrs. The
racist also placed himself in an illogical position by calling
our older folk "aunt" or "uncle"; one must assume they were
more willing to admit close kinship than render elementary
courtesy.   (*Livin'* 199)

However, in spite of the overwhelming racism in the South, Davis did not
neglect to recount the more surprising and positive experiences he had with
whites during his Southern sojourn.

For example, one weekend while coming back from Tuskegee,
Alabama, with his then-fiancée, Thelma Boyd, they were forced to stop for
gas in "some nameless hamlet." When the apparent owner who had been
loafing on the porch with "three or four crackers, including a shirt sleeved
deputy with a bright star" started to approach the other side of the car, Davis
tensed, fearing the worst, wondering how he might have "violated the ethics
of living Jim Crow," feeling that predictable psychological guilt which the
oppressed are used to experience as victims. To his astonishment, the man
called him "sir" as he referred Davis to another service station outside the
town limits which was authorized to sell gas "durin' church meetin' time"
(210). However, the respectful treatment he received in that area contrasted
with the racist abuse that African Americans were receiving just 20 miles
away. He recounts two separate incidents of racism in Georgia.

But a few months later . . . several members of Blanche
Calloway's band were severely beaten by infuriated whites
for attempting to use the rest room while their bus was taking
on gas. And in north Georgia, near the Tennessee border,
Juliette Derricotte and several companions died following
a car crash because no white ambulance would carry them
to a hospital. Miss Derricotte, internationally known and
the highest black figure on the national Y.W.C.A. staff, was
forced to lie critically injured on a public highway until a
black ambulance could be summoned from 30 miles away

> to haul her to a hospital with facilities for black citizens. By
> then it was too late.   (*Livin'* 210-211)

Davis critiqued the inhumanity of whites toward African Americans and
the insignificance of African Americans lives, regardless of how much they
accomplished.

Only once does Davis's writing reveal that he evoked the wrath of
southern whites and received threats. This incident was a result of his editorials
in defense of the Scottsboro boys who were on trial for allegedly raping two
white girls who later admitted that they had made false accusations against
the seven African American youths who were riding in the same box car in
order to avoid vagrancy charges. There was subsequently involvement, a
brilliant defense, and international publicity by the Communist Party; the
boys were finally freed after the case had reached the Supreme Court several
times. Again, in his "Touring the World" column, on October 2, 1932, Davis
used the black press to present an African American perspective of the news
and to attack America's racism:

> Mrs. Ada Wright, mother of two of the Scottsboro boys, who
> is now in Europe on a Communist-backed tour, represents
> in the flesh one of the most pitiful results of our present day
> American uncivilization with its clash of races and religions
> of capital and common people.   (1931-1933)

By inferring that America is uncivilized ("uncivilization"), Davis goes
on the offensive. Davis also tried to counteract the white lynch hysteria so
familiar at the time (*Livin'* 276-277). That his journalism was considered
a threat to the status quo is reflected by the letter which he received from
Birmingham signed Ku Klux Klan, which read:

> Lay off that junk in your little nigger paper if you know
> what's good for you. Them niggers is guilty and you know it.
> If you keep on printing that junk you'll die just like they're
> going to.   (*Livin'* 277)

By exploring the consequences of victimization and the unmitigated
struggle for equality, dignity, and self-determination in the life of Davis,
one discovers that he is indeed a good representative of authority and the
New Negro. This title, New Negro, was descriptive of a new archetype

in the African American Community: usually an educated, darker-skinned African American with an outreaching, assertive, and sometimes contentious personality.

The New Negro was also self-reflective and creative, and significantly often a defiant force against total assimilation at the expense of losing African American culture. By the 1930's, when Davis was still in his twenties, he fit the description and, like Scott, assumed the label of the "New Negro" or "Race Man." And, contrary to past tradition, he was proud of his dark skin, optimistic about the talents of the Negroes, and bold to attempt to organize a group of artists and assert their significance in defiance of a southern society which challenged the very humanity of African American people. His October 8, 1933, column emphasizes:

> I would like to see organized here a club of kindred spirits interested in writing and painting. Not so many years ago a literary renaissance was started in Aframerica. The nation went wild about Negro poetry, art and prose. Then decay set in. . . . It is obvious that an organization of kindred spirits will bring out whatever artistic qualities members possess. Here the brainchildren of each could be paraded before others for their criticism and helpful suggestions. . . . Who knows but what some youth residing right here in Atlanta needs only this sort of stimulus to rise to literary or artistic heights never before ascended by an American Negro.   (1931-1933)

His call to African American artists and youth to organize and help each other to excel and transcend to new heights was a part of his journalistic mission.

According to Hoyt Fuller, these New Negro men and women in the 1920's and 1930's, realized that the old edifices of white power were crumbling. They saw submission and poverty in the South and opportunity and optimism for African Americans in the North. For a brief time, it seemed no longer necessary to be white to be successful. Many of the writers of this period appealed to the moral conscience of America. Few dared to use scatalogical language--unwilling to tarnish their image as "spokesperson" for the race--preferring the Washington school of conciliation, appeasement, and accommodation. By contrast, Davis wrote critically of white power and hypocrisy in the 1930's and 1940's and served as a precursor to angry revolutionary writers of the 1960's (Bigsby, *Black American* 229-243).

The New Negro was independent, defiant, chauvinistic, and outspoken, especially on race issues. Typically, he or she chose democratic themes of the quest for justice, equality, and freedom--and ethnocentric themes such as mother Africa.

Like many other New Negroes, Davis favored a functional cultural and aesthetic program which Marcus Garvey and Booker T. Washington had ignored, as well as an effective economic and political base to which they adhered, in order to offset the psychological effects of victimization. Hence, like other Renaissance writers, Davis sometimes celebrated the rediscovery of his African heritage, but he equally celebrated his long history in America by exposing the racism and exploitation inherent in U. S. government policy. His gradual turn toward espousing cultural nationalism, organized labor, minority and oppressed causes, and non-traditional relationships was a natural consequence of daily rejection by the majority society.

Meanwhile, in Atlanta, Scott continued to warn Davis to be careful each time he heard about his controversial editorials, since he too feared that the newspaper would suffer economic reprisals from the whites of the community.

Davis balanced controversy with citizenship, and forever returned to the principles of democracy, the interconnectedness of the fate of America and all its citizens, striving to develop more consciousness in his readers, trying to make right the previous arrogant neglect of African American history and the effects of cultural genocide. He agreed with Alain Locke who said:

> Democracy itself is obstructed and stagnated to the extent that any of its channels are closed. Indeed they cannot be selectively closed. . . . We realize that we cannot be undone without America's undoing. . . . More and more, however, an intelligent realization of the great discrepancy between the American social creed and the American social practice forces upon the Negro the taking of the moral advantage that is his.   (Peplow and Davis 396)

Davis constantly exposed the discrepancies between America's moral code and the immoral reality of democracy.

Another area where Davis spoke out in his editorials was against capital punishment and what he called the legalized killing "long used against the blacks as an object lesson to 'keep them in their place,'" foreshadowing contemporary accusations of genocide and arguments by black militants that African Americans are expendable and victims of the ever-expanding corporate prison dynasties. He was particularly incensed by a case where a fourteen-year-old youth was tried and sentenced to death in the electric chair for entering the home of a couple in a rural community while they lay sleeping. He neither harmed them nor stole from them. Davis reported how the youth was "railroaded to the gallows and electric chair on evidence that would have freed white prisoners"; he fervently opposed this form of "socially sanctioned murder," commenting that "throughout Dixie, and in part of the North, lie the barren bones of humans who were put to death mainly because they were black and helpless; how can I support capital punishment when one of its major uses has been as a ready servant of racism?" (*Livin'* 188-189). He was outraged by the many brutal and senseless murders of African Americans who were killed sometimes by law-enforcement personnel because they dared to stand up against racism and discrimination, to fight for their human rights. He knew that the brutality against African Americans was not reported accurately, if at all, by the white press.

A case in point is another particular incident which evoked Davis's editorial wrath and attracted international attention: the 1931 Angelo Herndon trial concerning a young African American labor organizer and Communist.

> [Herndon] led a march of starving black and white Depression victims on the state capitol to demand food and shelter--an act of unbelievable courage. For this offense to the status quo he was arrested and sentenced to death by the white power structure under an antiquated anti-sedition law dating from the 1890's . . . This intended act of legal barbarism was so outrageous that even students and professors from white Emory University and Georgia Tech . . . actively joined in the Herndon defense.   (*Livin'* 194)

This episode reflects Davis's support for Herndon, although he was sometimes critical of the activities of the Communists during his stay in Atlanta. However, his later association with members of the Communist Party in Chicago, with the Honolulu labor movement, and his subsequent editorials in the union newspaper *The Honolulu Record* probably were influenced by the Herndon and Scottsboro affairs.

Such flagrant patterns of inequality and injustice toward African Americans propelled a considerable number of African American intellectuals to become extremely cynical and critical of democracy after the fall of the Negro (Harlem) Renaissance of the twenties. Scholars Michael W. Peplow and Arthur P. Davis note in *The New Negro Renaissance*:

> On the other hand, the "vision of despair" was fairly new. It suggests a kind of futilitarianism not found before in Negro literature. ...the kind of desperate rejection and repudiation of Western civilization that one finds in the literature of the new Black Renaissance of the sixties.   (4)

It is not surprising that a number were attracted to the egalitarian ideology of the Communist Party.

While he was in Atlanta, Davis assumed the role of the outspoken Race Man, using his words and fearless attitude to fight for justice, equality, and access to democracy and the egalitarian people's domain. As he affirms the African Americans' patriotism, his plea is for acceptance. Alain Locke notes:

> The Negro mind reaches out as yet to nothing but American wants, American ideas. But this forced attempt to build his Americanism on race values is a unique social experiment, and its ultimate success is impossible except through the fullest sharing of American culture and institutions.
>   (Peplow and Davis, 395)

Davis sees America as a social experiment which will fail unless the African Americans are included in its institutions.

In his editorials Davis called for unity of all African Americans, cooperation between African American leaders with different strategies, better public school education throughout the South, and more and better-trained African American teachers. By meeting these objectives, he believed that a psychological healing could occur:

> Up to the present one may adequately describe the Negro's
> inner objectives as an attempt to repair a damaged group
> psychology and reshape a warped social perspective. . . . In
> this new group psychology we note the lapse of sentimental
> appeal, then the development of a more positive self-respect
> and self-reliance; the repudiation of social dependence, and
> then the gradual recovery from hyper-sensitiveness and
> "touchy" nerves, the repudiation of the double standard of
> judgment with its special philanthropic allowances and then
> the sturdier desire for objective and scientific appraisal; and
> finally the rise from social disillusionment to race pride,
> from the sense of social debt to the responsibilities of social
> contribution, and offsetting the necessary working and
> common sense acceptance of restricted conditions, the belief
> in ultimate esteem and recognition. Therefore, the Negro
> today wishes to be known for what he is.
>
>   (Peplow and Davis 395)

In his columns, Davis also criticized the African Americans for imitating
the whites, and for being too dependent on their philanthropy. He attacked
the cultural imperialism and systematic destruction of African American
dignity and self-determination.

Although he admired the principles of equality of the Communist Party,
he resented a certain opportunism. He denounced the exploitative character
of the Communist Party, using African American issues and problems to
gain a foothold in the African American community. His October 2, 1932
"Touring the World" column criticizes the Party in the context of the
Scottsboro Boys trial.

> It is not at all amazing that the little Scottsboro mother fell for
> the sweet bunk of oily tongues Red. Mrs. Wright was used
> to being treated as a Negro, not as a woman. Until the Reds
> came along, the white people she knew called her "Ada"
> or maybe "Sal" or maybe they spoke of her as "that nigger
> woman." With the Communists came respect. She became
> "Mrs. Wright" and the white man and women who carried
> high the Red flag were not too proud to even sit at the same

table and eat with her.   (1931-1933)

He gently criticizes an African American mother for being seduced by the "sweet bunk" and "oily tongues" of the Communists, understandably seduced by politeness and respect when all of her life she has only received the opposite treatment.

Davis tried to balance the perspective of the African American struggle. He sought equality in different areas: socio-economic, political and cultural. In his editorial columns, Davis said that the vote alone would not lead to the race's salvation. Instead, he called for a program of African American economic development and self-sufficiency modeled on those of Booker T. Washington and Marcus Garvey, and articulating those of the Black Muslims. On September 25, 1932, "Touring the World" announced:

> The real honest to goodness truth is this: Neither the Republicans nor the Democrats, the right to vote or disfranchisement, will [sic] must come from within. That solution must be founded on dollars and cents. Until the Negro can find himself financially and get a foothold, even a million votes in the hands of each Duskymerican will avail him naught.   (1931-1933)

He critiqued the police force--as later the Black Panther Party would do in the 1960's--the chain gang system which was often dependent on the labor of illegally arrested and innocent African American men who were then used by the state and private industry for hard labor "to pay off their bail," which many took years to do.

During his stay in Atlanta, Davis critiqued the Presidential "black cabinet" (Robert Weaver and Mary McLeod Bethune, Roi Ottley, Ralph Bunche and William Hastie [Katz, 427-428]) for their submissive and accommodating attitudes, and he even used the word "terrorism" in describing the treatment against African Americans by whites (Katz 427-8).

He discussed the controversial spectrum of racial attitudes and strategies within the African American community itself: the gradualists, the accommodationists, the chauvinists, the educationalists, the assimilationists, the individualists, and the radicals--all striving for a more equitable society, each separately losing force and effectiveness due to their lack of unity.

Like Alain Locke, he called for more progressive solutions to contemporary problems.

> For the younger generation is vibrant with a new psychology; the new spirit is awake in the masses, and under the very eyes of the professional observers is transforming what has been a perennial problem into the progressive phases of contemporary Negro life.   (Peplow and Davis 387)

The optimism of the period was evident as African Americans reached to improve their lives.

Davis critiqued black-on-black violence, calling for a ban on concealed weapons, especially knives, which evoked a furor of response from the African American community, many justifying the knives as weapons of self-defense against whites (*Livin'* 192). The irony was that most African Americans caused casualties on each other and not whites due to the segregated communities, oppressive conditions which caused people to lash out against those closest to them, and the many restrictive laws including those prohibiting being in many white communities after dark. He attacked the daily injustices experienced by African Americans, as black lives seemed to be worth less than white lives in the judicial system.

> I pointed to the unwritten code which seemed to guide white officials: if a nigger kills a white man, that's murder and automatically means the death penalty; if whitey kills a nigger that's justifiable homicide, and if one nigger kills another, that's good riddance.   (*Livin'* 192)

At times, Davis was discouraged when he saw the mass acceptance of the ideology of white supremacy and racism in Dixie in the early 1930's, but he never gave up his attack. He used journalism as a weapon to expose the white power structure, a countermeasure to the white press, a vehicle to instruct the public on African American history and to provide a support system of racial pride and dignity.

Davis wanted radical change in the South, and although the masses were listening more to the voice of the New Negroes, the leadership was not prepared for social revolution. Society was not yet ready to accept on a large scale the radical measures and actions necessary to create a new order.

In writing in *The New Negro*, Peplow and Davis comment:

> It [race work] has not abated, however, if we are to gauge by the present tone and temper of the Negro press, or by the shift in popular support from the officially recognized and orthodox spokesmen to those of the independent, popular, and often radical type who are unmistakable symptoms of a new order.   (392)

Even the National Association for the Advancement of Colored People (NAACP), already famous for its legal fights for justice and equality, was considered a radical group in the thirties, and not then permitted to exist in most areas of the South. Davis critiqued the fear and inertia in the African American community and then considered options:

> Nevertheless, we did have the right to start legal action against murderers in official uniforms. Whether we obtained convictions was not the key issue. What we would have demonstrated was a willingness to fight back, and even if it were no more than an inconvenience to the accused, it would have served as a deterrent, with the strength of the deterrent determined by the numbers of those who pooled their resources to take action. There was no way to convince me that several thousand outraged blacks would not have had a sobering effect on future policies of the Establishment. Later in the 1950's and 1960's, it worked in Dixie. . . . But instead we did nothing.   (*Livin'* 193)

Davis espoused views of unity and organized resistance in his columns when he reported and exposed the "slaughter" (murder) of African Americans by law officers.

He hated the lies of silence, and lamented the inaction, fear, and intimidation of the African American second-class citizens who did nothing but accept oppression and exploitation overwhelmed by their sense of powerlessness and shame:

> As a group in 1931 we were black defeatists. When you stuck your neck out, you did it alone. We were grateful for any victories, but if you lost, the reaction was "you shoulda known you couldn't do that in the South."   (*Livin'* 194)

However, his fearless and outspoken editorials did not go unnoticed by the National Bureau of Censorship whose agents followed his writing career on an almost weekly basis for more than 20 years.

Despite intimidation from the government agency, Davis was not thwarted and remained persistent in his efforts to rip the veil of polite tolerance from the democratic system. In his editorials and his poetry, he exposed the neurosis and collective mass psychosis of a society conditioned by patriarchy, cultural complexes, legal practices, and social customs that resulted in aberrant behavior, misdirected animosity, hate, and all manner of inequalities.

Other African American writers were also criticizing America's hypocritical democracy at this time. A contemporary of Davis, Saunders Redding wrote *On Being Negro*:

> I should have probably been an unquestioning worshipper at the shrine of the social order and economic development into which I was born. . . . What was wrong was that I and people like me and thousands of others who might have my ability and aspiration, were refused permission to be a part of this world.   (123)

Redding, also addressed the oppressive racial creed and its consequences describing

> Negro-ness as a kind of super consciousness that directs thinking, that dictates action and that perverts the expression of instinctual drives which are salutary and humanitarian: the civic drive, the societal drive, the sex and love drive.
>
> *Negro* 222)

The pervasive injuries of a racist society were felt and commented upon regularly by African American writers.

Living in the South, Davis missed the live music of Chicago, the blues and jazz which portrayed so vividly the feelings of powerlessness, rage, frustration, and the saving humor of the African American experience. Music traditionally offered one of the few avenues through which African Americans could express their protest and themselves. Fortunately he found a radio station to which he could listen at nights which sent broadcasts of such greats from the North as the Mills Brothers, Cab Calloway's band, Jimmie Lunceford, Count Basie, and Louis Armstrong. He recalled one day the lyrics of a blues tune which "sardonically pictured relationships in Dixie, especially in rural areas: 'Nigger an' a white man playin' seven up, Nigger win the money but scared to pick it up" (*Livin'* 199).

It was also in Atlanta that Davis began to drink regularly and he reports that the Georgia bootleg was "good and hearty". When he describes the bootleggers, he portrays them as members of the secondary economy, extremely skilled at staying out of jail by keeping the police well-supplied. He notes with irony how although illegal, they functioned as an almost legitimate business, providing delivery of their moonshine, and even recycling their bottles. Davis said, "I was always ready for it [moonshine] long before it was ready for me" (*Livin'* 205).

Practically and economically speaking, because of limited employment opportunities, many African Americans joined the dual labor market not reporting their earnings to the federal government, since they had to devise alternative means to make ends meet. Women who were untrained took in laundry, ironed, and worked as cooks and maids. Men often resorted to bootlegging. Davis also discovered that "the numbers game was popular in Atlanta just as it was in New York. . . . Chicago, of course, was a policy town" (*Livin'* 206). The hopes of hitting it lucky and making a relative great deal of money was alluring to many African Americans who had no other possibility of ever earning more than two dollars per day.

This atmosphere of intimidation carried over into the social realm as well. The sexual mythology, which originated during the days of slavery and which continued to mushroom, created a sickness in society which carries over until today. Miscegenation, the mixture of races through sexual intercourse, was identified with immorality. Redding speaks of the perversion:

> The unrestricted use of the Negro woman as sex mate and mammy during slavery did a strange thing to the white man's mind. It filled it with anxiety, guilt and a grotesque exaggeration of the Negro male's sexual equipment - an equipment from which the white male has felt compelled to protect white womanhood ever since.   (*Negro* 112)

Similarly, Gunnar Myrdal says in his work *An American Dilemma*, "The necessity to protect the white female against this fancied prowess of the male Negro is a fixed constellation in the ethos of America" (114).

Indeed, the fundamental expression of human inequality to which the Negro was subjected struck at the deepest roots of personal dignity and self-respect, for the white woman with the African American man was considered morally depraved and sexually abnormal, whereas the white man with the African American woman was accepted. In speaking of miscegenation, Davis writes:

> Miscegenation was still primarily a one-way street in the South. A white man could bed black women with impunity, but the reverse was a signal for violence. In fact, more than one black man has been murdered for consorting with a black woman looked upon by some honky as his private possession. Conversely, there have been lynchings because some white gal literally threw herself at a brother and, to save her own hide when the relationship was exposed, yelled rape.   (*Livin'* 199)

These myths of Negro-white blood mixture resulting in alleged biological, moral, and social inferiority applied to anyone having a single drop of Negro blood. They served as an effective restraint, especially regarding white women, against miscegenation.

Davis analyzed the vicious dialectic of sex and power in which some southern whites felt they must even arm themselves against the enemies of racial purity and white supremacy:

> This widespread belief in the sexual prowess of "black bucks" was undoubtedly a major reason why Southern white males might murder a soul stud if he was heard to make even a verbal pass at a white woman; they did not really feel they must "protect the honor of white womanhood," but they had an almost pathological fear that by comparison they would be judged sexually inferior.   (*Livin'* 200)

African American men and women lacked rights of sexual freedom, self-defense, and protection of their families, and were thus victims of white dominance, whims, desires, and fantasy. Davis wrote of the resulting psychoses:

> Because it was against both the law and custom, relationships between mahogany males and chalk chicks had an almost irresistible fascination for many Southerners. Rick Roberts, the *World* cartoonist who could draw fabulous females, picked up sizeable fees from leading white Atlanta businessmen for creating large pictures of gorgeous nude blondes and gigantic well-tooled black males engaging in every imaginable kind of sex activity. These high priests of Nordic supremacy perversely got tremendous erotic kicks from looking at pictures of intimacies that would have made them pop their blood vessels had they witnessed them in the flesh.   (*Livin'* 199-200)

Police were quick to intimidate African American men for even being with lighter-skinned African American women who looked white. To escape these intrusive racial pressures, some African Americans chose to leave the South or cross over into the white world.

Because of the rigid segregation practices in the South, even travel was an ordeal for African Americans. Whenever they traveled, it was prudent to establish a network of connections just in order to maintain some dignity and have a decent place to eat and sleep. Thus, Davis met many distinguished African Americans passing through the South who shared their experiences of discrimination and racism in the system of "Dixie Etiquette" while staying overnight at the homes [hotel] of friends or "contacts." For example, George Schuyler, who was later to favorably review Davis's poetry books, was an "iconoclastic columnist" of the *Pittsburgh Courier* who defied the "Southern Etiquette of Mississippi" with impertinence and earned the dangerous, if respected by African Americans, label of "sassy nigger." He was the kind of Northern black to whom Southern whites liked to teach a lesson (*Livin'* 200-201). For his part, Davis tried hard to avoid confrontations with southern whites.

As for Davis's personal life with women, love, and sex, Atlanta was the place of initiation, where he met Thelma Boyd, the woman he married and with whom he would spend several years and who would introduce him into a new world of sexual pleasures, multiple partners, and erotica.

Before arriving in Atlanta, Davis had been engaged to marry a young teacher of chocolate complexion named Gladys back in Kansas. After his first year, when Roy Wilkins (later head of the NAACP) offered him an editorial position at the Kansas City *Call*, "one of the nation's largest and most influential weeklies," Davis accepted the job with the idea of marrying Gladys. But, as soon as Scott heard that Davis was planning to leave the *World*, he immediately offered him another raise with the promise of a third, thereby changing the fate of Davis. Davis remained in Atlanta, told Gladys, his fiancee in Kansas, that he had an incurable disease (he always had a flair for the dramatic as well as the manipulative), and finally, when she volunteered to come to Atlanta and nurse him until the end, confessed to her that he was going to marry another woman, Thelma (*Livin'* 203).

However, in spring 1933, Davis's life took another turn when he received a letter from Chicago from a woman patron of the arts named Frances Norton Manning. When he opened it, he later said, the experience was like opening "Pandora's Box" and he was introduced to "the most fantastic female" he had ever known (215). Frances was a wealthy white woman who had seen and been impressed by Davis's poem, "Chicago's Congo" and wrote him a letter of praise. Although Davis had written no poetry since he had arrived in Atlanta, he quickly became inspired to write again, and sent the poems to Frances. Before long, they were corresponding often, and Frances proposed to find a publisher for Davis if he readied a collection. Davis was flattered and soon sexually curious, especially when she sent photos of herself and informed him that she was "married to a yachtsman who was `a husband in name only.'" (*Livin'* 215)

Although the relationship began with a mutual appreciation for poetry, his autobiography explains that it rapidly changed character:

> Frankly, I was completely vulnerable to the overtures of an aggressive white woman. Raw from the biting lash of Dixie racism, it soothed me to smile to myself and think, "you crackers believe I'm some kind of ape, but emotionally involved with me is one of your own precious women, and a woman of obvious culture at that.   (*Livin'* 216)

The work contains Davis's admission that "revenge against the white world

. . . was originally a major ingredient in my relationship with Frances. But as I came to know her, this angle vanished" (*Livin'* 216). When Davis went to the World's Fair in Chicago that Spring 1934, he met Frances, her son, and friends, and she met Davis's step-father and his wife (Davis's mother had passed away). However, he returned to Atlanta to the *World* and Thelma, instead of accepting Frances' offer to go with her to France (*Livin'* 216).

Shortly after Davis's return to Atlanta, Scott was fatally shot. The heir who subsequently assumed control of the paper "lacked the daring and vision of W.A." (*Livin'* 217), and Davis lost interest in the *World*.

Soon thereafter, the Depression arrived in Atlanta, and Davis decided after some soul searching to return to Chicago for a visit. When he arrived and visited Frances, she revealed that she had hired a private investigator to follow his wife, Thelma. The detective had uncovered information on Thelma's "amorous escapades" and unconventional liaisons. Davis was angered to discover her infidelities and admitted to a chauvinistic response, being "hung up on the double standard". He adds, "I felt perfectly justified in owning a harem, and also righteously indignant if my spouse looked twice at another male. . . . I decided to remain in Chicago and sent a wire to the *World* and Thelma" (*Livin'* 218).

From this time on for many years to come, Davis would seek to affirm his manhood through his job, women, writing, and politics. In certain aspects of his life, he assumed the role of the picaresque hero, an African American intellectual, poet, and journalist, trying to chart a course of blackness. He was to become a key figure in the Chicago Renaissance, using the politics of journalism and sex to effect political and social change.

CHAPTER 3
Revolutionary Aesthetics: Davis and African American Writing

Let the jazz stuff fall like hail on king and truck driver, queen and laundress, lord and laborer, banker and bum/ Let it fall in London, Moscow, Paris, Hong Kong, Cairo, Buenos Aires, Chicago, Sydney/ Let it rub hard thighs, let it be molten fire in the veins of dancers/ Make 'em shout a crazy jargon of hot hossanas to a fiddle-faced god/ Send Dios, Jehovah, Gott, Allah, Buddha past in a high stepping cake walk/ Do that thing, jazz band!

(Davis, *Black Man's Verse* 35)

The tradition of an emancipatory aesthetic organized around themes of protest and freedom has been a reality for most African Americans since their arrival in the New World. In the early days, this empowering aesthetic was largely manifested through an oral tradition which included music, folklore, and religion, and later through written literature, most of which was added in the twentieth century. Frank Marshall Davis writes within and contributed to this tradition.

To Davis and other African American writers, African American literature is often a literature of survival and necessity, a literature produced to perform a political function as much as, if not more than, to embody an aesthetic one. As Henry Lewis Gates argues, this political function has been to critique white racism and, simultaneously, to demonstrate the intellectual capacity of all African American people through the agency of the artistic products of the writer who becomes a voice of the group, presuming a collective I or we (xviii).

During the 1930's and 1940's, the African American writer like Davis, was often considered a pariah, devalued by the white literary world because of his/her non-traditional writing style and content subject matter, and separated from other African Americans, both the masses, and the *bourgeoisie* as well because of his portrayal at times of the Black world. He has been a co-victim of race and class.

Intermittently, African American writers have found small audiences for their books. For example, since early in the twentieth century, African American writers have been in the vanguard in terms of using experimental forms, rhythms, topics, intonations, phonological elements, dialect and unique cultural unpredictable similes, metaphors, themes, often breaking the barriers between poetry and prose, as in Jean Toomer's revolutionary book *Cane*. However, rarely does such a writer enjoy the national acclaim, prestige, and economic success of even mediocre white writers. Rather, whites, as publishers, writers, and producers have usually profited the most from stories portraying the African American experience.

Nonetheless, the role of the African American writer remains pivotal and essential, not only to African American history, but to American history, culture, and political science as well. The African American writer is the maker and carrier of myths, fables, tales, riddles, poetry, novels, plays, and songs for the community and now the world. In Davis's time and before, names and egos were less developed than values and/or a moral message. Davis, like other African American writers, tells of the tension and struggle between the oppressor and the oppressed, the strong and the weak, the wealthy and the poor. Typically, the oppressor is most frequently represented by the white male and his institutions of privilege, sometimes portrayed metaphorically as large animals who are outwitted by smaller, weaker, quick-witted ones.

Davis, like most African American writers, acts as a chronicler and a catalyst for change, apart from the mainstream American experience. The separation is born of necessity in order to more accurately observe, impartially record, and when appropriate, imaginatively recreate the life and cultural experience of Black people and their community, issues, and ideals. It is a double alienation, that of being African American and that of being apart from the group. The African American writer has the responsibility of proclaiming his/her truth, and simultaneously recognizing his or her Otherness, in order to render the most objective yet original presentation possible. The writer's alienation and/or isolation is also due to the knowledge and understanding, particularly privy to the intellectual, of the ironies and tragedy of the African American experience over the last 350 years. Indeed, to stand apart and write is another way to wrestle with the phenomena of pain of exclusion and disrespect, in order to empower oneself and to affirm one's being in a hostile environment.

Thus, according to C. W. E. Bigsby in his collection of essays entitled *The Black American Writer*, a unique connection exists between (1) the African American writer like Davis who is the observer/chronicler of life and (2) his personal life experience as an African American. Life in the Black community reveals a constant socioeconomic and political tension in the struggle for self- determination and dignified survival, and the writer is a witness to this conflict. Consequently, the African American writer in his or her portrayal of life often feels a personal responsibility to reaffirm the self and society, and to quote Eldridge Cleaver, "to reclaim the shattered psyches and culture" (27).

A sincere writer like Davis can write his vision, enable analysis, and produce an interpretive rendering of the gap between the truth of African American culture and the biased illusion of non-African Americans. Davis seeks to move beyond the superficial, minstrel, silhouette mask of African American people and culture toward a positive black aesthetic vision and model, in order to represent the humane features of the black face, heart, and spirit. He sees and understands the necessity to create the whole person, not just a cameo of an exotic other and/or a happy if oppressed past (*Black American* 28).

James Tuttleton writes that the dilemma of the African American writer is multi-faceted. The major issues are various, and any one writer could not be reasonably expected to be the spokesperson for the group. Diverse writers such as Frank Marshall Davis, Richard Wright, and Langston Hughes discussed common issues in their writing such as: the nature of integration, assimilation versus nationalism, the African American family and relationships between black power and political power, the role of the African American as redeemer of American society, non-violence versus militancy as a strategy of African American progress, the specialness of the African American personality and culture, the debt or reparations owed the African American by white society, the relationship between African American art and propaganda, and the rate of historical process versus freedom (246).

The voices of African American writers like Davis have also reflected similar tones of frustration and outrage. Common themes range from racism, violence (overt and covert), the politics of color, miscegenation, corruption, crime, and the exploitation of blacks by the powers of big business, government, and the military. According to Bardolph, other common themes include slave insurrections, folk tales, "passing," gender issues of African American men and women, upper and lower class urban life, the West Indian Caribbean environment, education and poverty, discrimination, and the plight of the much darker-skinned person in a color-conscious Black community (204). The voice and themes also reflect the social origins, education, writing styles, preoccupations, employment, and attitudes of the writer like Davis toward the problems of living and writing in an often powerless black community surrounded by a dominant white patriarchal society.

One task of the African American writer that Davis does well is to explore the dynamics and philosophy of black culture and to contextualize his perceptions of reality. His will to balance a concept of dignified identity with the faults and flaws of humanity is admirable as he strives to create a variety of images of Black people and to deconstruct the national paradigm of white superiority. It is his way to help heal the distortions and wounds of racism, a destructive force, sometimes invisible, in the fabric of democracy that was historically incorporated and institutionalized into American literature.

Davis felt that a writer must see and transmit the particularity of his or her own cultural values and the self which is constituted by those values. This approach can be liberating and permit the writer to participate in the reconstruction of a more realistic democratic paradigm of pluralism says Abdul Jan Mohamed (83). Another function and responsibility of a writer like Davis was to create a post-modern narrative of democracy as global harmony and unity following the model of equality of Dr. Martin Luther King, Jr. "based on the content of their character, not the color of their skins," nor on creed, gender, or religious preference.

In terms of the Third World's literary dialogue with western culture (which includes African Americans and other minority groups), Davis exemplifies the writer's attempt to transform the Europeans' prior negation of colonized cultures through a creative synthesis: the adoption and modification of Western language and artistic forms, using culture, indigenous and dialect languages and oral literary forms. Jan Mohamed maintains, "The domain of literary and cultural syncretism belongs not to colonialist and neo-colonist writers, but increasingly to Third World artists" (84-85). He also addresses the writer's problem of identifying positively with an alterity, and the necessity to "overcome barriers of racial difference," particularly because the canon of African American writers during the 1930's and 1940's was especially limited and full of barriers for people like Davis, creating excessive friction and lending exacerbating frustration to the creative process (Jan Mohammed 78). "Difference" to some African American writers of the period may have meant dependence, subordination, subservience and inferiority, but Davis rejected anything which supported and justified a mythology of metaphysical difference based again on the colonialist ideology of racial hierarchy and white supremacy.

Davis saw the necessity to rescue "native", i.e. Black, culture from prejudged allegorical closure of "imaginary" texts which exploit stereotypes and trivialize the lives of those with darker skins and little education. He believed it is the responsibility of the black writer to destroy the colonialist discourse and negative stereotypes sometimes embodied in the plantation tradition and picaresque tales, thereby achieving what Jan Mohamed labels a transcendent or metaphysical identity that places all characters and subjects in the drama of humanity.

Davis understood and explored the consequences of emotional demands on the minority writer when it comes to confronting the phenomenal difference of the Other. He sought and wrote of the value that Jan Mohamed describes "in the pluralism and syncretism of the American experience" (76-77), and tried to eschew the temptation to represent the "Other" as superior or inferior.

After his sojourn in Atlanta, Davis became a labor activist in Chicago and later Hawai`i where he attacked capitalism and its alienating power of regulating wages and exchange value when it takes the forms of corruption, competition, greed, and the desire to control at the expense of the Other.

Indeed, many African American writers like Davis write directly or indirectly about how the values of democracy are subverted almost daily by callous competition, the ruthless upper class, and the profit motives of capitalism, especially visible in black and minority communities in all institutions in American society. As members of an oppressed minority, these writers have witnessed and experienced the pain, frustration, and anger as their communities have been poisoned by exploitation, discrimination and environmental waste, tainted by poverty, and humiliated by the enforced conformity to the Anglo-American models of patriarchy, competition, individualism, aesthetics, physical beauty standards, and materialism. Davis, the writer, bears witness to the blatant rejection of collective empowerment.

As Bigsby notes in *The Black American Writer*, the African American writer like Davis is acutely aware of the need for a rigorous new analysis of contemporary reality, because he or she is an archetype of the identity crisis and alienation experienced by many Americans. The metaphorical role of the African American writer can thus give integrity to and rejuvenate the national psyche. "To say this is not to suggest that the black writer is pandering to a fashionable universality but rather to acknowledge that in modern times and particularly since the Second World War the black writer as pariah has gained a painful relevance." (26) The works of Davis for example are not anguished cries for integration but dispassionate analyses of contemporary reality.

Davis, as African American writer, weaves his poetry atonally through the aesthetic labyrinth of Western literature creating new designs, styles, sounds, tones, and rhythms to incorporate the ethnic, historical, and cultural traditions and orality into a transformative alternative aesthetic.

In the Foreword of *The Transforming Power of Language: The Poetry of Adrienne Rich*, Miriam Diaz-Diocaretz speaks of the aesthetic spectrum of poetic discourse as including the following: links with tradition, originality, and the de-territorialization and re-territorialization of language (10). The African American literary tradition creates an aesthetic discourse transformed and personalized by seizing the traditional language and recreating it from a particular cultural historical perspective of being in the world, thereby making a blueprint for a unique aesthetic and positive sense of identity.

Bearing in mind this aesthetic spectrum, Davis, by re-visioning and reinterpreting the world from a new and active perspective, formulates a narrative of collective hope and survival in his writings. He puts aside the "victim" mentality, and explains and sometimes interprets the African American reality and calls for survival against a modern background of oppression. He uses themes of courage and overcoming obstacles in face of exposure to environmental racism, destruction, and decay, political repression, and economic stagnation. He addresses the Black community writing of the declining role of religion and the church, the debilitating effects of poverty, the disorder and decay of cities, the threat and effect of war on the American values of democracy, unity, perseverance, patience and the eroding influence of race on the national character.

Davis builds a sense of empowerment within his readers through deconstruction of traditional metaphors, paradigms, and ideologies, connected with the word "black" and its derivatives which he explains function as a metonym for evil, negativity and as an "ontological symbol" that is the quintessential signifier of what oppression means in the United States." He replaces the negative associations with positive ones such as black is beautiful, strong, creative, the Earth, and Africa. He also deconstructs the word "white" and its derivatives which traditionally function as a metonym for purity, goodness, patriarchy, power, and Christianity. Thus, the responsible African American writer like Davis can reconstruct reality and a negative self-image and portray African Americans as active, dignified and positive forces. bell hooks, on the findings of black theologian, James Cone, comments on his call for the deconstruction of whiteness, and writes:

> Encouraging readers to break with white supremacy as an "epistemological standpoint by which they come to know the world, he (Cone) insisted that "whiteness" as a sign be interrogated. He wanted the public to learn how to distinguish that racism which is about overt prejudice and domination from more subtle forms of white supremacy... Whether they are able to enact it as a lived practice or not, many white folks active in anti-racist struggle today are able to acknowledge that all whites (as well as everyone else within white supremacist culture) have learned to over-value "whiteness" even as they simultaneously learned to devalue

> blackness. They understand the need, at least intellectually,
> to alter their thinking. Central to this process of unlearning
> white supremacist attitudes and values is the deconstruction
> of the category of "whiteness."   (*Talkin' Back* 12)

An African American writer like Davis constantly deconstructs whiteness by choosing new images and themes, deviating from the traditional tenets of white superiority. He pushes language beyond the reified limits traditionally acceptable by the national academic community and society, for example, he uses the word "black" in the tile of his first book of poetry, *Black Man's Verse*, in spite of its pejorative meaning at the time.

Davis and other African American writers recognized the need to create a language devoid of the racial negativity typically directed toward African Americans throughout society. For example, Davis sifted through old intellectuals' words such as savage, black, heathen, power, love, friendship, community, and sexual to understand and critique their contextual and habitual usage in relation to African Americans. Davis found it necessary to explore the worlds of white supremacy and black inferiority to better understand the reasons for continuing oppression through writing and word usage.

Davis recognized the need to move from stereotypes to a fuller more complex approach to representation and characterization, in order to express the complex experience of which he himself has been a victim (Tuttleton 248).

Davis, like many other African American writers, uses language as a weapon to fight against inequality and to aggressively assert his place as a citizen of the USA and a valuable contributor to the literary canon. Since the African American experience has traditionally been largely a socio-political experience of alienation and exclusion based on color, a writer such as Frank Marshall Davis uses the written and spoken word to expose and break down the political and social walls of inequality. The black writer must be observant, analytical, and sensitive. Themes and sympathies are often with the economically and racially oppressed, the dispossessed and suffering masses, and the revolutionaries. The indictment of white America as imperialistic, paternalistic, and racist is not surprisingly a common theme.

Davis chooses the white male as a metonym of power, violence, government, control, exploitation, war, politics, and patriarchy. The dialectic between black and white, rich and poor, powerful and powerless reappears often in the lives and literature of Black writers.

The resolution is freedom and self-determination, a collective empowerment for African Americans. Thus, the tasks of the writer become: to break down barriers; to destroy the preordained African American place as subordinate in society; to create and cultivate consciousness, a will to change, a shield against violence, and a positive self-image. Davis as writer portrays and seeks to transform the alienation and suffering of poor blacks, minorities, and laborers into a successful united community. His aim is to transform and transcend racism, but sometimes the consciousness which he evokes does not go beyond one of resentment and rage toward the oppressors. The consequences of such rage and consciousness led to a surge in Black Nationalism, a consciousness of victimization, and a defensiveness founded on mistrust. Bardolph writes in *Vanguard*:

> It is true, however, that in time, some exploited groups attempted to overcome the effects of racial oppression through cultural revitalization and nationalistic movements, which frequently develop in conjunction with efforts to establish some degree of political and economic autonomy. And the more minority members press for their independence, the more likely racist views toward the dominant group could mature.   (40)

Davis wanted to educate his readers to the forces that activate and perpetuate status, wealth, and power and he wrote to offer solutions. A half century later, scholar Henry Louise Gates said that there is still a great need in America to develop the history of African American thought, because the relationship of African American literature to history is not like the art and prose of either the dominant Euro-American group or other less-oppressed groups. Recalling that African American literature is unique in that it arose from purpose or necessity (Gates, xxix), Gates echoed Davis saying the voice of African Americans is an affirming voice signaling survival in spite of the institutionalized efforts at exclusion and cultural genocide. By presenting the African American experience, Davis, as African American writer, creates a new writing and ideology that valorizes the black experience.

The tone of Davis as African American writer ranges from anger to frustration, from despair to racial pride, from compassion to a call for unity. He vaunts themes of compassion, empathy, strength, courage, and survival. His modus operandus is often evangelical, to use a term of Jean-Paul Sartre (11), because it announces the good news of blackness and reveals the hitherto hidden rich black soul. Davis follows the evangelical model in his search to awaken a commitment to a proud black identity, a new race consciousness, a sense of empowerment and transformation.

Traditionally the African American writers assiduously avoided the themes of violence and sex in the African American male characters in order to deconstruct the mythological stereotype of the violent black male, until the works of Richard Wright during the forties and Davis in his novel *Sex Rebel Black* written under a pseudonym in the fifties. Both men addressed sexual and racial issues that were not published in their early works, speaking of their hostility toward the white world and white males in particular, and the use of sex as a weapon.

In *Black Man's Verse*, *I Am the American Negro*, and *47th Street*, Davis uses a sardonic and sometimes angry tone in many of his poems. One cause for the angry, negative tone often found in African American writings, according to Cornel West, is the continuing cultural and political strife in the daily life of the African American that is a result of white supremacy. West affirms that the writer not only describes and represents the African American experience but also aspires toward a "demystifying hermeneutic" of that experience (11). Although West is primarily concerned with African American religious philosophy and theological socialism, he expresses concerns in other areas relevant to the physical, spiritual, and psychological well-being African Americans and their community. For example, he sees that there are two basic challenges confronting African Americans and the black writer: self-image and self-determination. The former he describes as the perennial human attempt to define who and what one is, the issue of self-identity. The latter is the political struggle to gain significant control over the major institutions that regulate people's lives. In other words, according to West, culture and politics must always be viewed in close relationship to each other (22), a perspective shared by Davis and many African American writers.

A quarter of a century after Davis's death, West affirms Davis's perspective that the major function of African American critical thought is to reshape the contours of American history and to provide a new self-understanding through the African American experience. The intellectual attempts to describe and demystify cultural and social practices and offer solutions to the still urgent problems of race and class besetting African Americans (22).

When West describes African American literary thought, he writes:

> Critical in character and historical in content, whose aim is to uncover old blindnesses about the complexity and richness of the African American experience. Its first task is to put forward an over-arching interpretive framework for the inescapable problematic of any such inquiry: What is the relationship between the African American and European elements in this experience....Look at the intricate transactions between marginalized Africans for the most part excluded from behavioral modes and material benefits of European life and the American culture in which these dark people were both participants and victims.   (22)

West speaks of the continuing need for genealogical inquiry into the cultural and linguistic roots of African American thought, in order to provide a theoretical reconstruction and evaluation of African American responses to white supremacy. He encourages a dialogical encounter between blacks and whites in order to demystify the deep misunderstanding and ignorance each side has of the other, with an aim to provide a political prescription for specific praxis in the continuing struggle for liberation (23).

Therefore, in addition to the economic, political, and psychological roots of the ideology of white supremacy which has shaped the African American encounter with the modern and postmodern world, the African American writer must continue to find and destroy the complex configurations of controlling metaphors, categories, and norms which shape and mold this paradigm of white superiority in the media, institutions and all aspects of American life. In so doing, the writer affirms an alternative black aesthetic which includes aspects of what West labels the "prophesy" tradition.

Like Frank Marshall Davis, Locke, Redding, and later West and Gates refute the assumption that there is no black aesthetic. Davis is committed to privilege the African American aesthetic in all of its neglected complexity and ideological commitment in the ethnic history of African Americans.

Davis writes in the Introduction to *47th Street* that he wants to capture the heart, authenticity, and soul of the African American community. In describing the poetry of Davis's friend and contemporary Langston Hughes, Gates demonstrates how Hughes experiments with the African American vernacular and reveals and maintains "soul," i.e. that racial or ethnic character, which often reflects the depth of suffering, energy, and transformative power contained in the collective experience and memory. Indeed, Davis also embodies the black aesthetic as he expresses racial rhythms, dialect, and as West would say, "the dark perturbation of the soul of the Negro…as the iteration of the drum rather than the exposition of the piano" (xxiii).

In Davis's "social realism" poems, one can find the aforementioned elements, as in his well-known poem "47th Street," named after the street that defined the boundary of the Black section of Chicago.

> Remember in 1942 the dark waving wings of war/ Remember a barrage of talk on corner, in barbershop, saloon/ "I ain't mad at nobody I ain't seen. If I gotta shoot somebody,/ Make it Ol' Man Cunningham down in Mississippi an'/ I's ready. Wuhked on his plantation ten long yeahs/ with no payday and' when I left I finds I owes him money"/ Hitler? I knows a dozen white men's worser'n Hitler/ just in Oglethorpe County, Georgia. Hitler/ ain't done nothin' to me'/ "Well, I been cut off WPA, relief ain't nothing an' I/ ain't smaht enough t' land a defense job. If I can eat/ regluh an' don't hafta dodge no landlawd, I'd take a/chance on fightin' Mistuh Christ:/ Th' white folks started it, so let the white folks end it./ If Uncle Sam don't know me in peace, I don't/ know him in war' . . .   (*47th Street* 24-25)

Many African American poets have created a poetic diction that is a vernacular-informed and vernacular-derived expression (Gates, xxiv). One half century later Gates counsels African American writers not to follow the often pale imitations of forms and languages alien to them.

Frank Marshall Davis was ahead of his time. As a New Negro and social realist in the 1930's and 1940's, he kept the colorful, vibrant ethnic speech forms, idea patterns, and rich racial flavor. In several of his poems, he wrote indications that they were to be read aloud and accompanied by musical instruments like drums. He also encouraged his public to turn inward, return to black language, African American forms and an Afrocentric cosmogony "which will yield the most splendid results, a spiritual and physical return to the earth . . . for pride, strength and endurance." This is the black aesthetic, which valorizes indigenous African American creative expressions. Decades later, Gates urges writers to continue the quest to create, define, expand, refine, and articulate a black aesthetic (xxiv), as Frank Marshall Davis illustrates in his writing.

The political aspect of the African American aesthetic can be seen and characterized by an ideological and moral quality found in the poetry and journalism of Frank Marshall Davis. Moreover, due to style and rhythms, his writing has also included a unique aesthetic component, self-referential in notions of taste and beauty, ideological because it has been a search for a foundation of a world where African Americans and their culture can be accorded dignity and meaning.

During the 1930's and 1940's, African American writers like Frank Marshall Davis aimed at creating poetry, sometimes using rhetoric, in order to disown and sometimes destroy the lying figures of speech, and the disguise of "civilized, artistic" forms that excluded and alienated Blacks. These "civilized" forms involved the insidious masks of poetic diction which openly denigrated and hence segregated African Americans from the rest of society. To counter the subversive and invasive verbal attacks by most white writers, Davis and other revolutionary African American writers constructed a critical and emotionally charged language which was a counterforce to the dominant discourse, a direct challenge to abusive white authority and to the tradition of patriarchal power (Diaz-Diocaretz 29) and sacrosanct American institutions. Davis attacked institutional racism, the politics of domination, injustice, and the patriarchal assumptions found in Christianity in his poem

"Christ is a Dixie Nigger" as an illustration of his irreverence and challenge to what he deemed hypocritical institutions.

> You tell me Christ was born nearly twenty centuries ago in a
> little one horse town called Bethlehem . . . your artists paint
> a man as fair as another New White Hope. Well, you got it all
> wrong . . . facts twisted as hell . . . see? . . . I don't want any
> of your stories about somebody running around too long ago
> to be anything but a highly publicized memory. . . . Your pink
> priests who whine about Pilate and Judas and Gethsemane
> I'd like to hogtie and dump into the stinking cells to write a
> New Testament around the Scottsboro Boys. . . .
>
> (*American Negro* 28-29)

This process of constructing new aggressive metaphors included the transvaluation of received judgments and assumptions (Diaz-Diocaretz 29) as the African American writer, Davis, in this case, rebels against traditional subservience. According to Diaz-Diocaretz in *The Transforming Power of Language*, the revolutionary writer sets forth a new discourse reflecting and recreating the social organization in representing the minority voice; the feminist Adrienne Rich says "western culture is a book of myths in which our names do not appear" (32), an omission which the writer must rectify. Davis creates a new myth inserting black identity and experience as he deconstructs the old in his poem "Christ is a Dixie Nigger."

Hoyt Fuller, in his essay "Contemporary Negro Fiction," speaks of the failure of the public and critics to understand the necessity of the African American writer to demystify the old myths, to "endow these actions (myths) with meaning" for Blacks, to interpret and empower the African American experience. This hermeneutic process of challenging old assumptions empowers many writers like Davis. Fuller affirms that "they (Blacks) will no longer be victims" and "are determined finally to destroy the power of white-perpetrated myths over their lives" (Bigsby 234).

The act of writing in a new way is for many African American writers like Davis a political action, a protest, and condemnation of Eurocentric domination. African Americans have always sought to affirm their own humanity through writing in overt and sometimes covert ways. They have aimed to provide new interpretations of the themes of equality, pluralism, reconciliation, humanity. They have brought a psychological healing through literature, at the same time striving to maintain ethnic integrity and to preserve positive cultural differences.

Davis saw the challenge of the African American tradition to critique the relation of indenture and control, even while using the Other's Euro-American language (Audre Lorde speaks of using the master's tools). He urges the writer and reader alike to not renounce one's own culture. For writers like Davis, to write is to give birth to an African American literary tradition, a black canon of literary excellence and self-definition.

In speaking of African American poetry, the critic and philosopher Alain Locke speaks of the particular qualities of the new African American poetry: rich language, inventive imagination, jazz and blues rhythms and imagery, fullness of scene, and complexity of historical, political, mythical, musical, and sociological references. Davis's jazz poem "Billy Holiday" illustrates all of these qualities:

> I think I'll/ be going now, So long./ And the transparent lizard/ with the blue blue gizzard/ and the candy striped/ bone/ wailed and went/ mourning/ her opaque scent/ By the presto of electronics/ I reincarnate Lady Day/ Listen as her rum-brown rope of a voice/ Fastens flannel strands/ around stiff sides of staid notes/ Sitting properly/ On their oh so proper scale/ She pulls/ Notes fall/ Into her molten mould/ Of flaming sounds/ Burning/ Bright as a hungry sun/ She sings/ And her words taste/ Of lavender butter/ Spread with a unicorn's horn/ How easy it is/ A switch turns/ And the dead breathes again/ How easy/ And no mosquito swarm/ of biting responsibilities/ No pushers now/ Peddling a promise/ Of pilfered peace/ In return/ For a dawnkilled soul/ Arrogant amphibians/ Proper in their prim dull scales/ Sinned and sunned/ "My man he don't love me/ He treats me awful mean. . ./ And the transparent lizard/ with the blue blue gizzard/ moaned/ and went.   (*Black World*, 25)

Because of the enormous influence of jazz and the blues on African American life and Davis's life in particular, it is not at all surprising that he entitled his autobiography *Livin' the Blues*. In fact, the blues often express an African American perspective of life full of contradictions and suffering. And yet the blues also include the transcendental notion of freedom, accepting or transforming one's state of mind, if not one's physical reality. The blues are intimately tied to the search for empowerment as they confront the painful socio-political and economic realities of life. The blues is about praxis. The blues is representative of the Chicago Renaissance in the 1930's and 1940's.

A decade earlier, during the Harlem Renaissance period, jazz and poetry as genres best represented the complex world of the African American. Locke speaks in *The New Negro* of the assigned role of the African American artist in the 20th century Harlem Renaissance as an exotic being, with an aim of cultural self-expression of his or her own separate ethnic reality; he or she portrays an evocative, colorful realism, using rhythms and originality which inspired many white avant-guard writers, dancers and musicians who were already being influenced by the new jazz (Chapman, 524).

Frank Marshall Davis and his contemporary African American writers wrote many musical poems during the Harlem and Chicago Renaissance periods, some of which were in honor of jazz musicians and singers: "Charlie Parker," "Duke Ellington," "Louis Armstrong," " and perhaps his most famous "Jazz Band." These poems reflected the staccato rhythms, tempo, dialect, and strident protest of the new jazz, and included references to the continuing power of African influences on African American culture. He used poetry as a form of protest against poverty and cultural imperialism. He also used poetry as a means of affirmation of the black aesthetic. In what he calls social realism, he used his poetry to describe the ennui and deception of black immigrants and youth caught in the vise of gender, race, and class.

In his poems, Davis also speaks of the natural grace and undefined hope of those everyday folk who inhabit the city. However, unlike many other Black poets, the depth and scope of Davis grows international as he reaches beyond the United States to Africa and India for his metaphors, rhythms, and images. He seeks correspondences between American Blacks and oppressed people of color in other parts of the world, people who are colonized, dissatisfied, and full of madness and sadness, striving for freedom or escape at home and abroad. In "Dancing Gal" he writes:

> Black and tan--yeah, Black and tan/ Spewing the moans
> of a jigtime band/ What does your belly crave?/ A brown-
> sugar brown/ Slim gal sways/ Pretzel twisting/ Beneath a
> yellow thumb/ of steel-stiff light/ Amid a striped rain/ of
> red-note, blue-note/ Jazz-hot jazz/ Gazelle graceful/ lovely
> as a lover's dream/ silken skinned, stillwater soft/ Young
> girl breasts in gold encased/ Scant gold around her lower
> waist/ Red lips parted/ Dark eyes flashing/ She dances/ Dips/
> whirls/ undulates/ Her body a living chord/ Set loud and
> sweet/ Against the bitter quiet/ Of drab and muted human
> shapes/ I see a long lean god/ Standing in painted splendor/
> Motionless in scented air/ of Tanganyika/ I see a frozen idol/
> Set free from a single stone/ His world in Hindustan . . . /
> Africa's madness, India/s sadness/ Wedded in Chicago/ By a
> Midwest gal/ In a Jew's cafe . . ./ Black and tan--yeah, black
> and tan/ Drenched in the jazz of a swingtime band/ Is this
> what your belly craves?   (*American Negro* 23-24)

The new racial consciousness celebrated blackness, music, sensuality, even third world people of color, and uncustomarily lacked apology.

Davis and the African American writers of the period, the New Negroes, accepted race as a category of classification and were proud to be called Race Men. In speaking of African American poetry, Locke says it "represents many strains, having only one common factor, - the fact of reflecting some expression of the emotional sense of race or some angle of the peculiar group tradition and experience" (Chapman 527-528). The new African American poetry of the twentieth century expressed the folk-life, folk-types, and idioms of thought, feeling, and speech of the masses. It also reflected the tone and temperament of dissatisfaction, the social protest, the social life and exhortation against poverty and discrimination. Some critics said it was radical political propaganda of African American writers in America. Nonetheless, this new social realism poetry rang of a new rhetoric. It was dramatic and melodramatic, expressing the anger, grief, suffering, and frustration of the insulted and injured African Americans. At times it even reflected a nihilistic despair.

Another contemporary of Davis, Sterling Brown, described African American poetry as a creative expression and battleground, where literature becomes a weapon of propaganda used to expose injustice and reveal the deep cultural roots of African Americans. He describes it as hortatory and lyrical, with an aim to refute stereotypes and deepen portrayals of Negro character as rightly human (1968, 566). Davis's poetry certainly reflected these qualities.

Unfortunately, during this time, most black poetry written in Standard English was devalued and relegated to a limited race based appeal, not to be categorized with "real" poetry written by white academics and intellectuals. Most whites preferred the dialect poetry written by people like Paul Laurence Dunbar that was non-threatening and did not challenge the social and political inferior position relegated to blacks. Bardolph writes:

> It was only . . . when it preserved the "tang" of Negro speech . . . that their poetry was said to be "successful." Fiction writers were also under pressure to confine themselves to Negro themes, on the plausible ground that their enforced isolation disqualified them as commentators on other facets of American life.   (203)

The new African American poetry written by Davis and his contemporaries expressed color, music, gusto, and free improvisational expressions of exhilarating or sometimes desperate moods. It also expressed the psychological effects (overt and covert) of racism on the black population. The unforeseen emotional explosion in African American poetry caused an imbroglio for the traditionally more formal, reserved, conservative, and intellectual whites. Even many middle class blacks misunderstood the new Race Men writers, and discredited the impassioned poetry which spoke so deeply of the joys and suffering of Black people.

> The distinguished Negro, to be sure, still felt constrained to confine himself to Negro themes, working usually in the ghetto and under Negro auspices, but the standards of excellence began to match those of the whites.
>
> (Bardolph 133)

Frank Marshall Davis, Sterling Brown, and Langston Hughes used dialect and free verse to set an ethnic tone and attack racism in varying degrees, whereas writers Countee Cullen and Claude McKay wrote poetry using more traditional literary forms like rhyme, sonnets, and conventional images to portray Negro themes. McKay sometimes attacked racism ironically using the sonnet form and always paid attention to Euro-American standards of excellence having been raised under the British educational system in Jamaica.

The African American writer as exemplified by Davis can be considered as a mirror critic and conscience of American morality. Davis turns the dominant white discourse and arguments used against African Americans to confront the hypocrisy of white morality which, from an African American perspective, can be described as destructive, barbaric, oppressive, and ruthless in relation to white attitudes and behavior toward African Americans, women, and other minorities.

Throughout his adult life, Davis exposed this cruel and immoral behavior which has been historically whitewashed and sanctioned by the church under the so-called noble rubric of Manifest Destiny and patriarchal government. Using the written word, he exposed the scientific theories used to support and justify white supremacists and other defenders of the status quo who perpetuated the subordination of African Americans.

Davis felt compelled by conscience to invoke the mystique of blackness and saw himself as a political vehicle writing a *literature engagée*. He was the messenger delivering a written representation of the daily African American experience and the collective effort and experience to survive in a racist environment. His work reflects the discourse on disfranchisement and inequality.

In choosing his subjects, Davis provides a challenge to the literary theory of "art as beauty" which required the subordination or exclusion of any political message (called propaganda) in acceptable prescribed art forms and reified European aesthetics. For the masses of African Americans, the political reality of oppression permeates all aspects of life and culture. Any efforts to preclude or exclude the literary expression of its existence and struggle would be to silence African Americans, exclude them from the voice, the art, and the audience as well. Davis felt that artistic material must remain relevant so that the audience can be interested in and able to relate to the subject matter.

The audience of the African American writer varies. Often the message is directed toward the African American masses and not toward the literary elite of the academy, where universal words tend to have more value than a particular expression of ethnic identity and experience. However, one should not be misled by that statement, since the African American experience like any human experience includes protest, suffering, courage, and transcendence, as well as the more traditional themes of nature, the world and the universe; all of humanity can find a familiarity in the themes, if they look beyond color.

An important function and service of many African American writers like Davis has been in their literary contributions to the struggle for freedom, identity, and consciousness in which other minority groups have found inspiration and role models. Some writers like Davis were also at the same time involved in other forms of protest, for example, especially those who were in academia, politics, entertainment, labor, social activism, and journalism. Bardolph notes:

> Newspapers had made a modest beginning toward becoming a major influence in Negro America before 1900 and then multiplied rapidly. By 1920 there were some two hundred, and thereafter growth was principally in the expanding circulation of existing papers. Like other professions, Negro journalism owed its sudden burgeoning to the maturing of free, separate colored communities in the new century, and particularly in the wake of the great northward Diaspora after 1914. After World War I the circulation per capital was at least four times as high in the North as in the South, and perhaps a third of the country's colored families subscribed. The papers passed from hand to hand before they were discarded, for their cost was comparatively high, and their influence was increased because those Negroes who took the papers were the most ambitious and literate third of the race.   (202)

However, what dignifies the voice of African American writers is that, by describing the struggle to survive and the anguish associated with it, the writer portrays universal subjects in a dynamic, creative, and accessible way, comprehensible to the masses of oppressed people anywhere and of any color. Theirs are the voices of experience, suffering, and transcendence, and include a real understanding of the ironic tragedy and comedy of life. Unfortunately, words used by many literary critics to describe African American writing have too often been limited to "anger, hatred, rage, protest," thereby trivializing the worth and significance of its very existence: a power, sometimes raw, is contained therein. But with modifiers, the same descriptions can become "beautiful anger, black hatred, painful rage, exquisite protest" says John A. Williams in "The Literary Ghetto" (227).

As a consequence of the former descriptions, much of African American literature, including works by Davis, has been dismissed as "protest" or propaganda for two reasons: (1) it deals honestly with African American life which often includes an experience of oppression and protest; and (2) because it is often accusatory toward whites, and nobody likes to be accused, especially of crimes against the human spirit.

Along with his political, economic and social commentaries in the news, Davis developed an active social life when he returned to Chicago from Atlanta in 1933. He met or became re-acquainted and wrote about many out-standing African Americans in his columns including entertainers, athletes, artists, writers, musicians, contortionists, and social activists, such as Jack Johnson, Richard Wright, Langston Hughes, Paul Robeson, and Gwendolyn Brooks, to mention a few.

He was especially happy to return to the music of Chicago. There was an abundance of musicians with whom he had become familiar before leaving for his two year job in Atlanta. Indeed, Chicago during this renaissance was considered a haven for musicians and a national center of jazz and the blues. According to Davis, one could listen to Louis Armstrong, Fletcher Henderson, Jelly Roll Morton, Teddy Wilson, Lionel Hampton, and W. C. Handy, "the father of the blues," all in one night by visiting the many clubs, theaters, and cabarets on Chicago's predominantly black South Side.

The 1920's to the 1940's was an extended period popularly called the Jazz Age which included Hot Jazz, Chicago and Kansas City Style Jazz, the

Boogie, the Swing, the Blues, and Bebop. Jazz had a pervasive influence on writing styles, use of language, theatrical presentations, the way people walked, talked, danced, and even the variety of music which developed from it. It was a time when new rhythms were commercialized, reflecting the pulse of transition even reflected in a few interracial marriages. It was also an era when the anger, frustration, and rebelliousness of an alienated mechanized society in the discordant throes of change soared on the dissonant music, reflecting the discordant throes of change.

Davis described jazz as "musical militancy" in an age when African Americans found it hard to speak out openly about the oppression of whites. In his poem "Jazz Band," he writes:

> Play that thing, you jazz mad fools!/ Boil a skyscraper with a jungle/ Dish it to 'em sweet and hot - / Ahhhhhhhh/ Rip it open then sew it up, jazz band!/ Thick bass notes from a moon-faced drum/ Saxaphones moan, banjo strings hum/ High thin notes from the cornet's throat/ Trombone snorting, bass horns snorting/ And the short tan notes from the piano/ Plink plank plunk a plunk/ Chopin gone screwey, Wagner with the blues/ Plink plank plunk a plunk/ Got a date with Satan - ain't no time to lose/ Plink plant plunk a plunk/ Strut it in Harlem, let Fifth Avenue shake it slow/ Plink plank plunk a plunk/ Ain't goin' to heaven nohow--/ Crowd up there's too slow. . . . / Plink plank plunk aplunk/ Plunk . . . Your music's been drinking hard liquor/ Got shanghaied and it's fightin' mad/ stripped to the waist feedin' ocean liner bellies/ Big burley bibulous brute/ Poet hands and bone crusher shoulders --/ Black sheep or white? Hey, Hey! Pick it, papa! Twee twa twee twa twa/ step on it, black boy/ Do re mi fa sol la ti do/ Boomp Boomp/ Play that thing, you jazz mad fools!   (*Black Man's* 34-35)

Davis reveals his command of language, imagery, world culture and history in this poem as well as his perception and understanding that music transcends individual and national differences. The ironic tones "Got a date with Satan", the cultural references "Wagner with the blues", and the use of sounds to imitate jazz were common to African American writers of the period, especially his colleague Langston Hughes. Such juxtaposed themes were evident in the jazz and blues music as well as in poetry: the bittersweet tones, the staccato anger, and the raging riffs.

Indeed, much of Davis's life and writing reflect the notable and revolutionary influence of jazz and its trans-cultural magic to unite people from different cultures. Growing numbers of whites, mostly new immigrants, were also disaffected with American society, the blatant inequalities, the injustices of capitalism, and brutal racism; they too found new freedom and rebellion against the establishment, status quo, and tradition in the strident tones of jazz.

Davis called jazz "one of our major weapons," because it upset and offended many whites and upper class blacks due to its discordance, its disconnect from classical "proper music." and inaccessibility (*Livin'* 235).

He distinguished between New Orleans Jazz as African American and Dixieland as white jazz. Nonetheless, he felt strongly that this period of history was one of the first stages of equality, integration, and true democracy in America. Davis credited John Hammond, a white liberal who fought against discrimination in the music industry, for helping to integrate the jazz bands.

> The democracy inherent in the jazz band and the equality of all its members became a national nose-thumbing at the royalty and rigid class structure of Europe. Its new devices of tone, interval poly-rhythms, and innovative use of various instruments with the revival of improvisation (long a lost art in the music of Western Europe) shocked American traditionalists. At the same time it stimulated European composers who borrowed heavily from jazz and recognized it as the chief American contribution to the world artistic stream.   (*Livin'* 235)

During the renaissance, Chicago was the center for the blues and jazz, and music venues became a neutral ground where African Americans and whites could socialize, enjoy the music, and exchange ideas and feelings. African Americans used the rhythms, discordant tones, and improvisation in jazz to express their alienation and pain, to assert themselves, and become active subjects, not objects. Davis wanted to assert himself as a Black Man and in *Black Skin, White Masks*, Fanon writes what Davis might have felt:

> I resolved, since it was impossible for me to get away
> from an inborn complex, to assert myself as a BLACK MAN.
> Since the other hesitated to recognize me, there remained
> only one solution: to make myself known.   (115)

Jazz spread like a wildfire across the country and around the world, affirming the active, creative, and rebellious presence of African Americans in face of discrimination. Davis himself moved in this neutral ground of integrated circles, in contrast to the segregated settings and sometimes nihilistic themes of his militant and nationalistic-seeming poetry.

In 1944, Davis began an annual series of lectures on race relations again at Northwestern University to the sociology classes of Dr. Herskovits, renowned anthropologist, and author of *The Myth of the Negro Past* (1941). His autobiography records that he even introduced Dr. Herbert Aptheker who on three different nights came to address the class (*Livin'* 290). Davis also wrote book reviews and made innumerable speeches about town. Slowly, he was able to gain more legitimacy and respect in the white community, expanding his voice and empowering himself through his writings and lectures.

In 1945 Davis also taught one of the first classes in the History of Jazz at the Abraham Lincoln School in Chicago, commonly known as the Little Red Schoolhouse, because so many controversial events occurred there. He writes in *Livin'*:

> The course was planned not only to give the effects
> resulting from this revolutionary music but the socioeconomic
> factors which caused its creation. My continually growing
> knowledge of our history here and in Africa enabled me
> to isolate those strong and persistent elements of African
> culture which survived slavery and were the heart and soul
> of jazz.   (284)

Ironically, due to the location of Northwestern University in the city, his students were almost all white, because the course was only offered at night and most African Americans were afraid of getting harassed for being found in a white community after dark. Therefore, the African American community was largely denied access to Davis's courses because of the unspoken barriers and politics of race and place.

Jazz soon fell victim to exploitation as white musicians appropriated, copied, and softened the rebellious rhythms and tones of the African American musicians, rendering the new jazz more palatable and less offensive to the white public. Soon, with a modified product, white jazz artists were making much better money than most of the African American composers, musicians, and performers. Redding writes in *The Lonesome Road*,

> The jazz age, which the new Negro fathered, named, and gave a voice, was an age of momentous trifles: the new Negro was a bauble in it. He became a commercialized fad. His talents were likely to be sold and his integrity rifled by slick gangster types who, for one thing, dominated a few of the theaters, more of the music outlets, . . . a place loudly trumpeted as "Nigger Heaven." There could be found the exotic, the primitive, the virile. There life had "surge and sweep and pounding savagery." There gaiety was king, but . . . not for Negroes. . . . Disillusioned and fear driven, those Negroes fled who could.   (244 245)

Although Saunders Redding wrote the preceding passage about Harlem during the 1920's Renaissance, it was equally applicable to trends in Chicago through the 1940's.

In spite of the taboo of miscegenation, Davis acknowledged in his writing that African Americans were "culturally and biologically . . . a goulash of Europeans, Africans, and American Indians, with African dominant" (*Livin'* 290). Imprisoned by the politics of color, he was understandably most fascinated by the carryovers of surviving Africanisms, represented in rhythms and atonalities.

> Since traditionally African music is functional, it was only logical that an oppressed minority blend what it valued of the music of the majority with its own concepts and extended the personal protest of the blues into the united protest of what came to be known as jazz music.   (*Livin'* 234)

The connectedness of traditions and experience were not lost on Davis. In his jazz poetry, he connects the European instruments and the

African American rhythms and tone to create a syncretic expression. In his lectures, he enjoyed explaining how the African musical traditions blended with European melodic concepts. He was well aware that composers like Stravinski and Bartok were influenced by jazz. He attributed the uniqueness of African American expression called "soul" to the emotional content which was created by a people who had suffered, both economically and racially: "This music vividly illustrated how these Baptist hymns originating in England had been completely transformed by African musical patterns retained" (*Livin'*, 290). Davis also wrote about and taught the functional aspects of African and African American music, the role of the work song in slavery, the blues in Jim Crow and the political role of spirituals in the Underground Railroad, the psychological release and transcendence with the blues with the addition of humor. In the clubs and cabarets of South Side Chicago, he witnessed and recognized the creativity and genius of the often poor, self-taught, and unacknowledged African American musicians, whose music was repeatedly appropriated and used by white musicians who almost always gave no credit to the black creators.

Davis also recognized causes for affinities and correspondences between poor whites and blacks. He understood race and economics, differences and boundaries (real and imagined) and why people came together and communicated through music. Despite most whites' initial rejection of jazz music as uncivilized, strident, and unprofessional, it eventually caught on as an edgy revolutionary cultural form. Many white musicians, especially those who were members of oppressed minorities like Jews and Italians, flocked to African American clubs to study the musicians who were playing there.

> Since it violated all their precious rules and originated among an "inferior" people, this new music itself had to be "inferior." But so strong and insistent was its assault against the boundaries of white culture, which tried to reject any values not established by itself, that shortly white musicians themselves turned to its radical new devices and began imitating black bands. Despite opposition from critics, . . . the revolutionary concepts of jazz forced their way into the mainstream of American music.   (*Livin'* 234-235)

Creative and oppressed people were interested in these new sounds and wanted to learn and listen to more.

By 1948, Davis had added three more books of poetry: *I Am the American Negro* (1937), *Through Sepia Eyes* (1938) and *47th Street* (1948). These books, with themes of race, class, and gender with many poems featuring jazz rhythms, were hailed by many critics as contributions of worth and significance to the new African American protest literature, although the financial rewards were insignificant. Davis received excellent reviews nationally by such writers and critics as Langston Hughes, William Rose Benet of the *Saturday Review*, William Allen White, philosopher Alain Locke, and George Schuyler. Ralph Matthews reviewed *Black Man's Verse* in the Baltimore *Afro-American*: "Mr. Davis definitely established himself as one who possesses rare creative genius." In 1937 George Schuyler wrote a review of *I Am the American Negro* in the Pittsburgh *Courier*:

> [It] is a fitting successor to his notable `Black Man's Verse' which created much stir last year. It further stamps him [Davis] as the ablest Negro poet in the country. He is keen as a razor blade, as penetrating as an ice pick, as modern as television. (n.p.)

While Alain Locke in *Opportunity* (Jan 1938) said, "*I Am the American Negro* becomes thus the outstanding verse effort of the year", William Rose Benet in the *Saturday Review* (June 19, 1937) said, "I regarded him [Mr. Davis] as the most promising Negro poet of recent years" (1937). Sterling Brown wrote in *Opportunity* (July 1936) of Davis's "strong and vivid revelations of the American scene" (1936). Davis enjoyed the positive reviews, but remained broke, since financial recompense did not accompany his literary successes.

> As for me, I wanted critical recognition. Luckily we got both, particularly after several influential critics including Harriet Monroe of *Poetry Magazine* and William Rose Benet of the *Saturday Review* of Literature printed high praise. I was now an Author with a certain prestige -- but my wallet was as flat as ever. (*Livin'* 226)

As had other African American writers before him, Davis also experimented with his use of images, borrowing from the visual arts, music (especially jazz and jazz rhythms) and musical instruments, science, and philosophy in order to explore the self and to speak to others with whom he might not ordinarily be able to converse. The subject and persona became one. For example, influenced by Carl Sandburg and Vachel Linsay, Davis often used the city as a metaphor of urban life, a locus which he captured, personified, and bestowed with character, personality, moods, and authority--a giant dwarfing human beings. In the poem "Chicago Skyscrapers," he writes in *47th Street,*

> Here in this fat city
> Men 72 inches short
> Have frozen their dreams
> Into steel and concrete
> Six hundred feet tall
> Thin fingers
> On the hard hand
> Of Chicago's Loop
> Are these skyscrapers
> Rubbing bright sides
> Of rainbow stars
> Tearing the gray gauze
> Of low clouds. . . . (45)

The pathos of frozen dreams and the insignificance of people dwarfed by large steel and concrete cities depersonalizes individuals who live alienated lives amidst the strangely beautiful "rainbow stars."

While Davis was in Chicago in the 1930's and 1940's, African American intellectuals as a group were still grossly underrepresented in American society, since education remained essentially segregated and sub-standard in most areas. Moreover, because many African American schools lacked adequate funding, and only a few spaces for African Americans were available in professional schools, the African American intellectual struggled for more than a century after the Civil War to gain equal access to professional training.

Fortunately, most African American intellectuals were strongly motivated by hope, courage, and a belief in the race's ability to endure and transcend the persistent historical legacy of discrimination in education, economics and employment. However, as was mentioned in previous chapters, many middle-class Blacks strove to assimilate and imitate white ways and values. They did not know, or neglected the significance of African Americans' contributions to America, science, history, politics, and culture. Some were embarrassed by the shameful history of slavery and the devalued blackness and perceived inferiority associated with it. Others went so far as to denounce much of the traditional African American folk culture and music as offensive expressions of ignorant people.

However, Davis, like Langston Hughes, belonged to a small group of intellectuals who had a deep appreciation for the common people, their colorful and original music, art, and lifestyles, their resilient spirit, dynamic and diverse energies, and unexplored oral histories. These intellectuals worked to keep the history of struggle and overcoming alive and to promote and support other African American artists and intellectuals. Davis himself deemed the music of jazz and the blues valuable and unique as well as culturally and historically significant.

> African musical concepts, differing radically from the musical traditions of Europe, were the only ancestral art permitted to survive under slavery. With a distinctly different approach to rhythm, timing and tonality, African music was basically functional, and this carried over into hymns, work songs, and play songs.   (*Livin'* 234)

This valuation in turn accounted for Davis's development as a specialist in the history of African American music. In Chicago, not only did he write poetry, give lectures, teach classes, and write columns about jazz, but he also developed and hosted a popular radio show, "Bronzeville Brevities."

During his time in Chicago, Davis was professionally and socially in contact with other African American intellectuals and activists like Langston Hughes, Arna Bontemps (who headed the WPA Writer's Project at the time), Countee Cullen, Richard Wright, Paul Robeson, A. Phillip Randolph, and Margaret Walker with whom he shared friendship, correspondence, panels, committees, and/or literary events. In *Livin' the Blues* he writes:

> On one of his infrequent trips to Chicago, I met Langston

Hughes. . . . Although we never developed a really close
friendship, we did correspond, and Lang frequently went out
of his way to see that I received the honor that he felt was due
me. . . . In those days Lang was looked upon as Communist
by the establishment. . . . And while he was so often highly
controversial, his longtime friend and close associate, Arna
Bontemps, was not. . . . I first met Arna during this period,
when he headed a WPA Writer's Project. . . . During this
period I became associated with Richard Wright. I first heard
of Dick when the National Negro Congress was organized
[1936]. . . . I was invited to join another of those writers'
groups which shoot up, burn brightly, then plummet back
to earth. In addition to Dick, the group had another member
destined to achieve fame in literature: Margaret Walker, later
winner of a Yale award for her brilliant book of poems, *For
My People*.   (238-239)

Most of these people were concerned with the material and emotional
lives of ordinary working people in African American communities which
in turn influenced the content of the African American aesthetic. It was only
after the publication of Davis's first book that he met many white creative
writers and activists who held to a radical approach to culture and art as he
did and who were not afraid to speak out. Angela Davis comments:

Artists not only felt compelled to defend their right to
communicate the real pains, joys and aspirations of the
working class through their art, but many went on to become
activists in the labor struggles and in the fight for the rights
of the unemployed and especially of black people.   (206)

CHAPTER 4
Creative Empowerment: the Black Chicago Renaissance

I personally edited or rewrote every item released. In addition I read each week virtually every black newspaper in the nation, from 35 to 40 key dailies from every section of America, leading magazines, foreign publications printed in English and the ambitious efforts of would-be journalists. It was essential that I know what was happening to black people everywhere as well as remember names and past events; I needed to be an ambling encyclopedia as well as a writer.

(Davis, *Livin'* 227)

Davis was a Renaissance man, a courageous writer, and journalist in the Black Chicago Renaissance experience (1930's-1940's) from 1934, when he returned from Atlanta, until his departure for Hawai`i in 1948. This Renaissance followed on the heels of the Great Depression and the fall of the Harlem Renaissance. Davis is primarily remembered as editor of the Associated Negro Press (ANP), but he also "worked on a succession of black and labor newspapers, including the *Chicago Evening Bulletin*, the Gary (Indiana) *American*, the Chicago *Whip*, and the *Chicago Star* (Tidwell, Intro. *Livin'*: xx).

Historically, the lifestyle and communication venues of an African American intellectual, like Frank Marshall Davis, has extended far beyond the lofty towers of academia and the sacred territory of Euro-American art to include the streets, formal and informal institutions, and poor communities themselves.

Davis's writing and activities during this time in Chicago reflect his important role in the relentless socio-economic struggles of African American and poor folk. Davis's multi-dimensional communication modes and his process of empowerment using the word as a tool for change enabled him to transform the public ideas and organizations through writing. Political activism, economic reform, and even sexual politics were his topics of choice because of and in spite of the corruptive forces of racism and discrimination.

Because Davis was a man with an intense social conscience and with a deep sense of commitment to several communities (racial, labor, writing, sports, and entertainment), his life reflects the many masks that he wore and the acts and responsibilities in general that an African American intellectual must juggle to survive. In Chicago, during the Depression and turbulent 1930's and 1940's, Davis experienced simultaneously significant roles as a newspaper reporter, editor, columnist, an activist in labor and Civil Rights, a photographer, and a spokesperson and respected figure in the African American community.

By 1933, the Great Depression had taken its toll nationally, and especially on the black people in Chicago's South Side community as well as in other urban centers. There was little work in the factories and slaughterhouses. African American skilled workers had been mostly replaced by whites, and many European immigrants had taken the traditional service jobs usually considered the domain of African Americans; immigrant whites displaced African Americans as garbage collectors, street and gutter cleaners, ditch diggers, barbers, and domestics. Indeed, once again racial tensions grew as African Americans earned about one tenth the wages of whites, if they worked at all.

Davis, in his poem "47th Street," describes the harsh, cruel, and devastating effects of the Depression on the street (personified as a scarred prostitute), the at-risk families, on the hardened children, and on the many residents who escape to the taverns to drink in order to forget their poverty and suffering.

> This street is a woman of bulging bust and ready hips/ Many scars cover her body, for the depression was a cruel lover/ Her breath shouts of gin, for she and the taverns live as man and wife/ Speak to her softly, and she will tell of her dark children/who have grown hard and strong as any others/ in this broad city from the thin milk of her brown breasts (30).

Davis personifies the city as a woman, battered and poor, yet still seductive.

Poverty is the antithesis of freedom, and Davis addresses the continued state of economic inferiority of African Americans. Indeed, when workers cannot reap adequate profits from their labor, are unable to accumulate surplus, and are poorly trained for promotion and advancement into the hierarchy of the powerful, they become increasingly hardened, discouraged, and disillusioned, often seeking drink, drugs and crimes like theft to change their mood.

During this Depression period, hoards of African Americans, former tenant farmers, sharecroppers, and service personnel from the South continued to migrate to the North, pushed to escape from the extreme poverty, lack of jobs, poor farming, racist intimidation and pulled by the lure to seek better-paying jobs with benefits in the urban centers which they had often heard about through relatives who had gone North and the African American press. As economic and agricultural conditions in the South worsened, especially for African Americans, due to a series of droughts and plagues, the mostly young adults sought hope in the North, many believing they would find there a more just and democratic society. The majority surely did not realize that they would be stirring resentment and animosity from the whites and other Blacks in the North who were also feeling the economic squeeze of the Depression. The African American newspapers, in particular the Chicago *Defender*, ran huge ads encouraging them to move north, and featured stories of success.

> Those blacks who could scrape enough together came to northern urban centers where they wrote back that even relief recipients lived better than those breaking their necks for coolie pay in Birmingham, Jackson and Little Rock. So they started saving until they got enough for bus tickets out of Dixie.   (Davis, *Livin'* 251)

In fact, Davis commented in his editorials on the irony of people "on relief" in the North having a higher standard of living than people working as tenant farmers and servants in the South due to the "racist wage differential" (1931-1933). The Depression brought movement, migration, and a new meaning to liberation for blacks along with social, economic, and political change if not opportunities.

Davis understood that for African Americans who made it to the North, a chance to escape poverty, a new beginning, and a space to protest segregation seemed like starting a new chapter in their lives. Not surprisingly, when subjugated people sense the possibility of change for the better from dire situations, they are most likely to take aggressive and radical steps to improve their situation. Militancy and migration both require at least some degree of hope and morale, which although linked with dissatisfaction, offers an escape from despair.

As the Depression wore on, Franklin D. Roosevelt, a Democrat, in his inaugural address in 1933 announced his New Deal Program which was full of experimental social programs and new opportunities: unemployment benefits, welfare, and many other public projects supported and funded by the government, designed to make hard times more bearable for the jobless. These programs of social reconstruction assisted poor men, women, and children--including more than a million African Americans.

Davis documents in his editorials how many African Americans benefited directly from the vocational training programs, work relief projects, fair labor standards, social security benefits, housing, education and employment acts, and safeguards against discrimination. Numerous agencies such as the Federal Public Housing Authority (FHA), the Federal Employment Relief Administration (FERA), the National Recovery Administration (NRA) later called the Works Progress Administration (WPA) which brought art to the people on a massive scale including sculpture, music, murals, theater, and literary works, the Civilian Conservation Corps (CCC), the National Youth Administration (NYA), the Tennessee Valley Authority (TVA), the Agricultural Adjustment Administration (AAA), and the National Youth Administration (NYA) touched the lives of African American people, particularly those immigrants from the South. These programs and agencies ignited the energy of the cities--Chicago, Detroit, and New York--like a catalyst for constructive change.

Davis writes of the hope offered by Roosevelt's programs:

> Roosevelt's New Deal experiments made hard times more bearable among the jobless. With the end of prohibition, bootlegging was no longer big business. Some of those who had operated speakeasies now ran taverns at the same locations and with the same customers.   (*Livin'* 223)

However, since most college educated African Americans were denied access to administrative and professional jobs outside of limited African American institutions, many of the most gifted intellectuals found themselves in alternative careers which were open to them in entertainment and sports. Only a few chose traditional careers in medicine, science, teaching, the arts, and journalism. Jobs and times were exceptionally difficult for Blacks and Whites during the Depression. Davis writes:

> That summer I tried railroading again. . . . I was assigned to a friendly and helpful crew. It included a couple of college men, one a dentist. . . . A similar pattern existed in Chicago. . . . During the Depression and its drastically reduced incomes, a number of South Side doctors and lawyers kept regular daytime office hours but at night donned overalls to work on city garbage trucks. . . . Black college graduates in general were grateful for the lowest menial jobs in order to eat. Virtually any large railroad station had enough well-educated Afro-Americans with degrees working as porters and redcaps to staff a first rate college.   (*Livin'* 174-175)

National and local politics became more interesting as a result of Roosevelt's efforts at restoration. Many African Americans, traditionally Republican since the Civil War and Abraham Lincoln, moved to the Democratic Party, bringing to it a new and revolutionary spirit.

> Blind support of GOP candidates among us was dead. It was not that the Afro American had decided to reverse itself and go democratic; it was due instead to the personal appeal of Franklin D. Roosevelt and his New Deal Administration which had put bread into the mouths of starving people.
>
> (*Livin'* 250)

However, Davis stayed with the Republican Party longer than many because of his job.

In 1935, Davis's first book of poems *Black Man's Verse* appeared "beautifully bound and printed" a few months before he joined the staff of the Associated Negro Press, where he worked until 1948.

Between 1936 and 1948, Davis documented the great economic and social changes that took place for African Americans in the United States, especially in cities like Chicago. Living standards were rising, wages improving, stereotypes diminishing, violence declining, and white attitudes changing in a slow, steady drift toward the mainstream, although race stratification, differentiation, and discrimination were still a part of daily reality.

A new ameliorative social philosophy replaced Social Darwinism. People were on the move from the south in large waves of northward and westward migrations. Urbanization was the national trend, and African Americans benefited from this social and economic diversification. They even found more political power through voting rights. By the forties, Davis clearly recognized that half of African Americans were living in urban areas, divided evenly between North and South, in contrast with the seven decades after the Civil War when 90% of African Americans were in the South and in rural areas. He witnessed the changing patterns of employment and status as some Blacks found work during World War II in industries, in clerical positions, and in government jobs. The numbers of Blacks slowly increased in the professional fields as well. However, Davis clearly understood that the majority of African Americans still found it difficult to attain adequate training for promotions and cultivate support networks for meaningful employment.

He observed that Blacks in the growing middle-class were still way short of acceptance into the social fabric of the white bourgeoisie and stayed in their own social groups due to segregation and prejudice. Moreover, residential segregation kept breaches in the color line to a minimum. To ease the pain of exclusion and 2nd class status, many Africans Americans sought refuge in the church and various forms of entertainment.

Davis skillfully wrote newspaper columns that reflected his personal connection to the arts and entertainment circles. Communities like Chicago's South Side had an abundance of cabarets, clubs, and liquor stores, most owned by outsiders who took the money spent by blacks out of the community. Of course, it was almost impossible for African Americans to obtain conventional loans or credit to establish their own businesses due to institutional racism.

> [M]any adjusted themselves to their catastrophic rejection
> either by flight into unreality and the world of make-believe
> that, Franklin Frazier has described in Black Bourgeoisie, or,
> … capitulated to frustration, or were broken by the tensions
> that accompanied the "Mark of oppression." (Bardolph 279)

In the forties, Davis understood that social integration and equality still remained the most difficult obstacle for African Americans, in spite of the progressive New Deal Programs and great numbers of African Americans registering with the Democrats during Roosevelt's presidency.

However, the Republican Party (GOP) continued to make deals with African American leaders, like Davis, to maintain some foothold in the African American community. Republican administrations continued to give African Americans posts and perks such as money, advertising in the Black press, free tickets to events, and some connections to the white ruling class that were coming to be regarded as traditional African American plugs. Strategic party offices were still held by African American politicians in urban districts like Detroit and Chicago where Blacks were a clear majority in some precincts. Indeed, in the North, civil rights had progressed to the point that when, by 1936, a dozen states were sending a select few African American members to state legislatures. This phenomena of black office-holders representing black precincts excited little notice, even in the African American press. The highest political position held by an African American in this Renaissance period was a seat in the United States House of Representatives held by Oscar DePriest of Chicago who was elected in 1928 to the first of three terms (*Livin'* 196).

Curiously, despite his reformist attitudes, Davis stuck with the Republican Party a bit longer than most Blacks, always aware of continuing discrimination and wage discrepancies between African Americans and Whites in many of Roosevelt's New Deal programs due to local customs of discrimination and white privilege. Davis was also realistic about the pressures and vagrancies of basic survival: food, housing, and especially his job. It is therefore understandable how he was seduced by GOP perks, advertisement revenues, and promotional and publicity fees, not to mention the cash payoffs given to GOP publicity in the black press.

> Each Saturday we whipped out GOP propaganda for all the weeklies. Heading the Negro division were Dr. Redmond and Perry Howard, national committeemen from Mississippi. The positions of Perry Howard and Ben Davis Sr. during this period were a paradox. In both states the scant Republican Party membership was composed almost exclusively of

those few Afro Americans who voted in national elections.

(*Livin'* 250)

Davis, working at the ANP at the time, was primarily interested in the survival of the black press during hard economic times. He understood too well the value of having a privately owned African American press to balance the white press and its supremacist themes and perspectives of success, wealth, power, status, and the blatant exclusion by the white press of positive news about Blacks and other non-white Americans.

Davis always chose to offer through the black press a variety of news articles, editorials and analysis about and for African Americans and their community. Like other African American editors and activists, he chose to construct an alternative paradigm to white supremacy. His columns were based on the principle of and struggle for a just democratic society that he fought for with each column he wrote. But how could he do these things if the newspaper and black press fell silent and folded? Indeed times during the Depression and Renaissance were hard.

In spite of Jim Crow laws, policies, and practices, Davis continued to firmly believe in and support the principles of democracy and to regularly publish news to promote it. When an African American student, Lloyd Gaines, with the help of the NAACP, sued for admission to the law school of the University of Missouri in 1938, Davis characteristically covered the story.

> The U. S. Supreme Court in 1937 rendered its historic Gaines case decision, establishing the precedent that a state must provide equal educational opportunities for all citizens within its borders--a break in the dike of discrimination paving the way for the high court decision seventeen years later outlawing segregated schools. . . . However, the 1937 edict was generally ignored by Dixie commonwealths. . . . And again I want to stress that this drastic change came about only through militancy on the part of Afro-Americans.
>
> (*Livin'* 258-260)

Davis recounts how he was approached by segregationists to help establish and possibly head a professional regional school "for Nigras" even though it was in direct violation of the recent decision.

State officials had the choice of admitting Gaines to the law school or establishing a completely equal separate law school within Missouri borders. They chose the latter and shelled out taxpayers' funds to start a law school at Lincoln University, the state's Jim Crow institute of higher learning.

(Livin' 259)

Davis deplored the role of the legal system as a whore to social tradition in the perpetuation of inequality; he was sympathetic with political and civil rights groups like the N.A.A.C.P.

Political issues brought people together to work for social reform such as integration in the armed forces, the fight against fascism, the struggle against poverty, and the various federal work programs. By joining their voices and efforts, African American strength and political clout grew. Intellectuals and community leaders met at workshops, rallies, conferences, jazz clubs, and the Allied Arts Guild where they discussed strategies. They participated in the National Negro Council, the National Negro Congress (a coalition of about 40 African American organizations), and the National Negro Exposition in Chicago which included many distinguished African Americans, including A. Phillip Randolph, Ralph Bunche, Richard Wright, and Davis. There was a sense of excitement and solidarity between artists and political activists. Fanon observes: "Each time a man has contributed to the victory of the dignity of the spirit, every time a man has said no to an attempt to subjugate his fellows, I have felt solidarity with his art" (*Black Skin* 226). The Communist Party encouraged a proletarian art which did change American cultural history by publishing and promoting working class and African American artists. The Communist Party's influence rendered the thirties and forties a very exciting, creative, and *avant garde* period in the development of diversity in culture and the arts.

During the forties, Davis's slow, deliberate, eloquent, and intensely resonant voice made him a much sought after public speaker in Chicago at events both political and cultural. His network of African American and white radical friends was as extensive as an African American *Who's Who*, ranging from those in the most influential communities to the regulars at Mojo's Cafe. Davis was known and respected as an outspoken editor and a critic of Jim Crow, white supremacy, and the inequalities of capitalism. He managed to live fairly well during this period in spite of many obstacles, not the least of which was his low salary, standard for the African American newspaper business.

Empowerment of African American intellectuals also manifested itself in national communications with the expansion of the African American press and the beginning of *Negro Digest* (1943), the first successful African American news and culture magazine; according to Davis, it became the prototype for many other African American magazines and periodicals, and subsequently developed into *Ebony* magazine (1945) which in turn successfully established and maintained an ethnic readership (*Livin'* 274-275).

Davis believed that perhaps some of the most significant empowering creative contributions of African Americans to America and the world were in music. Jazz, bop, the blues, and innumerable dances and rhythms were quickly adopted by creative whites and spread throughout the society. In discussing the rapid spread of African American cultural influence in the United States, Ishmael Reed in *Mumbo Jumbo* calls it the "Jes Grew" phenomena, because it seemingly like magic touched and transformed all in its path starting in the 1920's. "Jes Grew" included an attitude of irreverence which was visible through the music, style and fashion, body language, and slang, and included an impertinence toward authority and disrespect for tradition which was invisible in precise origins. "Jes Grew" infected the whole country, threatening the racist institution of segregation and the entire social fabric, as whites from all levels of society turned to African Americans for rhythms, inspiration and even intimacy. "Jes Grew" was a consequence of liberation praxis. It was a product of the African American creative imagination and political acumen manifested in artistic expressions revealing their visceral indignation at injustice, and fearless, militant convictions coupled with the courage of self-expression against injustice (*Mumbo Jumbo* 13-32).

Another area of creative empowerment was journalism. Davis played a clear and decisive role in the history of Black journalism in the United States. The long history of journalism in the African American community springs from the early 1800s and the abolitionists who stressed the need to protest for freedom and equality by using the printed word and the power of circulation to communicate the message to many people (Bardolph 62). As an African American journalist, Davis, in the tradition of protest, documented the emancipatory movements of individuals and the community, reporting on oppression and liberation, failure and success. He witnessed major race breakthroughs in sports, especially boxing, basketball, and football, all of which he recorded and commented on in his editorials in the Associated Negro Press (ANP), public forums, poetry, and prose.

Journalism also provided Davis with a forum for his ironic commentaries, analysis, and critiques of society. Although his salary was often minimal, he survived and thrived with journalistic perks, status, relative power, and privileges. The press card gave him access to almost any event, as well as free drinks, invitations to parties and dinners, and even bribes which ranged from booze and cash to women and clothes, all "customary" in Chicago, a city known for its graft and corruption.

In the 1930's, the combined circulation of African American newspapers had reached well over 1.25 million, much of it accounted for by a dozen leading periodicals in Pittsburgh, Chicago, New York, Baltimore, Norfolk, and Philadelphia, all of them weeklies designed for national circulation. Working in Atlanta, Davis knew that individual papers strongly reflected the personalities of their editors and publishers, though the day of personal journalism was beginning to give place to standardizing influences such as columnists, other "chain features," and the emergence of the Associated Negro Press (ANP).

Davis and his contemporaries affirmed that the African American press was above all a fighting press, offering mainly "race news". It included materials, in short, which the white press either did not present at all or offered in minuscule quantities and often with distortion. "Be ready!" was a constant, almost apocalyptic, refrain, for the press never doubted that the triumph of full justice--soon--was inevitable in the logic of American history. In short, the church in these years was losing to the press and the "race agencies" or social clubs (*Livin'* 190-191).

African American journalism was a bootstrap operation, because the men and few women who built and ran the press faced the usual lack of opportunity for training, experience, and acquiring much needed capital to survive and expand. National advertisers usually passed the African American press by, for they knew that the buyers of African American papers bought white papers, too. Even the large department stores withheld advertisements, since they were reluctant to invite African Americans to come in and shop. In fact, African Americans usually were not even permitted to try on clothes, shoes, and hats in most stores, North and South.

Thus, it is not surprising that, in the 1920's and 1930's, African American papers were obliged to take subsidies from politicians and other interest groups just to meet their production costs. Ironically, the principal advertising income came from vendors of what Davis would call dubious "race" products: hair straighteners, skin lighteners, lip reducers, good luck charms, patent medicines, hair pieces, and flamboyant sartorial oddities, feeding upon the national stereotypes that colored skin tones and hair were inferior. These products created a desire to look white and encouraged a superficial assimilation, playing upon low self-esteem, ignorance, and self-hatred.

Because of the lack of revenues from advertisements, two-thirds of the money for the African American newspapers had to come from subscribers, which meant a selling price five times above that of the white daily. Perhaps the compensation to all of this financial struggle and injustice was that this freed the African American press from advertiser domination.

The black editors like Davis could print stories and editorials with less censorship than the large national dailies that depended on advertisers' money and politics for their survival. Unfortunately, it also compelled many African American publishers and editors to sometimes print sensationalism, sports, and society news and to appeal disproportionately to lower-class interests in order to boost circulation.

The move toward sensationalism was especially visible after 1910, when Robert S. Abbott, founder of the powerful Chicago *Defender*, demonstrated its appeal. The new trend was toward mixing the paper's sober crusading content of race pride with lurid headlines, heaping portions of scandal, sex, crime, and vulgarities, to attract the attention of readers with a weak literacy and no literary tradition.

The African American press maintained a highly personal journalism far longer than the white press. When Davis was writing in Chicago, it was not yet dominated by the business mentality that would, in the next generation, make the African American newspaper an increasingly faithful facsimile of the white tabloid (*Livin'* 192).

Like many African American publishers, Abbott, owner and publisher of the Chicago *Defender*, was obliged to recruit his staff from porters, barbers, waiters, musicians, entertainers, and assorted bright young persons, most of whom were male college graduates, and a rare few, specifically trained in journalism. Fortunately, despite Abbott's lack of technical training, he had a remarkable knack for recognizing talent, like Davis. His techniques for building circulation among the working-class people with unsophisticated tastes, while keeping close to the role of the race's "defender," revolutionized African American journalism according to Davis.

Between 1935 and 1945, Davis was a features editor and later Executive Editor of the Associated Negro Press (ANP). He also had several columns: his editorial column, "Behind the Headlines" was popular. He wrote on the theater under the name of Franklyn Frank "enabling me to again chronicle the show world and bathe in hot jazz" (*Livin'* 228). J. Edgar Tidwell writes in his excellent chronology that Davis wrote another column on jazz under the titles of "Rating the Records" and "Rating Hot Records", and yet another column on sports. He used the names Frank Boganey and "The Globe Trotter" for his sports columns (*Black Moods* xviii). Davis writes he simultaneously often handled publicity for other organizations, such as the National Negro Congress and the Republican Party. As a columnist, he had access to famous musical and sports personalities like Ray Nance, Cab Calloway, Oze Simmons, and Joe Louis. He also penned stories on popular dancers, and even a few impersonators (*Livin'* 228).

During the hard times of the Depression, Davis occasionally acted as a promoter for several up and coming arts and entertainment stars. For example, he arranged the debut of Frank Yerby in Jack Conroy's *The New Anvil*, and granted exposure to Chester Himes in the *Atlanta World*. He was proud to include columns from black correspondents and supporters from and throughout the African Diaspora. Davis states in his autobiography:

Nationally known leaders in various fields submitted regular columns to ANP but most of our material came from correspondents all over America, the Caribbean, Africa and some parts of Europe including London and Moscow. Usually small space rates were paid, although some such as Nancy Cunard, maverick heiress to a steamship fortune, wrote because they had ideas that begged for exposure. ANP prided itself on mirroring black activities everywhere.

(Livin' 227)

He prided himself on including stories concerning blacks around the world, whenever he could find them, by reading extensively 35 national and international newspapers on a daily basis. The significance of the ANP was its connections with the African American papers all over the country. Davis's particular responsibilities were enormous, and he was by all accounts an excellent editor.

One of his more significant contributions as an editor was Davis's input into the 1942 National Conference of Negro editors in Washington D.C., ironically scheduled the day after the attack on Pearl Harbor. Although Davis was unable to attend, his associate and colleague, Claude Barnett, carried his important suggestion for volunteer integrated fighting units during World War II to General George Marshall, chief of staff, in the presence of representative editors and members of the N.A.A.C.P. who had gathered from all over the country. Even though the proposal was initially vetoed,

... the question of an integrated army was officially on the record before many witnesses. Immediately after the close of the conference, the N.A.A.C.P. launched a nationwide petition campaign, creating strong sentiment for the proposal and obtaining thousands of signatures demanding mixed army units. ... With the pressure mounting from many areas, the big Brass in the Pentagon finally had to take action. During the Battle of the Bulge, the American army at last broke with custom and inaugurated the radical innovation of an experimental voluntary fighting unit, just as I had proposed through Claude Barnett. Although those who signed for this special outfit knew they had to give up their ratings and be reduced to private, there were more than enough men of good will who chose to make this sacrifice on behalf of practical democracy to fill the initial quota. This was the beginning of the end for two separate and distinct armies. . . . Undoubtedly had I not been able to have the concept of voluntary integration brought up before General Marshall in front of reputable and influential witnesses, the change to mixed units would have taken place as a fact of evolution. Nevertheless, it was presented to the highest soldier in the armed forces, the day following Pearl Harbor, and under circumstances where it could not be shunted aside or ignored. I cannot think of a more strategic moment this century.   (*Livin'* 270)

All in all, Davis's talent, timing, and commitment to the African American community were most evident when he was working as editor of the ANP. It was a part of his life that he was very proud of.

As years passed I prided myself on my versatility as a newspaperman. I served not only as straight news reporter but as rewrite man, editor, editorial writer, political commentator, theatrical and jazz columnist, sports writer and occasionally news photographer.   (*Livin'* 231)

The dedication of the African American press to the elimination of racism, its denunciation of the status quo of Jim Crow, and its growing national circulation assured its wide readership and financial success for many years. Even the Pentagon and Executive Branch recognized its power and yielded to some of its editorial demands. However, Davis writes that what brought integration most readily was the desperate need for manpower.

Our support was essential to victory. Barriers crumbled. At the beginning of the war, we could rise no higher than mess-man in the navy (despite this, Dorie Miller was a hero at Pearl Harbor), and we were completely barred from the marine corps and from flying war planes. Other ratings were opened in the navy, black marines came into being, a pilot training school was established in Tuskegee, Alabama, and for the first time in history we could point to a general.

(*Livin'* 272-273)

As a result of efforts to de-segregate the armed forces spearheaded by black journalists, today some of the nation's outstanding African American military leaders, pilots, and cavalry are remembered for their bravery and outstanding service in numerous books, documentaries, and movies.

As was previously mentioned, Davis documented the segregation in most sports, especially football, basketball, and boxing. He covered the first annual National Professional Basketball Tournament in 1939 in Chicago between the two best African American teams in the nation, the New York Rens (Renaissance) out of Harlem and the Globetrotters out of Chicago. He wrote of the outstanding players on the African American teams, how they met their demise once the teams were integrated, and how they were lured away to the formerly all-white teams due to higher salaries, better publicity, and a wider power base.

> I think the initial success of the Rens and Trotters in a national test of strength was the first step toward the breaking the color barrier in this pro sport. Until then teams were usually all black or all white. After the first few annual tournaments, they started showing up with mixed personnel. . . . Meanwhile the interest aroused by the annual tournament revived the pro league and resulted in integrated teams and the spectacular kinds of games familiar today.
>
> (*Livin'* 232-233)

Ironically, this is a fate now being experienced by many traditional African American colleges.

Like other African American intellectuals in the 1940's who had read Carter G. Woodson's *The Negro History of America*, Davis was familiar with much African and African American history and recognized that many gains in Civil Rights were but a restoration of rights that African Americans had earned after the Civil War. He took pleasure in discovering and writing the facts about outstanding and unrecognized contributions of African Americans in history, such as the 5000 African Americans who fought side by side with whites in the American War of Independence in 1776. He took pride in breaking the story about the pioneer woman soldier, Deborah Gannett, when the Women's Army Corps was created in WWII.

> I took great relish in pointing out that a black woman,
> Deborah Gannett, fought the entire Revolutionary War with
> a New England outfit which, of course, saw her color but
> did not know her sex until she was mustered out. Then in
> gratitude, she was granted a pension for the rest of her life.
> She deserved the rating of first WAC in American History.
>
> (*Livin'* 273)

He included an African American historical context whenever possible in his editorials which were informed and occasionally erudite, and he included women in his columns as well.

During this period, labor and political coalitions were encouraged as means and tools of empowerment, and cultural foment produced abundant creative expression. The momentum of the New Deal gave birth to an optimism in the "big, burly town of Chicago" felt by workers and artists alike.

> Never before had I worked closely and voluntarily in equality
> with a number of whites. At this period I had already rid myself
> of the worst elements of my teen age inferiority complex by
> studying black history. At last I had come to possess what
> is called race pride. Still, I doubt whether anybody reared
> under the constant hammering of white superiority can ever
> fully free himself of its personality crippling effects.
>
> (*Livin'* 248)

Eventually, despite his independent efforts as a journalist, Davis came to believe that an individual, even through poetry and editorials, was not strong enough to effect change in American society's racial politics. Then he decided to join hands with others fighting racism.

> I knew of course, that the Establishment tolerates the
> solitary protester. It smiles and points to him as proof that
> free speech does exist in America. The unwritten rule is
> that you can yell as loudly as you please, by yourself. But
> when two or more of you get together, you become a threat,
> even though you speak only in whispers. Two or more
> automatically become a conspiracy which endangers "Our
> Way of Life" and those agencies, such as the FBI or House

> Committee on UnAmerican Activities, which ignore the
> injustices triggering your protests, now began hounding you
> as dangerous radicals. I had seen this happen over and over
> again.   (*Livin'* 276)

When Davis joined the powerful Chicago labor movement, he took a large
risk by calling attention to himself in a period rife with suspicion and
censorship by the federal government.

> From now on I knew I would be described as a Communist,
> but frankly I had reached the stage where I didn't give a
> damn. Too many people I respected as Freedom Fighters
> were listed as Red for me to fear name calling. (*Livin'* 276)

Although involvement with the labor movement was Davis's
opportunity to work to bring about better wages and conditions for both
African Americans and whites, perhaps most significant about this period
in Chicago was that Davis and other African American intellectuals had
a chance to mix freely in interracial situations, thereby opening doors for
those who came after. It was also a chance to heal some of the wounds of
racism.

Davis understood more than ever that the problems in America caused
by class inequities were intricately woven with racial inequities. The Chicago
Renaissance was a period when it was possible for interracial friendships to
form and new levels of communication to occur.

> I felt equal to my white peers. Around them I could not sniff
> the offensive odor of condescension. You see, I like people
> despite being basically a loner, but experience had taught
> me never to immediately trust anybody white . . . and in a
> determined effort to become cosmopolitan, I participated in
> all. . . . I still have warm personal feelings for those with
> whom I worked. This is a big reason why I cannot support
> the African American extremist postulate that all whites
> are our enemies. . . . Unless you have allowed yourself to
> become completely dehumanized by American racism, you
> value and retain your proven friends, no matter what their
> color.   (*Livin'* 248-249)

Davis recognized strengths and weaknesses of the African American group. He was neither nationalist nor separatist but rather a humanist and an integrationist. He did not want to forsake the culture nor history of African Americans, because it was particular to his cosmology, but he did want to have the freedom to act responsibly with whomever he chose, and that included friendships with people of diverse ethnic and cultural backgrounds.

In Chicago, there was yet another arena besides music, labor, and government where African Americans and whites could meet and exchange on intellectual and social levels. This was in liberal political circles and coalitions which often included socialists, communists, university types, and representatives from labor unions.

Many African American intellectuals lacked authority, status, and money, and had little to risk or lose by censorship of the white power structure since they were already considered pariahs. Some like Davis, Wright, and Robeson listened to the Communist rhetoric, honed their intellectual skills in the many discussion groups and activities, supported rallies, conferences, petitions, and other organizational efforts, often simultaneously sponsored by the liberals, socialists, and Communists. Because they had little to lose, informal affiliation with the Communists did not seem to matter at the time.

Like many creative and intellectual African Americans of the thirties and forties, Davis circulated in what the government and white society considered radical political groups, which sponsored rallies, forums, poetry readings, signed petitions, disclaimed the existing inequalities of class and race, and proclaimed what they felt ought to be a true democracy. These activities served in the long run to effect a change in the national political consciousness of the diverse public, heighten the awareness of the values and issues of democracy, and lay the groundwork for the Civil Rights Movement which was yet to come.

Occasional members of the Communist Party were also connected to these groups and one cannot ignore their influence on the thought of many progressive African American leaders and intellectuals, although it has been documented that relatively few African Americans actually joined or remained with the Party. Curiously, when Davis was in Atlanta, he disclaimed the "Reds" in his editorials as exploiters of poor African Americans, particularly when a cause was involved such as the famous

Scottsboro Boys' trial. In his *Touring the World* column, October 2, 1932, he wrote:

> The Reds have placed her [the mother] on exhibition in much the same manner as a quack medicine show doctor would a diseased person when he wished to impress his audience that unless they bought his cure they would surely end up like his exhibit.   (1931-1933)

However, by the time he returned to Chicago and the Renaissance, Davis inevitably associated with people connected with the Party since they were most likely to be involved in civil rights, labor, art, and the fight for equality. From an interview it seems that Frank did join the party for a short time, although on other occasions he strongly denied it. Were there repercussions due to his association?

Because of the unwillingness of the Party to recognize the value of religion in the African American experience, and inconsistencies in their ideology, at times appeasing the white workers, at times trying to attract the African Americans, their erratic platform of nationalism was not sufficient to ever draw large numbers of converts from the African American community. Cornel West argues that Marxist theory has been inadequate for grasping the complexity of racism as a historical phenomenon due to its failure to probe the psychological and cultural spheres (49-50).

When considering Davis's personal life during the Chicago Renaissance period, especially his relationships with women, one cannot ignore two primary texts: his memoir/autobiography, *Livin' the Blues*, and an earlier novel, *Sex Rebel: Black*, written under the pseudonym Bob Greene and which is purported to be largely autobiographical.

In his early years, Davis was somewhat traditional in his attitudes about sexual activity, even wanting to marry a virgin, and believing that "nice girls didn't" engage in sexual activity before marriage. However, by 1937, predating and predicting the sexual revolution of the 1960's and the women's liberation movement of the 1970's according to his autobiography, Davis writes he was becoming bored with his marriage to his first wife, Thelma Boyd (*Livin'* 230), and was contemplating separation after six years of marriage. He fictionalized their marriage experience in *Sex Rebel: Black* using the names of Bob and Doris.

Beginning in a southern setting, Bob is satisfied with his sexual life with Doris, but feels little intellectual stimulation. Whereas Bob enjoys jazz, the blues, good literature, satire, and lively discussion, Doris prefers partying, romance novels, and her friends. They both share the pleasures of sex and drinking, which become liberating paths to escape the painful problems of race, class, confinement of daily life, and self-worth that Davis would follow for a long time. When he receives offers to publish his poetry and work for several newspapers, Bob and Doris move to Chicago. They set up house, although Bob is no longer satisfied with their marital relationship.

However, once Doris introduces him to "swinging," Bob stays married to her for eight years longer, although for a period of time they reside in different cities, both leading sexually active and independent lives. Davis says:

> Bluntly I can enjoy coitus with unlimited partners but I have met few women who have these essentials for the long, intimate relationship of marriage. Also, I have no interest in the double standard. But I do know I would wither and die if I confined my sexual outlet to one woman; I need the transfusion of other flesh. (*Sex Rebel* 19)

Compared to his sheltered adolescence, the interest in multiple partners seems like an escape mechanism for Davis to experience freedom and gain power.

Doris introduces Bob to the "swinging" life which includes multiple sex partners (of her choosing), sex parties, and non-conventional practices to stimulate their faltering marriage. However, she constantly refuses to consider whites as possible partners, due to her previous personal negative racial experiences growing up in Alabama.

> Doris, coming from a small town in Alabama where Negroes didn't have a chance, was bitterly anti-white. . . . But even my wife's overwhelming desire for variety could not overcome her rabid antagonism toward whites.   (*Sex Rebel* 67)

Bob explains the politics of race and rejection by using Doris's Alabama experiences to illustrate how the power of racism can delimit one's most personal of choices, even into the bedroom. Bob comments:

> Prejudice . . . is both rotten and senseless. I don't sanction it
> in anybody. But at the same time, with us (Blacks) it's usually
> defensive. It's a reaction to the prejudice we experience.
> If you ever heard my wife tell you how she and all other
> Negroes were treated in her home town in Alabama, you'd
> understand.   (*Sex Rebel* 92)

He cites Doris's opinion:

> I don't want a goddamn thing to do with any stinkin' ass
> paddies. I haven't seen a white man yet I'd let put anything
> in me--well . . . You know how I feel 'bout peckerwoods
> anyways.   (*Sex Rebel* 67)

Doris's derogatory southern terms for whites reveals the gulf between her
world view and Bob's. However, the naming of the *other* (the white man)
illustrates the creative responses to African American oppression, as blacks
(Doris) seize the words and a subjective feeling of power by creating new
words to render their oppressors powerless as "paddies" or "peckerwoods".

The need for power and control in the lives of people who have
historically been disempowered is evident throughout Davis's writings. He
writes of extra-marital affairs, multiple partners, and other orgies within
and crossing the color line. As mentioned before, Doris also likes to be in a
position of control over her husband's sexual activities. She does not mind
sharing Bob with other African American women and men, but she prefers
to be present, responsible, and in control for providing pleasure and variety
to her husband. For example, since some of Doris's friends, due to loneliness
or monotony, are sexually unfulfilled, she offers to share Bob's techniques
of "frenching" (cunnilingus) with them. The free-love complicity of the
husband/wife team creates surprise and approval from some of their friends.

> Yes, I told Clara how talented you are," Doris went on.
> "So don't let me down. Don't you wanta help out our close
> friend--specially since she's crying for relief? Remember,
> you're supposed to love thy neighbor.   (*Sex Rebel* 21)

Davis's irony is abundant throughout the book; in the preceding passage the
sardonic reference to God's commandment to "love thy neighbor," means

to have sex (eros not agape), and it somehow seems to surpass the other related commandment of "thou shalt not commit adultery."

Even Doris participates in the sexual acts which become an integral part of their "swinging". Her sexual proclivities and activities with other women, both with and apart from Bob, reveal her bisexuality which Davis does not judge or condemn. Again Davis is bold and courageous to write about another taboo subject, lesbians, before the women's movement.

Although male chauvinism was common during the forties, Davis basically believed in liberation on a political and personal level, which included the liberation of women. He had long recognized the role of the independent African American working woman in the community who through her work outside of the house had contributed in large part to the survival of the African American family. Davis does confess to having a double standard with regards to sexual behavior. He became angry with his wife, Thelma, for her amorous escapades, but he quickly overcame that lapse of jealousy, and as he grew older, he became more tolerant.

> It had also occurred to me I could not logically oppose one kind of discrimination and support another. If I fought privilege based on color, I could not conscientiously demand privilege based on sex. To a modern, emancipated woman, male chauvinism is as offensive as white chauvinism to a black American. If I objected to being treated as if I were owned by Caucasians, a woman could rightfully object to being treated as a male possession. From then on, I rejected the double standard. (*Livin'* 230)

Regardless of his commitment to the personal freedom of women, Davis is seemingly chauvinistic in his vocabulary in *Sex Rebel, Black*, probably reflecting the time and culture he lived in. For example, he often refers to women by such terms as dolls, chicks, and good-time girls; he utilizes over forty terms for the vagina and its parts such as slit, sheath, portals, quim, and gash. This usage compares to less than half the terms in his writing for the penis, such as lance, staff, pole, and sausage. He also uses a wide variety of terms when speaking of female breasts such as, globes, dairies, knockers, dinners, and jugs. Nonetheless, Davis insisted that he did not have a double standard for men and women, and prided himself for being pro women's liberation: physical, psychological and sexual. The character Bob says:

> Personally I prefer emotional fidelity and honesty. As long as my mate remains hooked on me, I don't give a damn if she has discreet sex with another. I want companionship, affection, rapport, similar intellectual interests and emotional involvement along with erotic compatibility. (*Sex Rebel* 19)

Davis did have a historical consciousness of gender equality which was uncharacteristic of the times, i.e. uncommon for most whites. However, gender equality had historically been the thinking and reality of many outstanding African American women and men such as Sojourner Truth and Frederick Douglass from the earliest days of slavery, probably due to the break-up of the family and subsequent active roles of nurturer and provider for the family that many African American women were obligated to assume. Davis writes:

> With Afro-American males customarily the last hired and first fired, with vast numbers both underemployed and underpaid when they have jobs, prospects of marrying for security are far fewer. Our women, knowing for generations that usually they must work to help make ends meet and because they often were forced to raise their families alone, long ago developed sexual independence. (*Livin'* 221)

The African American woman was often less constrained by African American men and the community in the personal realm of the body and sex. Promiscuity was generally frowned upon, the family structure was respected, but circumstances (historically and contemporarily) often created a more independent attitude toward sexual expression. Therefore, Davis was not surprised to have an ample supply of African American women models when he began to develop his passion for photography. He was later to distinguish himself in this field and win several national awards.

Davis became interested in photography thanks to his friend and neighbor, Leo, who provided him with inexpensive equipment and a camera, he quickly learned how to develop and print proficiently. He recounts in *Livin' the Blues* that he soon turned his attention to the human body, especially nude women.

> As I gained confidence behind the lens, I turned to nudes.
> Obviously the female body fascinates me, both aesthetically
> and emotionally. The steatopygian aspect (I use the word
> advisedly) of black women pleases me; . . . I was amazed at
> the number of gals eager to strip and stand unclothed before
> the all-seeing eye of the camera. Sometimes husbands
> brought their wives to pose nude -- Thelma (wife) was
> helpful in getting models. She had no hesitancy about asking
> a shapely gal to have her picture taken with nothing on her
> but lights. Usually Thelma was present, but it would have
> made no difference anyway. . . . I forget personal sex when
> I photograph a nude woman. . . . [N]o matter how appealing
> the model under normal conditions, I become a robot back of
> a camera. I have no male reaction until I develop negatives
> and make prints.   (*Livin'* 230)

Davis enjoyed the power of controlling people's images and observing their vanity and desire to be seen, remembered and possibly immortalized in film. His preference for African American women at this point in his life seems obvious, or perhaps it is no more than his appreciation of the beauty of the human form.

In *Sex Rebel, Black*, when the character Bob moves to Chicago from Atlanta, Doris comes to visit him in Chicago, but returns alone to Washington where she has already taken a job. Other female characters in the book also move to other cities to seek work and/or education, not allowing their relationships with men to determine or influence their career choices and goals. Davis admires this independence of African American women, born of the hard necessity of the past, and writes in his autobiography:

> The economic facts of life dictated that the soul sister should
> satisfy her natural desires for sex just as she took care of
> natural desires for food and sleep instead of waiting for some
> knight in shining armor to carry her off to a castle where she
> could live happily ever after, sheltered from the cruel outside
> world.   (*Livin'* 221)

Davis was a social realist, and he recognized that there was little chance that an African American woman would ever meet her "knight in shining armor," a wealthy man who could provide her with the proverbial castle. He knew that as long as racism existed, one could never be happy for ever after, sheltered from the outside world. It was practical and realistic according to Davis's perspective that African American women should seek their brief pleasures and satisfy their needs when the moment and person were right, rather than live in a fairy tale dream world.

He also saw perhaps some African carryovers which reflected what he thought to be a more natural, instinctive response to the body and its needs and desires. He compares the independence of black women with the security bound white women, alienated from their bodies and sex until the sexual revolution of the 1970's and he states in his autobiography:

> Generally speaking, black women have long been more sexually liberated than their male counterparts. During slavery they were not only forced to bed their masters but breed with powerful studs, like cattle, in the hope of producing physically strong offspring, but this was forced behavior. I refer instead to a more realistic attitude toward sex as a surviving Africanism and to the economics of black existence. Traditionally white women have married for security after being taught coitus was a dirty ordeal to which they must submit. This systematic repression of natural urges resulted in frigidity from which white women have escaped in sizeable numbers only since the spread of the continuing sex revolt.   (*Livin'* 220)

Davis did not agree with the Christian tenets of original sin, fornication, abstention, and "sex-for-reproduction-only" (*Sex Rebel* 16). He felt that women and men should both enjoy sex.

> I cannot imagine a Supreme Being, supposedly compassionate and all-loving, instilling in mankind the persistent drive for sex activity and then telling us we cannot satisfy this consuming desire when we need to, but instead must wait only for those times when we want offspring. Such a God would of necessity be the Supreme Sadist laughing his holy ass off at, first, daily tortures inflicted on those who abstain through fear of His displeasure, and second, at contemplation of eternal punishment in hell. . . . I, for one, refuse to accept

such an insane idea of a God.   (16)

Again he spoke of the illogicality of a Christian God.

Davis also wrote of a man's watching another man make love to his wife, an act which the husband finds sexually arousing, revealing the erotic recurrent theme of voyeurism in *Sex Rebel: Black*.

> [N]ot only did I anticipate sessions with other of my wife's friends, but I might eventually be able to realize a dream so fantastic I hardly dared think about it. That dream was to watch another man make out with my wife. Because she was my wife and there was emotional involvement, the thought excited me far more than watching any other two persons copulating, as stirring as that, too, was.   (23)

As Davis moved within liberal and radical circles, he soon discovered that many white women and men both secretly and openly harbored desires to have sexual contact with an educated and large African American man. This was perhaps due to the stereotypes and disfigured images about African Americans' sexual prowess which was a carryover from slavery time when blacks were used as breeders, and sexual objects—alternately feared and idealized for their "primitive passions".

Davis himself was curious about sexual contact with whites, and this inquisitiveness led him on a path which was eventually to end in exile when he married his white wife Helen Canfield, a student in his vanguard and exciting jazz class.

CHAPTER 5
The Precarious Freedom of the Cold War African American Intellectual: Race, Poverty, and Exclusion

Negro writers are now moving into new areas of involvement with fundamental social issues that go beyond the race question into an awareness of the tragedy, irony and absurdity of American and twentieth-century life.

(Hill xxi-xxii)

The cultural denigration of African Americans in U.S. society had a decisive effect on Frank Marshall Davis and the black psyche. His fiery rejection of Eurocentric ideology lead Davis, consciously and unconsciously, to use writing, activism, public speaking and sex as means of gaining status and power in an unrelenting pursuit of freedom.

He witnessed far too many African Americans who had been abused and/or abandoned by society. He refused to ignore the enormity of this racial dilemma and tragedy.

An interpretive analysis of certain events of Davis's life in Chicago which affected his psyche, hopes, and understanding, points to the limited choices available to a supra-conscious Race Man during the first half of the twentieth century. Davis's reactions to inequality, the failures of democracy, and the monumental injustices of race and class can be a mirror to various historical forms of African American protest, civil disobedience, and resistance: nationalism, separatism, and various civil rights movements for integration, assimilation, justice, equality, and forbidden sexual activity.

Moreover, northern white attitudes towards African Americans who migrated to Chicago reveal many whites' overwhelming commitment to racial segregation, and the preservation of their economic status and social privilege.

The politics of racial estrangement has the effect of creating a metaphorical black orphan in a hostile environment: social, economic, political, and cultural. The victim, be it an individual or a community, becomes like a blind person wandering aimlessly and alone in a treacherous storm looking for shelter and acceptance. Over an extended period of time, in face of closed doors and repeated rejection, the compelling desire to assimilate and be accepted can create frustration and/or neurosis in the rejected and alienated victim.

However assimilation was not the goal of Frank Marshall Davis. His was not a narcissistic quest to be a white status African American man, but a quest to simply be an American citizen in a functioning democracy, free to fulfill his personal potential and participate fully in society by making his own responsible choices.

Davis's dedication to social justice and personal freedom can be traced to a sense of insecurity and lack of self esteem that he experienced as a child and adolescent in Kansas due to forced and segregated isolation. It is likely his early observations and experiences of injustice led him to his unwavering commitment to the struggle for democracy, respect, dignity, and participatory politics. Perhaps his dedication was also fueled by his conscience. Indeed his writing reflects his frustrations and simultaneous hopes for the world he lived in; it also incorporates the history and legacy of African strength and greatness. Nor does he ignore the more thorny topics of racism, resistance, and poverty. Davis relentlessly tries to educate his readership and inform them of a noble African past in order to create more pride, unity, and power in the individual and community.

During the lifetime of Davis, throughout the USA, most black men were limited in terms of education, status, and success; they were ignored and/or thwarted from competition by dominant yet sometimes insecure whites. The gulf between the two groups was ever reflected in the divergent lifestyles, cultures, attitudes, economic and political realities, and a national sense of the inferiority of blacks in relation to whites. Fanon describes this pathological state of self-loathing from a black man's imagined perspective:

> I begin to suffer from not being a white man to the degree that the white man imposes discrimination on me . . . robs me of all worth, all individuality, tells me that I am a parasite on the world, that I must bring myself as quickly as possible into step with the white world, "that I am a brute beast".
>
> (*Black Skin* 98)

The heinous stereotype of black man as beast is the epitome of the myth of black inferiority and savagery, and has continued to haunt African

Americans even into the 21st Century. This mythification of the black man has had tragic consequences, often ending in conflict, social pathology, and violence, overt and covert.

Davis experienced the conflict between the desire to integrate and the desire to be apart from white society for self-protection and survival. Yet he tried to stay in step with the world, always with an aim to benefit the African American community, to bestow knowledge, self-esteem, valuation, and also to encourage self-reliance. As he matured, he recognized that hostility between the races was most often caused by a conflict in cultural expressions, values, and identities. Many values held by the African American community were misunderstood or feared by whites and often included cultural carryovers such as: the extended family, a strong sense of community, expressive emotional and sensual behavior, a holistic approach to life and living, an oral tradition, African-influenced music which was played at most ritual celebrations, flamboyant adornment, dramatic and vociferous communication, beliefs in spirits, ancestors, invisible powers, and their connections with humans, and a prophetic tradition.

Davis could clearly see that these carryovers were frequently in opposition with the more conservative, traditionally white protestant values of mind over body, materialism, modesty, discipline, competition, individualism, abstinence, fear of God, success-oriented status based on money, and a European aesthetic of beauty. Indeed, Western Europeans and Euro-Americans were the so-called authorities on aesthetics, science, and civilization. Davis thought that whites appropriated others' cultural expressions, art, and history in order to elevate and celebrate their white power, knowledge, and dominance. They used the privilege of white power to include and exclude whole groups of people, countries, continents and their histories from the so-called legitimate and civilized realm of whiteness.

> There appears to be a definite correspondence between the African ethos and the Afro-American world view in terms of the focus on emotional vitality, interdependence, collective survival, the oral tradition, perception of time, harmonious blending, and the role of the elderly. . . . The African world view begins with a holistic conception of the human condition. The human organism is conceived

as a totality made up of a series of interlocking systems. This total person is simultaneously a feeling, experiencing, sensualizing, sensing, and knowing human being living in a dynamic, vitalistic world where everything is interrelated and endowed with the supreme force of life. There is a sense of aliveness, intensity, and animation in the music, dance, song, language, and life styles of Africans. Emotions are not labeled as bad; therefore, there is no need to repress feelings of compassion, love, joy, or sensuality.

(White and Parham 15)

Unfortunately, because of this conflict in values, most African carryovers, especially those which touched on the emotional sphere, were labeled by whites as inferior, savage, or feminine compared to those Christian ideals of reason, self-denial, obedience, submission, and humility held by the dominant patriarchal society. This sense of white superiority created in many blacks a kind of cultural and social shame. Cultural *rapprochement* with EuroAmericans was generally discouraged in order to maintain a sense of cultural degradation in the blacks rendering them impotent.

Davis sought to educate, affirm, and celebrate the differences between the two groups rather than repudiate black values. He understood the denigrating assumptions and labeling by the majority who thought that African Americans who tried to assimilate--for example, by appreciating classical music--were considered "cocky niggers" who needed to be reminded of their place. Davis might have also been considered a "bad nigger" when he wrote his outspoken editorials; he was big, strong, outspoken, and fearless.

Many whites thought that blues, jazz, and so-called low-down, low-class music was the true cultural domain of Blacks. Oliver Cox writes that their need to maintain an illusion of superiority created severe states of social pathology among both groups (366-367).

The idea of "improvement" or "progress" by blacks is looked upon with apprehension by whites. Hence jails are always more tolerable than schools and Old Testament preachers more acceptable than social-service workers.   (377)

Indeed, if jails, religion, and punishment were deemed preferable for

African Americans to schools, knowledge and rehabilitation, then those whites in control could regiment and pre-determine the success and/ or failure of great numbers of African Americans. Consequently, it was extremely difficult for black people to find a positive identity, since they were systematically stripped of most of their African culture, heritage, and dignity upon arrival in America, and at the same time they were deliberately excluded from Anglo-American society and culture.

Fortunately, some blacks remembered and passed on fragments of indigenous African values, practices, rituals, and remnants of religion which Davis observed and wrote about. These carryovers were retained in songs, dances, tales, legends, and myths.

The African ethos also stresses a variety of values at the personal level including various interrelationships and balance between humans and the universe and an acknowledgment of and respect for the forces which affect lives, both visible and invisible. It includes an understanding of scale and connections: human, planetary, and universal; an appreciation for the body and physical pleasures; the connected roles and responsibilities of the individual and the group in society; the importance of the extended family, the valuation and requests of the ancestors, and the rituals of Nature's seasons, moon cycles, and fertility; the use of intuition, music, rhythms, and dance in rituals. There is a strong emphasis on collective survival strategies, mechanisms and solutions in face of poverty and the impersonal city.

Some carryovers from the African ethos and cosmogony found expression in African American life styles, values, culture, and writing, but for urban dwellers, a certain respect for a balance with the earth and the environment was often lacking. An example of some of these variables can be found in Davis's poem "Notes on a Summer Night" in *American Negro*:

> Past wood and water, over steel and stone/ Through the forty-room mansion of a millionaire/ Into the one-room cabin of a cotton picker/ Dark purple runners of darkness run -- / Today is another grain of sand/ And the shore is long and smooth. . . . / Twenty brownskin babies suckle the wet teats of gin bottles/ at Mojo Mike's in Chicago/ Twenty gin guzzling gals gone to the dogs with a grin/ at two bucks a throw/ The hot air staggers under the heavy smell of beer and / bourbon,

> dead tobacco and dripping sweat/ A five cent phonograph
> flings vermillion streamers of jazz/ through the atmosphere/
> Outside a mazda-bandaged night limps slowly along Forty-
> Seventh street in Chicago's Congo./ (Do you remember,
> Mandy Lou,/ When shadows of oak leaves danced a slow
> mazurka/ Plucked by clouds from a banjo moon/ Near
> Kanka-kee?)   (*Black Moods* 78)

In contrast, the Euro-American paradigm of culture focused then and now on individualism, competition, technology, and intellectual and commercial achievements. It sanctioned certain behavior patterns as civilized, rewarded competitive efforts of individuals such as private ownership, control and exploitation of nature, and the aggressive behavior and legitimized violence used to acquire these goals.

Davis saw that his role as a black writer was to affirm black identity and a positive historical and cultural presence, and to provide realistic pictures and analysis of blacks' current and past status in America and the world. Davis's writing, consciously and/or unconsciously, re-flected not only the African American experience, but also included his deepest dreams for the Black American. His personal experience typifies the struggle of Blacks and people of color in the United States who seek love, acceptance, and status as authentic Americans while maintaining their own minority group cultures.

Davis consistently focused his attention on the African American community, socio-political issues, cultural carryovers, and the inequalities and contradictions of democracy. When he published *I Am the American Negro* in 1937, he included a Forewarning to the reader:

> Fairy words . . . a Pollyanna mind/ Do not roam these pages.
> / Inside/ There are coarse victuals/ A couch of rough boards/
> Companions who seldom smile/ Yet/ It is the soul's abode/
> Of a Negro dreamer/ For being black/ In my America/ Is no
> *rendez-vous*/ With Venus. . . .   (*Black Moods* 57)

Davis's personal sense of alienation, discontent, and loss often produced unhappy satirical themes and topics and very few smiles, as almost all photos of Davis affirm, although he did have an ironic sense of humor that came through in certain of his poems and editorial columns.

White and Parham observe that ". . . White America provided no positive images through which Blacks could see themselves reflected in a positive way" (43). The images of African Americans provided through U. S. institutions were most often of uneducated, angry, violent, and unsuccessful people. For the African American, it was a constant struggle to transform a feeling of socio-economic inferiority into a competitive focused hope of escape from poverty and for equality. Davis offered words and images of hope to his readers as he explained that the economic security of the white community was inversely proportional to the economic insecurity and poverty in the African American community.

During the first half of the 20th century, the dominant white group systematically erected a system of legislation and practices to exclude the masses of African Americans from middle class status many of whom fled from poverty and Jim Crow in the South and flowed North to cities like Chicago seeking better jobs, opportunities, and status. Unfortunately, many of the small African American bourgeoisie, already victims of exclusion in the North, were unable or unwilling to help the tens of thousands of new, poor, uneducated immigrants from the rural South.

> For Negroes who moved North, the process of urbanization
> was complicated by the hostility of the older Negro urban
> folk, the Old Families who, when Negroes were still rare
> in great Northern cities, had made a comfortable modus
> vivendi but now saw their tranquility threatened by the
> "low class" Southern Negroes swarming into their peaceful
> neighborhoods, certain to bring squalor and strife and to alter
> the social attitudes of whites.   (White and Parham 136)

After the Depression and his return to Chicago from Atlanta, Davis tried to bridge the great gap between the working class of both races, accusing the wealthy as the enemy of both groups. He wrote in "Peace Quiz for America:"

> Say, Mister, you with the white face, you
>   toiler
> Come over here and let's talk.
> Maybe we both got the same disease
> But different symptoms;
> Mine pops out in humiliating race discrimination

Yours is a rash of class distinction and poverty
Coming from the same infection;
Fascism and profit grabbing
And we're both tired steppers to a dollar jazz. . . .
We are the people
And in a democracy the people run the country
Together we have whipped fascism in war
Together we shall whip fascism in peace
How about it, America?   (*47th Street* 63-64)

Unfortunately, for too many African Americans, the trauma and psychological damage of their cultural isolation and economic alienation manifested in a neurosis of inferiority and socioeconomic impotence, sometimes ironically juxtaposed with a fierce determination to succeed and assimilate into the dominant white society, despite repeated and catastrophic rejection.

The African American press was partly instrumental in encouraging the masses of poor blacks in the South to migrate north and seek better job opportunities and to join together in group solidarity, thereby redeeming the confidence, reputation, and status of the race.

It was the Negro press particularly that became the chief scold of the race, berating it for its shortcomings, exhorting it to greater exertions and self-confidence, and deploring what Carter Woodson, the race's foremost historian, called "the Negro's con-spicuous belief in his own inferiority . . . the . . . barrier between him and the progress he might now be making." The lack of "race pride" and of group solidarity which derived from the same inferiority feelings kept them from rallying to agencies like the NAACP and the Urban League, from supporting their own businessmen, and authors and artists from voting for their own candidates for public office. The shadow of the plantation still lay athwart Harlem and Bronzeville in the early twentieth century.

(Bardolph 138)

Davis's heuristic editorials constantly reflected the strident call to racial pride, pointed out the various race and class obstacles to democracy, and provided an analysis of second-class citizenship.

While in Chicago, Davis himself seemed to be often poor, or on the edge of poverty, but he could pay his bills and eat, most of the time. Like most other African Americans of the period, his access to money-producing resources and bank loans and credit was extremely limited. His relative deprivation, despite his many efforts to succeed, perhaps created in him a burning if unconscious psychological desire to pierce and shock the white world, possibly even to wound it for his institutionalized lack. He recognized on some level that through self-empowerment, one could enhance one's self-esteem if not status in the community.

The conscious beginning of Davis's pessimism and political war with society's limitations began in earnest perhaps around the time of his return to Chicago in 1934. He began to question the ethics and intentions of American democracy which seemed to favor some and reject others. He exposed its failures and hypocrisy of equality citing statistics in his columns which revealed the gross inequities between African Americans and whites reported in the 1943 Census in the areas of median income, types of jobs lacking dignity, benefits, advancement, poverty, education, and egregious shortages in housing and unemployment in predominantly Black Southside Chicago.

> As the line between the castes diminishes and economic competition increases between the subordinate group and lower-class segments of the dominant group, hatred and bigotry are frequently manifested. Physical segregation is introduced to protect the dominant group's position. Thus the amount of contact between the castes is minimized, and the society is increasingly compartmentalized. Segregation becomes spatial.   (Wilson 53)

One can point out many similar inequalities in the current U.S. Census. Davis's frustrations and feelings of impotence expanded as he began to understand the enormity of the problems of race and poverty. The tragic circle of domination and degradation encouraged whites to strengthen segregation and relegate African Americans to declining expectations of success.

Perhaps nothing so effectually choked off the young Negro's

ambitions as the constant reminder of the disability and
"inherent" incapacities by which both whites and Negroes
(and even his own parents) exhorted him to abandon his
illusions.   (Bardolph 138)

There were everywhere growing tensions within the African American
community itself due to pressures from both without and within.
Simultaneously, Davis's understanding of the dilemma of the African
American was enhanced as he saw the liabilities of a racial system with
few rewards outside the boundaries of "duskymerica" and the devastating
consequences to the country at large. According to Lemelle, "Therefore,
the social and economic characteristic of the Black population is a critical
assessment of the ethical health of the nation" (75). The fabric of democracy
and ethical health of the nation was flawed, and until African Americans
could become productive participants, Davis feared the polarization could
only lead to more destruction. His youthful optimistic vision of a liberated
future was clouded by his recognition of the real, tragic effects of alienation,
even among the various members of his own community.

During the Depression, class lines began to harden in the North between
the lower, middle, and upper classes, both within and between the races. For
African Americans, the lower classes were composed of recent immigrants
from the rural South; the middle class were usually lighter-skinned old-
time residents who sought to distance themselves from their darker-skinned
kin and aspired to skilled or professional versus domestic or service jobs.
The upper class consisted of a handful of professionals, black leaders, and
"stars" of entertainment and sports.

However, because most whites tended to ignore any class distinctions
between African Americans, there was overcompensation among African
Americans to create a hierarchical social society in imitation of whites. This
exemplifies the black middle-class rejection of jazz and the blues as "low
class," further increasing the distance between the educated middle-class
and the poorer masses. Yet as their education increased, many in the African
American community began to reject whiteness and Euro-American culture
as the definitive standard of excellence.

The disinclination of whites to take upper-class Negroes

> seriously, often led the latter to an exaggerated preoccupation with "Society", . . . and an insistence upon deference from their underlings . . . and to habits of conspicuous consumption. . . . After the 1930's, the importance of skin color seemed to decline as a status symbol. . . . The Negro masses exhibited a growing hostility to this intramural color prejudice, especially as more and more dark Negroes, through education, native talent, industry and marriage pushed their way into the upper class.   (Bardolph 284)

However, with the advent of darker-skinned, educated African Americans, and the growing consciousness of the New Negro and the international movement of negritude, the significance of color in the African American community declined in proportion to education.

Partly due to lack of illustrious family connections and his cinnamon skin color, Davis was neither a member of African American social clubs nor the sometimes pretentious middle/upper-class society. He seemed to exclude himself from the social gatherings of the African American bourgeoisie, perhaps because of his democratic idealism and global vision, his darker hue, his unwillingness to become involved in trivia, competition, and gossip, and his commitment to sociopolitical change. In discussing the politics of color, Bardolph says:

> In the upper stratum, again a shade lighter than those in the stratum below, were folk whose family connections, general culture, occupation, income, education or special achievement set them apart from their fellows.   (284)

The preoccupation of many black professionals with materialism, status, skin color, and social mobility, as well as their disdainful lack of concern for the masses, was antipathetic to Davis's cosmology of democratic inclusion of the working class. He clearly understood the divisive power of color politics and the pain of domination and exclusion. In "Giles Johnson, PhD.," he writes:

> Giles Johnson
> had four college degrees
> knew the whyfor of this
> the wherefor of that

could orate in Latin
or cuss in Greek
and, having learned such things
he died of starvation
because he wouldn't teach
and he couldn't porter.   (*Black Man's* 81)

In this poem, Davis attacks the false pride of the black bourgeoisie, although he usually refrained from criticizing this group openly. However, he did write some satirical poems in *Black Man's Verse*, and he did little to join the bourgeois social circles and formal traditions. Rather, he attacked in his writing their vanity, false pride, and hypocrisy. He satirized their desire to be white, their blind imitation of white ways and institutions, and illusions of self-importance, which crumbled in the path and power of institutional racism and white supremacy. In "Robert Whitmore," Davis writes:

Having attained success in business
possessing three cars
one wife and two mistresses
a home and furniture
talked of by the town
and thrice ruler of the local Elks
Robert Whitmore
died of apoplexy
when a stranger from Georgia
mistook him
for a former Macon waiter.   (*Black Man's* 79)

Usually, Davis preferred as subjects the raw, vibrant, and sometimes explosive energy and folk traditions of the masses, although he wrote poems about women, musicians, the policy man, and the exploited workers. He described the familiar warmth of community folk and places like the bars, poolrooms, barbershops, and other informal institutions in South Side Chicago. He respected the colorful dialect of the people, admired the new black music of Jazz and the Blues with its staccato rhythms and angry tones which he incorporated into his writing style.

In "47th Street," he uses dialect and standard English to show familiarity with both and offers commentary on a slice of life in the neighborhood whose residents have few hopes of escaping from poverty, except through the game of chance

> "Five cents 'll git you five dollars
> A dime brings ten iron men
> So gimme your gigs
> An' hope t' God you hits."
> This man
> long and brown as an earthworm
> crawling familiarly
> into barbershops, poolhalls,
> With pencil, pad, printed slips, jingling coins
> Is a policy writer.
> With him he carries
> Hopes and analyzed dreams
> Backed by pennies
> Of the trusting many.   (*47th Street* 15)

Being a Race Man, Davis saw the compelling need and responsibility to lift up the masses, and for the group to work together as a whole. However, this was not to occur on a mass level during his stay in Chicago, because too many Blacks, uneducated and unfamiliar with the urban north, were still arriving from the South; too many were unprepared for the de facto segregation and the violence of poverty and exclusion. With inadequate support from the educated African Americans who were themselves often recruited and struggling on a daily basis to survive and to create a social society based on a formal European tradition, many of the new immigrants were quickly seduced by the false glitter of freedom and fell prey to the tentacles of greed, power, and stratification.

> Distinguished Negroes were now recruited from all levels of colored society, but showed increasing tendency to derive from the emergent middle-class rather than from the humbler strata, for Negro society was undergoing steady stratification.   (Bardolph 137)

One group that was occasionally able to break down some racial barriers was the intelligentsia, of which Davis considered himself a part. It was not unusual to see the African American intellectuals fraternizing with the white intellectuals and social movement groups which tended to be integrated and comprised of people from different classes.

> Intellectuals were cheered to note that at least some members of the vanguard now stood on a wavering color line, making frequent contact with whites who were according them some tentative acceptance, especially in the arts, the sciences, religion and in the scholarly disciplines.   (292)

Through his creative writing, Davis joined the South Side writers group and the Allied Arts Guild which, he writes, included a variety of creative people from various fields including writers, dancers, singers, pianists, photographers, and painters (*Livin'* 241). Davis had met Langston Hughes, Margaret Walker and Arna Bontemps during the New Deal WPA writer's project. Hughes and Richard Wright were looked upon as Communists. Davis became associated with Wright after the National Negro Congress in 1936 which was alleged to be a Communist Front Organization. Although Davis did not see Wright very often after the latter left Chicago to be employed by the *Daily Worker* in Harlem, they maintained a friendship and Davis read the galley proofs for *Native Son* which Wright sent to him from New York. Indeed, Wright informed Davis of the policy of most publishing houses at that time to have on their lists no more than one African American writer at a time. Wright later used a photograph taken by Davis to accompany a book review of *Black Boy* in *Time* magazine which Davis also later reviewed for the ANP newspapers. Davis credits Wright for his first-time acquaintance with a number of white writers almost all militantly leftist, many of whom would become famous and who encouraged Davis in his forthright style (*Livin'* 239-244). Davis did not see Wright again after openly criticizing Wright's attack of the Communist Party following the latter's defection, although both men held on to the ideology of equality in face of the bitter, seemingly hopeless plight of African Americans. Both Davis and Wright called for a collective, positive socioeconomic solution to the poverty and poor education of the masses.

The quest for physical independence, economic power, and equality were predominant themes in the life and writings of Frank Marshall Davis. He refused to conform to reified roles of class behavior. He felt no obligation to illustrate the race's potential in his every move. He did not fear nor avoid gaucheries, vulgarities, and other behavior patterns typically associated with "black behavior." He ignored stereotypes and imaginary class lines. Instead he associated with the working class when he felt like it, and often frequented establishments which featured "low-down, vulgar blues" and non-conventional jazz where people went to forget their troubled-strewn lives. In "Tenement Room," Davis describes the bleak poverty and dark despair familiar to many inhabitants of Chicago's South Side:

> Dirt and destitution/ Lounge here in gaudy tatters/ Through the bright hours/ Forever shouting/ Its bony nakedness--/A crippled table, grey from greasy water;/ Two drooping chairs, spiritless as wounded soldiers/ shoved into a prison hole;/ A cringing bed, age-weary; Corseted with wire squats a flabby stove;/ In the corner slumps a punished trunk rescued from Jake's Second Hand Store;/ Through the lone window, broken paned, spills light/ and weather on the dust-defeated and splintering floor--/ Only night muffles/ Those visual cries/ of the despairing room.   (*47th Street* 47)

Faced with such enormous and seemingly unsolvable sociopolitical problems, Davis sometimes drank, caroused, shunned religious orthodoxy, and puritanical conduct. Davis foreshadowed the words of Fanon who said, speaking of the oppressed, "All I wanted was to be a man among other men. I wanted to come . . . into a world that was ours and to help to build it together" (*Black Skin* 113). Many African American intellectuals of the period identified with Fanon's later descriptions of being an outsider, and with Du Bois's description of the African American as pariah. They experienced the dialectic of double consciousness (the tension between being black and being American), the alienation, and the struggle for self-definition, empowerment, and recognition.

Cornel West discusses the historical alienation from the European ethos experienced by many African Americans such as Davis, ironic because the dominant Protestant European was suffering from its own identity crisis full of anxiety and provincialism.

> Black Americans labored rather under the burden of a triple crisis of self-recognition. Their cultural predicament was

> comprised of African appearance and unconscious cultural
> mores, involuntary displacement to America without
> American status, and American alienation from the European
> ethos complicated through domination by incompletely
> European Americans.   (30)

Confronted with hostility and rejection, lacking access to most power
organizations, the African American press and writers like Davis had a
critical role in the community. They had to analyze the situation, indicate
possible solutions, mediate between various factions, and transform a
negative self-image by educating the public to African American successes
and the pitfalls of failure.

Unfortunately white-superiority theories, advanced by leading white
anthropologists and sociologists, fed African American intellectuals'
discomfort. In addition, the many so-called legal tentacles of justice
attacked self-esteem and served to detract from a positive sense of identity.
Even in the havens of home, library, and job, there was no easy escape from
theories of black inferiority. Racism was always present and felt by blacks,
sometimes indirectly through glances, rejection, and isolation, sometimes
through laws, traditions, words, and actions. It is little wonder that African
Americans were often forced to the psychopathic edge: avoidance behavior
patterns, internalization of negative stereotypes, and submission to
segregation. Once again Fanon articulates the psychological consequences
of powerlessness and dehumanization.

> I came into the world imbued with the will to find a meaning
> in things, my spirit filled with the desire to attain to the
> source of the world, and then I found that I was an object
> in the midst of other objects. Sealed into that crushing
> objecthood, I turned beseechingly to others. Their attention
> was liberation . . . endowing me once more with an agility
> that I had thought lost, and just as I reached the other side, I
> stumbled, and the movements, the attitudes, the glances of
> the other fixed me there . . . I was indignant; I demanded an
> explanation. Nothing happened. I burst apart . . .
>
> (*Black Skin* 109)

Davis smoldered daily like most African American men, at his exclusion from the social order, the lack of economic opportunities and political power available to African Americans. He raged at the hypocrisy of a democratic "system" which bred corruption at all levels regardless of color.

Daily he observed that greed and the desire for power, bribes, and perks were as abundant as restaurants in the city, but he also recognized that it always seemed to be the whites who became wealthy.

One of the reasons he did not separate himself from the masses was that the only places he could listen to the music which he loved and which expressed his deepest feelings were in the clubs and cabarets in Chicago's South Side, the part of the city open to the black masses.

To sooth the barbs of racism and injustice, he turned to musical entertainment in the evenings where he found solace and others like himself, seeking to forget the pain and humilia-tion of daily living. The blues and jazz vibrated between the rhythms of exhilaration and despair.

Another way to help relieve the tensions and disparities of race and class was to write. Davis wrote but also began to drink more, and unconsciously laid the foundation for what later evolved into his Epicurean philosophy of life. In a poem called "Creed for Hedonists," Davis writes:

> Yesterday is a bucket of bones/ Picked clean by the tireless teeth of Time/ Tomorrow stirs in the womb of Now/ Felt and formed, but not yet being/ Only today is real!/ Today is a roasted pig/ Soft, succulent, savory/ Come, my starving friends/ Let us brighten our bellies now/ Let us feast our fill -- / For who can surely say/ He will be around/ To dine tomorrow?   (*Black Moods* 171-172)

He embraced or slipped into a *carpe diem* philosophy and a hedonistic lifestyle when he was not working, perhaps in part to erase the humiliation of exclusion, and to compensate on the individual level for the inequalities of a society where African Americans anchored the socioeconomic scale.

In large cities like Chicago, some African Americans who became too disillusioned with the system turned to various forms of hedonism. Others found hope in Black Nationalism and various brands of separatism, espoused by early emigrationists like Martin Delany (1812-1885), and later Marcus Garvey and the Black Muslims in the 1930's. Even the Communist

Party for a while advocated self-determination and a separate region for African Americans in answer to the strong nationalistic sentiment that was sweeping the masses in the community. Davis, no communist, disagreed. He wrote:

> Still another area of basic disagreement was the issue of "self-determination for the black belt." And as to whether those Southern counties with an Afro-American majority "constituted a nation" under Stalin's definition of nationhood, my frankly expressed reaction was that Stalin's criteria in the Soviet Union had no practical relevancy among us souls who couldn't care less about Stalin's view, and that at that time the prevailing goal was complete integration, not separation into a black nation.   (*Livin'* 282)

So Black nationalists sought to relocate African Americans somewhere away from whites, either in a separate state or country; some, like Garvey, preferred to think of returning to Africa.

> Blacks addressed inequality in historical phases which may be subsumed under the rubric of Black Nationalism. Five major historical forms emerged: political, economic, cultural, integral and moral.   (Lemelle 71)

The significance of the influence of Garveyism on the Harlem Renaissance and the African American intellectual cannot be ignored. Garvey's message to the urban masses was one of black awareness and self-esteem, and the Race men who followed in the 1930's and 1940's, including Davis, saw the necessity of the race to be aware of its history, heritage, and culture. Garvey's injunction, "Black man, know thyself," was a theme which was to appear in various ways in Davis's life and writings. However, Garvey's message of racial purity did not find a place in Davis's ideology. Davis wrote:

> By now I had learned considerable black history through the writings of Dr. W. E. B. Du Bois, Dr. Carter G. Woodson, and J. A. Rogers. This kind of education and sense of black identity I had to assimilate independently of the school system.   (*Livin'* 244)

Davis resented being deprived of full participation in the democratic system which had been so liberating for most Euro-Americans and so hypocritically oppressive and confining to most African Americans. Indeed, he was forever seeking different perspectives of history and more effective ways to fight racism and injustice in a system where the laws, angels, and God from which they came, seemed to be all white.

African American intellectuals sometimes used the concept of Black Nationalism to express their mistrust, rage, and frustration with white America and to capture the theological mood of the times. James Baldwin who followed Davis and Wright, was to express a similar sense of powerlessness and injustice in a conversation with the noted anthropologist Margaret Mead published in a book entitled *A Rap on Race.*

Mead:	We have both been told lies.
Baldwin:	But there is a difference in that you --
Mead:	Whether one was the lied about or not.
Baldwin:	-- you are identified with the angels, and I'm identified with the devil. We are living in a kind of theology. Therefore, my situation -- our situation really - presents itself as exceedingly urgent. I cannot lie to myself about some things. I cannot. I don't mean anybody else is. I mean that I have to know something about myself and my countrymen, and the most terrible thing about it, is not the looting, the fire burning or the bombings: that is bad enough. But what is really terrible is to face the fact that you cannot trust your countrymen. That you can not trust them. For the assumptions on which they live are antithetical to any hope you may have to live on. It is a terrible omen. . . . That is a bitter, bitter, bitter pill, but it is like that. (228)

The African American cosmology reflected in the discourse of the intellectuals became more and more urgent, bitter, accusatory and mistrustful of white America.

The Second World War and its aftermath produced peculiar new tensions in American race relations to which Davis was acutely sensitive. He continued on a regular basis to observe and comment on racism through both the news stories he covered and the editorials and poetry that he wrote. His topics included the economic exploitation of the community, and discrimination, with a focus on education, musicians, the defense industries, the military, sports, social activities, events, and housing.

Davis directly attacked the color bar in sports. Since African Americans could traditionally aspire to earning a decent living and a measure of success in only a limited number of fields, mainly sports and entertainment, Davis exposed the many difficult obstacles facing black athletes even in those fields for promising talent. He wrote about Joe Louis and how when he won the heavyweight championship, the national African American community celebrated, and how when he lost to Schmeling, the people mourned. Joe Louis like Jack Johnson before him was an early symbol of success and power to African Americans and both offered a hopeful model to many young men. It was generally understood that one must be "outstandingly superior" in one's field in order to be recognized or honored, and one had to brace oneself "against white spectators shouting `kill the nigger!'" (*Livin'* 257)

The irony of the color bar for African American troops serving in a war to combat (among other things) fascist racism struck Davis as particularly absurd.

In fact, the rise of fascism in Europe brought early concern to many African American people, especially after Italy invaded Ethiopia. In a poem entitled "Nothing Can Stop the People," Davis wrote:

> "Go back, go back!"/Shouted three sadistic voices/Not long ago,/"This is our private path./What right have you/ to walk this way?"/They were Mussolini in Ethiopia, Spain;/ Hitler in Austria, Czechoslovakia:/ Hirohito in China, the Philippines;/ And confusion danced among the climbers. . . ./Queer how three sadistic voices/ Believed they could stop a

march/ Curving the people back down the high mountain/ By condensing the hot red fog of war/ About the steep tight trail. . . ./ but they keep pushing on. . . ./ Buying newly packaged confidence/ From the cosmic counters/ of the democratic dreamers./ There is nothing - / Fog nor rain nor flogging wind-/ that can stop these climbing people.

(47th Street 70-73)

Feeling the heels of oppression from the war dictators who sought to control the lands and resources of the world, the common people, boosted by an international sense of democracy and dignity, fought back. A new spirit of brotherhood among the exploited arose, and a wave of Pan Africanism surged around the world with the attack on Ethiopia. Davis, always in the vanguard and fearlessly writing on a razor's edge, said:

Until the Ethiopian war, Afro Americans generally had little feeling of closeness with their kinsmen in Africa -- except for some followers of Marcus Garvey. Brainwashed by the racist propaganda system, by and large we were either indifferent or held ourselves superior to Those Savages inhabiting the big dark continent. But Il Duce woke us up. When his son spoke in public print of the "joy" of seeing black bodies hurled skyward when he bombed them from his planes, as a group we suddenly realized these were our ethnic brothers being slaughtered and for the first time felt mass ties from thousands of miles away.   *(Livin'* 244)

As time passed, the tensions of freedom grew in Davis's life directly related to his movement from a solitary attack on racism and inequality through his editorials and poetry to a developing deep commitment to organized group work.

I knew of course, that the Establishment tolerates the solitary protester. It smiles and points to him as proof that free speech does exist in America. The unwritten rule is that you can yell as loudly as you please -- by yourself. But when two or more of you get together, you become a threat even though you speak only in whispers. Two or more automatically become a conspiracy which endangers Our Way of Life and those agencies, such as the FBI or Un-American Committee,

> which ignored the injustices triggering your protests, now
> began hounding you as dangerous radicals. I had seen this
> happen constantly.   (*Livin'* 276)

When Davis decided to align himself with political groups, he knew
that his life was going to change from the comfortable immunity of being
a reporter to being labeled an agitator. Although he did not belong to the
John Reed Club as did Richard Wright, in conjunction with his labor union
work, Davis joined the League of American Writers, a national united
front organization which was mobilized by the fear of the alarming rise
of power of Hitler and Mussolini. The League published a controversial
booklet, *Writers Take Sides*, which soon drew the attention of the House on
Un-American Activities Committee (HUAC) to those involved, including
Davis.

> Of course we were all duly listed in Washington as "un-
> American" for opposing the Rome-Berlin Axis. We were
> "premature anti-fascists" for not waiting until the thief
> entered before trying to lock doors. . . . I did not know at
> the time I joined the League that it was created following
> a decision by the Communist Party to close down the John
> Reed Clubs and establish a broad, united front organization
> among writers. . . . Fact is, membership and supporters read
> like a Who's Who among U.S. writers.   (*Livin'* 245)

Davis considered himself a free thinker and was obviously not afraid to
speak out against what he thought was wrong in American Society. He did
not want to forget the struggle against racism at home for the sake of national
unity. Davis says all the writers in the League were listed in Washington as
"un-American" for opposing the Rome-Berlin Axis.

Davis was a bit different from the majority of white writers because he
wore the double label of radical writer and Black nationalist (*Livin'* 245).

> Of course, I could not accept the idea that the struggle
> against racism must be sacrificed on the altar of national
> unity. I was eager to aid in any program aimed at increasing
> intergroup cooperation and respect, but I held tenaciously
> to my basic belief that the war against fascism must run
> concurrently at home and abroad. I was called a "black

nationalist."   (*Livin'* 282)

Because he had lived and worked in the deep South, Davis could not see the relevancy of the Communist plan for self-determination and nationalism in the Black Belt. He knew that the majority of southern African Americans had never heard of Communism or Stalin. Indeed, the prevalent view at that time expressed by most Civil Rights groups was that the way to equality was through integration and assimilation, not through the Communist brand of nationalism and a separate black nation. Eventually, the African American newspapers became as anti-Communist as the rest of the white press, but Davis was not so quick to dismiss the Communist Party because of their persistent ideological call for equality and brotherhood.

During and after World War II, Davis's public activities were numerous, and he was often associated with activist groups considered by some to be radical. He spoke on anti-Semitism for the Democratic and Republican Platform Committees in 1944, was on the National Committee to Combat Anti-Semitism, the National Civil Rights Congress, and the Board of Chicago Civil Liberties Union which fought bigotry in the public schools. Bigotry was particularly bad in Chicago, since many European immigrants in the area adapted and maintained the national pattern of prejudice. They, being the lowest on the totem pole of immigrants due to their recent arrival, looked for a scapegoat to elevate themselves, gain status and favor with the dominant whites, and justify their usurpation of African Americans' jobs. In his autobiography, Davis comments:

> Thus I worked with all kinds of groups. I made no distinction between those labelled Communist, Socialist or merely liberal. My sole criterion was this: are you with me in my determination to wipe out white supremacy? Having some smattering of prestige as a writer, wielding some influence as an opinion maker in the black press at large, my active participation was welcomed.   (*Livin'* 278)

Davis also frequently spoke to young members of American Youth for Democracy, organized and chaired conferences on black-white unity, helped to organize white-collar workers, addressed mixed audiences on African American history, worked with the Boy Scout movement, and spoke before various CIO unions and more (278). Davis even shared panels with Adam Clayton Powell, Paul Robeson, Marshall Field, and Mike Quill, head of the Transport Workers Union. In his autobiography he goes on to say:

> I was positive that by now I had attracted the special attention of the House Un-American Committee. If so, I would accept any resultant citation as an honor for it would indicate I was beginning to upset the White Power structure. (*Livin'* 279)

Indeed, by 1944, the FBI agents were asking others about Davis, as they had previously questioned him about other African American leaders who were perceived as a threat to national security. Davis made a game out of misleading them, and when asked about specific individuals whom he considered conservative, for example someone in the N.A.A.C.P., he would tell the agents that they were "dangerous" and a "rotten security risk," whereas if the subject was a militant Davis would again mislead the agent as much as possible with his answers, labeling the latter in "glowing terms."

> From now on I knew I would be described as a Communist but frankly I had reached the stage where I didn't give a damn. Too many people I respected as Freedom Fighters were listed as Red for me to fear name calling. Actually I knew personally only a handful of genuine Communists, among them Angelo Herndon and Ben Davis Jr. in Atlanta, plus Richard Wright and William L. Patterson in Chicago. An attorney by profession, I was fully aware of Patterson's efforts on behalf of the Scottsboro boys long before I first met him in Chicago where he was actively engaged as an editor in addition to his many other endeavors. (*Livin'* 276)

As time passed, the FBI kept an eye on Davis, and continued to monitor his activities even after the "Red Scare" and his move to Hawai'i.

In 1944, Davis published a long poem in the N.A.A.C.P.'s *Crisis Magazine* entitled "War Quiz for America"--later republished in *47th Street* under the title "Peace Quiz for America"--which offended the white power structure and Communists alike, although most African Americans, even the more conservative ones like Roy Wilkins of the N.A.A.C.P., could relate to it because Davis attacked white supremacy, patriarchy, discrimination, the hypocrisy of democracy, fascism, poverty, sharecropping, perpetual debt, exploitation, violence, colonialism, and imperialism. Using a traditional African American cultural form of participation called call and response, Davis writes "Peace Quiz for America" (to be read aloud by Eight Voices). He satirizes the four freedoms of democracy using the leader as a black man and the respondents as white Southerners to expose the hypocrisy of American democracy.

> Leader: Are these the Four Freedoms for which we
>   fight? Freedom from want.
> Voice: ("So sorry but we don't hire Negroes. Our
>   white employees won't work with them. The
>   union, you know.")
> Leader: Freedom from fear.
> Voice: ("Nigger, take off yo' hat and say `sir' when
>   you speak to a white man in Arkansas. A
>   smart darky down here's a curiosity and
>   sometimes we embalm curiosities.")
> Leader: Freedom of religion.
> Voice: ("Of course you can't come in here! This is a
>   white church.")
> Leader: Freedom of speech.
> Voice: ("We gits along with ouah niggers, so unless
>   you want to leave here feet first don't be
>   puttin' none of them Red social equality ideas
>   in their minds.")
>
>   (*Black Moods* 132)

He challenges the illogicality of fighting a war for freedom abroad while blacks have little freedom at home in the USA.

> Leader: Did you hear about regimentation in
>   Washington? Ten men to run the war. A
>   hundred to ration black participation.
> First Voice:
>
>   Uncle Sam, Uncle Sam
>   Why send me against Axis foes
>   In the death kissed foxholes
>   of New Guinea and Europe
>   Without shielding my back

From the sniping Dixie lynchers
In the jungles of Texas and Florida.

(*Black Moods* 133)

He uses blacks and white dialect to express the conflicts between the
races and the exploitation by whites of even educated blacks.

Second Voice:
> Me? I'm from Paine, County, Alabama. Born black
> and I'm gonna die the same way. Went t' school three
> yeahs befo' it rotted down. By the time the white
> folks got around t' fixin it my first wife had done
> died.
> But you oughta see my brothah. Finished State
> Teachuh's College an' now he's makin' forty dollah
> un month back home. That's ovah half us what they
> pays white teachuhs. Been helpin' Pappy work the
> same fifty acres fo' Mistuh Jim his own pappy had.
> Pappy bought a single barrel shotgun from Mistuh
> Jim five yeahs ago. Paid ten dollahs down an a
> dollah a week an' he still owes twenty 'mo. Sheriff
> came 'round and told me they wanted me in the
> Army. Come heah to Fort Benning an' they give me
> a gun and a uniform an' three good meal a day. Fust
> time I evah knowed a white man to give me anything.
> This mawnin' I heard somebody on a radio say we
> was all fightin fo' democracy. Democracy? What's
> democracy?   (*Black Moods* 133)

Davis then uses the leader to critique democracy, imperialism, and the
hypocrisy of war abroad when the same conditions for war exist at home.

Leader: Nothing is so final as a bullet through heart or head
And a correctly thrust bayonet is an unanswerable
argument
For democracy against fascism
For Four Freedoms against oppression.
This you taught me in camps from Miami to Seattle
to use against Nazi, Jap
and it works;

It works in the Pacific Islands
In Africa, in Europe
Everywhere it works
You have convinced me completely
Even as I have become expert
In killing the mad dogs
Leaping high to tear
Democracy's soft throat --
And if that's the technique
If it works in lands I never saw before
Against strangers with faces new to me
Then it must be the right thing to use
Against all the foes of freedom
Against all the apostles of fascism
Against some people I know
Right here in America   (*Black Moods* 134)
                    *   *   *
If I'm going to clean up the Rhine
I might as well include the Mississippi
With the understanding
Of course
That it will be only
For democracy against fascism
For Four Freedoms against oppression
Say, Uncle Sam,
Are you sure you want me to have a gun?
                              (*Black Moods* 134)

In this lengthy poem, Davis exposes American race relations through the use of several voices to express cultural alienation, ignorance, and sharecropping in the South: poverty and suffering, pay inequities, the dehumanization of the black man, the respect demanded by whites in titles such as Mistuh Jim, and the irony of African Americans willing to fight abroad to protect freedom when fascism and oppression exist in their own land of America. He uses dialect and an accommodating African American man who starts to become conscious of his power and citizenship rights.

The radical edge of Davis comes out when he says it is now the time to fight those other Americans who oppress blacks and are the foes of freedom.

He finally switches to the first person and asks Uncle Sam if he really wants him, a black man, to have a gun.

Davis comments on the color bar which was also evident in the segregated troops in the military. He exposes the ill-treatment of African Americans: their lack of promotions, adequate training, and assignments for active combat duty.

When the American army integrated its first group of soldiers during the Battle of the Bulge, it was with a voluntary group of black and white soldiers willing to give up their rank and be reduced to private, a plan for which Davis likes to take credit.

During the World War II period, even the music of the day reflected the patterns of racism and inferior treatment toward African Americans. Davis writes:

> Of course the war and our inferior status brought into being many topical and realistic blues songs. In keeping with the bitter beauty of "Strange Fruit", first recorded by Billie Holiday, Josh White sang six stirring songs of angry protest in an album produced by Keynote Records called "Southern Exposure, An Album of Jim Crow Blues". Liner notes were written by Richard Wright. Under such titles as "Jim Crow Train", "Hard Times Blues", "Defense Factory Blues", "Uncle Sam Says", "Bad Housing Blues" and "Southern Exposure", an accurate picture of the status of Afro Americans was tellingly rendered. More than 35 years later, many of the complaints are still valid.   (*Livin'* 271)

In music African Americans could most easily express their true feelings of alienation; alternatively, the black press made government officials uneasy when its reporting of news of race riots in the military and police brutality threatened to rock the stability of white dominance.

During the war years, the Office of Censorship kept an eye on African American newspapers across the nation and scrutinized Davis's editorials, since he regularly reported on discrimination, race riots, inequality of promotions, inferior training, and disproportionate casualties in the armed forces. However, with the death of Roosevelt in 1945, the progressive coalition of liberals, leftists, and African Americans broke up.

Growing race pride and the rise of African American nationalism, led to instability between African Americans and whites that became increasingly evident, except in a few liberal and radical integrated circles. Even labor unions split under the pressure, as anti-Communist pressure started to build. Before long, Republicans regained control of Congress and national policy. Davis comments in his autobiography:

> This was during what was known as the Earl Browder period when the party's official position was to soft pedal harsh criticism of American racism for the sake of "national unity."   (*Livin'* 279)

The rapid deterioration of relations between the United States and Russia and the increased Red-baiting created tension and suspicion between former allies. Davis appealed to Ben Davis Jr. of the Communist Party, encouraging the effort to maintain a connection with the African American press, since both men opposed racism and supported civil rights, equal opportunities, anti-lynching legislation, and abolition of the poll tax. This idea of connection was apparently not accepted, and soon the African American press became almost as violently anti-Communist as the general press (282).

One bright spot amid the oppressive atmosphere of post WWII was the creation and promotion of *The Chicago Star*, a newspaper financed by various labor unions, progressives, liberals, and ghetto dwellers; Frank Marshall Davis became the editor while maintaining his editorial position at the Associated Negro Press. The aim of this publication was to heal the rift between the various aforementioned groups and to promote a policy of cooperation and unity between Russia and the United States. The paper backed Henry Wallace as an independent candidate for President in 1948 whose platform included full employment for all citizens in peacetime. However, when it seemed that too many Democrats would desert the party and vote on the Independent ticket, Truman spoke out for an innovative Civil Rights program, and many African Americans turned back to the Democratic Party (298-299) giving Truman a victory. Unfortunately, under Truman, old antagonisms at home and abroad flared and the cold war began. Conservative forces of the "industrial-military complex," a term coined by Eisenhower in his Inaugural Address ("Military-Industrial Complex"), regained control, and thus governmental support for Civil Rights subsided.

By the mid-1940's, African American people were fed up with discrimination and were willing to speak out and protest. Believing in the principles of democracy, they challenged their second-class citizenship through various groups and organizations. The NAACP, CORE and the Urban League became more active in the fight for equality and justice. They held to the principles of the Declaration of Independence and the Constitution and challenged what they thought to be a corrupt system of government. Many African Americans felt that the war against Fascism and later Communism abroad should not supersede the battle against racism at home; they had a stake in both. Davis draws obvious parallels between Nazism and white supremacy in the United States. He notes:

> In fact, our drive for equality was accelerated in the years immediately before World War II. Aware of the super race theories of Adolf Hitler, so like the ideas of our own white supremacists, we felt a vital stake in not only fighting the Nazi ideology abroad but in moving with all-out strength to combat similar beliefs at home.   (*Livin'* 261)

Because it had been common before the war for almost everyone with a conscience to associate with the Civil Rights struggle, labor, and/or leftist intellectual thought, after the war and at the beginning of the Cold War, the HUAC felt compelled to censor anything or anyone whom they could not control. Davis writes:

> With the rapidly deteriorating political situation and the growth of the witch hunts during the Joe McCarthy period, a number of libraries removed my books from their shelves and stored them in the basement along with other controversial literature until the nation began returning to sanity.
>
> (*Livin'* 304)

By 1946, in face of such threats to freedom of expression and meaningful democracy, the dominant mood of the liberals (*revoltés*) was defiance and self-righteousness, although they were often surrounded by a shroud of fear that their careers or lives were at risk as the government tightened the limits of freedom.

The FBI tried to curb Davis's controversial editorials about racism and violence in the armed forces, alleging that his stories eroded national unity and gave the enemy propaganda to be used against the U.S. They regularly questioned Davis's friends, producing their "dossier" on him and alleging subversive activities that Davis was to have attended--all in an attempt to frighten or intimidate him. Davis says he was quick to respond, "Stop the prejudice and the stories will stop themselves" (*Livin'* 272). He exposed the inefficiency of the FBI agents in his writing.

Frank Marshall Davis was not easily intimidated; however, most people cowered in fear for their families and careers and, if they found themselves on the blacklist, they sometimes sacrificed others for their own freedom. Hellman says, "Truth made you a traitor as it often does in a time of scoundrels, but, there were very few who stood up to say so" (*Scoundrel* 82).

Davis stood up, condemned the HUAC, and called their intimidation a fascist tactic. However, his irreverence and hard-hitting racial candor marked him for both the HUAC and the FBI, influenced his subsequent career choices, and eventually evoked in him a kind of nihilistic attitude toward the world of politics and activism.

CHAPTER 6
An Engaged "Ex-Patriate": The Returns of Davis's Hawai'i Writing

The local establishment, which evidently had been given a file on me by the FBI, flipped. I was a Communist and a subversive and a threat to Hawai'i.

(Davis, *Livin'* 323)

A focus on the changing career of Frank Marshall Davis will reveal how the Hawai'i experience influenced his ambition, status, and journalistic and literary efforts. When Davis began to write in Hawai'i, he returned to many of his earlier themes of race, class, and discrimination in new contexts. He added the international theme of imperialism, although few writers were using that term during that time. Because Hawai'i had not yet become a state, Davis could explore, critique, and develop the existing conditions and paradigms about race, colonialism and imperialism in his writing which were subject to different interpretations and understanding than those on the mainland. Davis could also write from a minority position since there were still so very few black residents in the Islands. One can note how he remained rooted in the Afrocentric tradition, how he adapted to the contemporary African American tradition, and how much of his writing was influenced by the Islands and residents.

During the 1930's and 1940's, a significant number of writers and musicians, including Davis, chose to live outside of the United States due to the climate of racism at home. Bardolph comments:

> Among the contemporary writers, Richard Wright became a permanent Paris resident; Frank Yerby and Wallace Thurman established homes in France; Ralph Ellison, James Baldwin and the late Claude McKay sojourned extensively abroad; Frank Marshall Davis settled in Hawai'i. . . . Several married white women.   (290-291)

Those who emigrated felt a similar estrangement moving to areas where there was a very small African American resident population. They were the voluntary exiles of African Americans who often were involved in the rare interracial marriages of that time. Many became acclaimed in their fields while in exile, whereas if they had remained in the United States, they might not have been able to succeed.

> Some highly talented, ambitious Negroes were broken by the disabilities laid upon them, and others were driven to a sullen despair or belligerency that effectually thwarted their rise to distinction. A few well-known achievers tried to flee their constraints by leaving the country, a resort available only to a few: a tiny core of writers, artists, musicians, and entertainers.   (Bardolph 290-291)

However, the vast majority of African Americans never considered emigration due to constraints of family, livelihood, and familiarity with their own communities, no matter how humble.

The obvious question is why a prominent African American intellectual, writer, and Race Man like Davis would choose to go to the territory of Hawai`i in 1948 and not to Europe like so many of his compatriots? In an interview shortly before his death for the television series *Rice and Roses*, Davis recounts how his friends, labor activist Harry Bridges, and political activist and internationally famed singer Paul Robeson--whom he knew from Chicago and the progressive movement there--influenced him to come to Hawai`i. His wife, Helen, encouraged him as well due to a feature article on Hawai`i in one of her magazines.

> He [Robeson] had been over here [Hawai`i] the previous year on a concert set up for the ILWU. And he was telling me how much he liked it and he said he was going to come back every year. He never did show up again. But anyway, he was instrumental in helping me to form my desire to come over. He and Bridges suggested that I should get in touch with the *Honolulu Record* and see if I could do something for them. So when I came over, one of the first things that I got involved with--well, I met all the ILWU brass, Jack Hall and all of them, and I went (they had both of us over) to various functions for them. Harriet Bouslog was also a good friend.
> (Conybeare, Davis 1986a 5:29-30)

By examining Davis's experience living in Hawai`i for almost four decades, and the subsequent changes in lifestyle which followed his inability to continue a career in journalism, one can begin to understand the existential gaps in Davis's life and the long-range repercussions of victimization on the psyche of a rebellious and outspoken African American Race Man in American society.

Unlike most African Americans who were leaving the Hawaiian Islands after the war to return to their African American communities, Davis was arriving. When Davis came to Hawai`i in 1948 and decided to stay, he concomitantly chose a life of isolation from the continent and all which heretofore he had considered valuable: his career and the African American struggle for freedom and equality.

However, he was tired of being hounded for his association with radicals, of hostile stares from those who opposed his interracial marriage, of the jeers and insults, the discrimination, the white supremacists, the African American nationalists, the Hearst press and other media, and of all the racist propaganda. He was fully aware of the confusion and jealousy caused by his marriage. Even Helen's own mother was not told immediately that she had married an African American man. Finally, Davis and Helen packed their valuables for an extended trip to Hawai`i.

To escape this defensive relationship with the whites, Davis reached out for something new. Were his reasons for not returning to Chicago any different from those of other African American expatriots? Did he feel a need to escape the race struggle in order to be recognized and accepted as an equal citizen by the Other, the white man? Fanon writes:

> Man is only human to the extent to which he tries to impose his existence on another man in order to be recognized by him. As long as he has not been effectively recognized by the other, that other will remain the theme of his actions. It is on that other being, on recognition of that being, that his own human worth and reality depend. It is that other being in whom the meaning of his life is condensed.
>
> (*PNMB* 195-196)

Perhaps he thought that a change of venue might help him to be accepted for his human worth.

Davis's experiences in Hawai`i can be compared to a significant number of African American writers, musicians, scholars and artists who went into exile during the 1940's, like his friend, Richard Wright, who moved to France. Both men became permanent residents in exile, both married white women, and both felt compelled to continue to write about America's racial problems although no longer experiencing them in the same way (Bardolph 290).

In December 1948, articles in the *Honolulu Star- Bulletin* and *Honolulu Advertiser* announced the Davises' imminent arrival, then their delay, and finally their belated arrival. A few of these articles were accompanied by photos of Davis and his wife. There were contradictory reports on the purpose of their trip. "Executive Editor of ANP Is Due Tonight" says that Davis is in Honolulu for a visit that will combine a vacation with business . . . [that he] is planning a story on racial groups in the Islands . . . [and that] Davis also plans to visit army and navy posts" (December 8, 1948). "Negro Press Executive Here" says that Davis "is here on an inspection and vacation tour of the islands . . . [and] will tour army and navy installations and other territorial institutions" (December 14, 1948, 10). "Davis Considers Hawai`i Advanced in Democracy" says that the Davises are in Hawai`i "for a visit of not less than four months. Davis will write a series of articles on his observations of the island scene and also will work on a book of poetry which he hopes will capture the spirit of the islands." However, the photo caption accompanying the article says the Davises are "in Honolulu for an indefinite visit" (10).

Ah Quon McElrath, deceased in Dec. 2008, a labor activist whose husband wrote for the *Honolulu Record*, said in an interview for the PBS *Rice and Roses* (KHET) program that she thought that Frank and Helen were tired of the constant struggle against racism and prejudice on the mainland and came to Hawai`i to rest (24:1).

The press presented Davis as a successful journalist, a poet, and a 1937 Julius Rosenwald Fellow who planned to "work on a book of poetry which he hopes will capture the spirit of the islands in verse" (*Honolulu Star-Bulletin*, December 10, 1948). Davis's wife, Helen, was presented as an artist, writer, and executive editor of a national press agency who planned "to do watercolors of the islands during her stay" (*Honolulu Star-Bulletin*, December 10, 1948).

As mentioned earlier, the extensive media coverage made them feel accepted and welcomed. They were even stopped on the street and greeted warmly by many local residents. Frank and his wife were offered rides when waiting for a bus, and were invited to dine at the Willows, which refused to serve most African Americans, especially military personnel, at that time. Davis says in a 1986 interview with Conybeare and Takara:

> I found that many of the people around here . . . were quite . . . on my side. And I would sometimes be in my car, and I would stop at a light and, this was after I was writing this column for the *Honolulu Record*, . . . an Oriental businessman . . . would tell me that he recognized me from my picture which accompanied my column, and he'd say, "You know, you're writing exactly what I would say if I could. I just don't know how to say it." So therefore I got a lot of friendships which grew that way. During this time when there was this controversy between the ILWU and the Big Five firms, I was obviously on the side of labor . . . and the strike was something that was opposed by virtually all of the *haoles* of importance around here and many of the Oriental businessmen . . . who had a vested interest in keeping things going with the Big Five.   (Conybeare 1986a 9:52)

The Big Five were five large corporations, whose wealth and power were based on the pineapple and sugar plantation economies. (American Factors, Theo H. Davies, Alexander & Baldwin, Castle & Cooke (Dole), C. Brewer and Co.). These companies represented the power elite in Hawai`i and the press was largely controlled by their money.

In a Dec. 14, 1948 interview for the *Honolulu Advertiser*, shortly after their arrival Davis said:

> Hawai`i has gone much farther along the democratic road than any other section of the world, but [he] suggested there has been a definite increase of anti-Negro feeling in the Islands since 1941.

Davis's perceptions were accurate about the economic exploitation of island and immigrant workers by the Big Five firms. He noted, "There is not the complete equality that the best of America is supposed to represent."

In the same interview Davis said that this widespread feeling of being discriminated against among resident African Americans was based on two things:

> 1. The influence of prejudiced Mainland whites who came here as civilians or servicemen during the war.

> 2. The willingness of some people to accept the conduct of the least advanced element of Negroes, some of whom came here during the war, as the standard of the whole race.
>
> (*Honolulu Advertiser* 14 Dec. 1948)

Davis also wrote of the increasing Negro participation in national politics, particularly due to President Truman's Civil Rights program which aided his 1948 election--although Davis said he felt most Negroes supported Thomas E. Dewey for president. Davis foresaw the anti-lynching legislation in 1949. He commented also on the growing pan-African identity of African Americans as a result of World War II and the Italian Ethiopian War which resulted in a more general third-world consciousness. He even commented on apartheid in South Africa, revealing his far-sightedness in global issues.

Before Davis arrived in Hawai`i in 1948, he had already contacted labor leaders Harry Bridges and Koji Ariyoshi. Upon his arrival, he felt optimistic, and assumed that finding a job would not be difficult, especially with all of his experience and expertise in journalism. Shortly thereafter, Davis tried to get a salaried job with the large local daily, *The Honolulu Advertiser*, but when word got around that Davis was prolabor, the newspaper, controlled by the Big Five, quietly ignored him. The huge International Longshoreman's Workers Union (ILWU) strike was imminent in 1949, pitting labor against the Big Five.

Economically, this did not bode well for Davis, since he would eventually have five children to support and his wife Helen's money was at risk, if her mother were to discover she had married an African American. However, Davis was slow to complain because he felt that, since his arrival in the islands, he had at last found dignity and respect as a man and as a human being. He resolved that politics would never take his dignity away from him again. Fortunately, he was soon offered a column, "Frankly Speaking," in the *Honolulu Record*, the local labor newspaper edited by

Koji Ariyoshi.

Although Davis realized that race relations in Hawai`i were not perfect, he enjoyed "the shifting kaleidoscope" of people. He became familiar with the subtle forms of discrimination and, on occasion, the more blatant ones as well, for example the segregated housing facilities for Blacks at Pearl Harbor, particularly with Civilian Housing Areas 2 and 3 (CHA2 and CHA3). He became familiar with the hostilities between Okinawans and Japanese, and various other inter and intra-ethnic group prejudices and discrimination.

His eye for class and race analysis led him to quickly discern the exploitative role of big business and landowners in the lives of the ethnic non-white minorities, and he wrote several strong poems expressing his observations and critical analysis. He had already written an editorial on the Massie case when he was living in Chicago, so he knew that Hawai`i residents had experienced virulent episodes of racism. He observed the discrimination in certain bars and restaurants, as well as the reluctance of the legislature to pass a Civil Rights law giving the excuse that by passing such a law, it would admit to having a problem. This insular attitude toward racism and discrimination which highlighted anti-black feelings would continue until the 21st century.

Nevertheless, after a few months' stay, Davis and his wife Helen decided to settle permanently in Hawai`i, and they bought their first house on Mt. Tantalus overlooking Honolulu. When the Davises purchased their 14,000 square foot property, some local people were surprised. He comments in an interview:

> . . . my being black theoretically I wasn't supposed to be able to buy things up there. But I got this land. Around here at that time, too, it was interesting. If you had the money you could buy anything . . . that was fee simple. But if you wanted a lease, that's where you ran into problems.
>
> (Conybeare 1986a, 5:53; 6:33)

Leases were most commonly held by the Big Five or old missionary families. Because his job as a columnist at the *Honolulu Record* did not include salary and benefits, Davis started a paper supply business on Sand

Island, but when the warehouse mysteriously burned, he lost almost all of his inventory and assets.

Undaunted by the mysterious fire, Davis turned to a new business enterprise consisting of operating a small wholesale paper business. McElrath says in an interview:

> When I first got to know him very well, was when he had started Paradise Papers when he sold office supplies: calendars, papers, carbon paper, mimeograph paper of very high quality, and this required a lot of work. Frank had to make the rounds of all the offices. He came to the ILWU because he had heard we were a very fine union. After all, there was an ILWU in Chicago and he was aware of the work that our union had done in eliminating race prejudice in bridging the gap among working people and the community. So when he came to us and I saw that the paper that he peddled was of very fine quality, we gave him our business . . . and when the babies came, I think he had five children, you couldn't very well support a family of five on the kind of money you were making selling office supplies.   (Conybeare, 1986 24:6)

Davis experienced the forced sale of his property on Tantalus to cover the losses.

This coincided with the labeling of Davis as a labor sympathizer and communist. He writes in his autobiography:

> Not too long before my arrival, all Democrats were tarred with this same brush by the ruling Republican clique.
>
> In my column I tried to spell out the similarities between Afro-Americans and local people, and local leaders thought my fight against white supremacy meant I was anti-white. I opposed any and all white imperialism and backed the nations seeking independence following World War II. I so incensed members of the White Power Structure that I became the constant radio target of an anti-labor organization known as IMUA, formed to combat the long waterfront strike in 1949, and whose membership was overwhelmingly haole. Even the two dailies were not above taking occasional potshots at me.   (*Livin'* 323-324)

Did Davis wonder if there was a correspondence between his political background, race, outspoken attitudes in the *Record* and the burning of his business? He rarely articulated his suspicions. He was certainly cognizant that the whites were still in control in Hawai`i: the acting Governor at that time was Gov. Stainback, a native of Tennessee, and his unofficial attitude often coincided with that of the many southern whites imported to work for the military (1992, 313).

After the fire and the Tantalus fiasco, to escape the negative forces pressing upon him in Honolulu, Davis and Helen invested in property on the Windward side of O`ahu, first in Kahalu`u, then in Hau`ula where the growing family remained for seven years. Since Davis's growing family soon required some financial security beyond the inheritance received by his wife prior to their arrival, Davis also began to work on a sex novel, *Sex Rebel: Black*, written under the pseudonym Bob Green, to earn extra money. Davis seemed to feel welcome in Hau`ula--and only moved to the leeward Kalihi valley in 1956 for its convenience and proximity to hospitals, schools, and work in Honolulu. He writes:

> For seven years Helen and I lived at Hau`ula, a predominantly Hawaiian village on the ocean some 31 miles from Honolulu. When I began driving daily to town and back, local boys who knew my schedule often waited beside the highway, sometimes for as long as three hours, to flag me down and ask questions about their personal lives, explaining, "you're not *haole* [white] so I know I can trust you." In Hau`ula I joined the Democratic precinct club, virtually ran the organization and was sent to the state convention by the predominantly Hawaiian membership who told me that since I was educated and articulate, I could speak for them.   (*Livin'* 316)

Ironically, even within the relative freedom of Hawai`i, in a world far away from Chicago, there were still tensions, again within the peculiar mixture of race and class origins. Davis and Helen struggled to survive in the lifestyle to which they had been accustomed before moving to Hawai`i. Because his job prospects grew no brighter as Helen's money dwindled, Davis worked on the sex novel to earn extra money. She went to work part time, as the children grew older, drawing illustrations for an advertising agency. Davis worked as a part time correspondent to the Associated Negro Press (ANP), wrote and published a few poems, and tried to complete his aforementioned manuscript.

Before Davis moved to the territory of Hawai'i in 1948, the major decisions of his life had been influenced and directed by the politics of race. To a certain extent, this pattern continued. Moreover, due to his involvement in various labor issues in the 1930's and 1940's in Chicago, his poetry and journalism had developed to include more rhetoric of the politics of race and class.

In remembering Frank Marshall Davis, Henry Epstein, a local labor leader, spoke in an interview about Davis and the post WWII optimism in the labor movement and progressive circles in Chicago and Honolulu.

> What I remember about Frank was that he was a very prominent and well-known black poet who was very highly respected in Chicago. You'd see his picture once in a while on the society page of the Chicago newspapers and when they had fund raisers for progressive organizations in Chicago, if Frank Marshall Davis was coming, you had a real attraction, a prominent person that would help bring people into the event. . . . [Y]ou saw him in what's now called civil rights affairs. . . . I don't think Frank was recognized [in Hawai'i] as the prominent person that he was back in Chicago.
>
> (Conybeare, 1986a, 2:1 & 5)

In fact, in Hawai'i, after Davis's arrival and initial enthusiastic welcome, few people accorded him the status and respect that was his due, because they were unfamiliar with his past and it was a time when most people were afraid to takes risks due to the shadow of McCarthyism.

When Davis became a columnist for the *Honolulu Record*, the newspaper was just beginning to document the imminent strike of the ILWU that lasted 178 days, and the subsequent breaking up of the monopolistic, economically exploitive power of the Big Five over the various immigrant labor groups: the Japanese--who were the most powerful and radical--Chinese, Filipinos and Portuguese. For Davis, this conflict between bosses and laborers was the kind of political ferment and struggle between the powerful and powerless that he thrived upon and enjoyed writing about. He writes:

> When we arrived in 1948, the Big Five [several wealthy
> white firms] had an iron grip on island economy. Organized
> labor led by the ILWU with Jack Hall at the helm was still
> struggling to break its hold. Groups of oriental businessmen
> were forming cooperatives and attacking from another
> angle.   (*Livin'* 313-314)

On the eve of the famous ILWU strike of 1949, the big issue was wage parity. Labor (non-white) was demanding from management (white) equal pay with workers on the West coast. The white executives and employers were starting to fight back against the union, and even their wives organized the "broom brigade," an anti-labor group to oppose the strike. They named themselves *imua*, a Hawaiian word which means to move forward, and they tried to convince the wives of the striking workers to side with management and join with them on the side of a presumed better life. The "broom brigade" also launched a publicity campaign, supported by the commercial newspapers, accusing the ILWU of threatening to starve the people of Hawai`i with the impending strike, because much of the food came from the United States.

In response to the "broom brigade," Helen Davis picketed with other labor wives to support the ILWU. In the end, the ILWU was successful in the strike, and a settlement was made for equal pay with workers on the West coast. The Davises' visibility during the strike did little to endear them to the power elite in the islands, who of course controlled public images and media jobs. McElrath explains:

> Generally, the community didn't look upon trade unions
> with a great deal of love and affection. Besides which the
> Izuka pamphlet about Communism in Hawai`i had just been
> issued, so there was fuel added to the fire which had started
> during the 1946 strike when they said that outsiders were
> coming in and taking over . . . Hawai`i and destroying the
> sugar industry as well as the pineapple industry.
>   (Conybeare, 1986 24:1)

The ILWU publicized itself and its opposition to the Big Five and management through a daily radio program and labor newspapers such as the *Honolulu Record*. It offered a pro-labor viewpoint to answer the conservative *Advertiser*, *Star-Bulletin*, and radio show by celebrity DJ Aku. In speaking of the origins of the Record, Epstein notes:

> The *Honolulu Record* was started by Koji Ariyoshi and Ed Robo with the help of the ILWU and the idea was to have an independent newspaper which was friendly to the labor movement and could present the other side of the news. . . . [T]hey had a lot of articles that you wouldn't read anyplace [else]. John Reineke contributed to the papers. Bob McElrath contributed and Frank Marshall Davis wrote for them. (Conybeare 1986a, 5)

The *Record* contained socio-political analysis which is still valid today, particularly in terms of land ownership, colonialism, and power in Hawai`i.

During this period before Statehood, most whites, commonly called *haole* in Hawai`i--descendants of missionaries, merchants, and/ or landowners--had a colonialist attitude and looked down on the local Hawaiian people and immigrants who worked for them. Class and ethnicity were well-defined and obvious. Epstein remarks:

> When I first came to Hawai`i, my understanding was the banks had dual salary schedules and that *Haoles* had one rate of pay and local people had another. I don't know whether it was justified by classification or how they covered it up, but it was commonly accepted.   (Conybeare 1986, 2:2)

Traditionally, *haole* were discouraged from seeking employment in subservient roles and were neither permitted to work as laborers on the vast sugar and pineapple plantations, nor (for the most part) to join the trade unions. Management kept the different ethnic groups in segregated housing areas with discriminatory salary schedules, playing one group against the other.

The ILWU sought to unify the workers and encouraged them to transcend their diverse ethnicities and cultures. Davis says in an interview:

> When the (local) ILWU started organizing . . . they were advised that they must have an inter-racial leadership or the ILWU would not charter them or would not help them organize. . . . [T]his spirit of all the people working together

is what built up the ILWU and it's what gave them a lot of
strength.   (Conybeare 2:9)

In his column for the *Record*, Davis openly airs his views on imperialism
and colonialism. He compares Hawai`i with other colonies around the
world and attacks the local press for its racist propaganda. He identifies and
connects the non-white people of different cultures and colors as victims of
exploitation. One "Frank-ly Speaking" column dated Jan. 12, 1950 states:

> To the people of Hawai`i, Africa is a far-away place,
> almost another world. And yet in many ways it is as close as
> your next door neighbor. The Dark Continent suffers from
> a severe case of the disease known as colonialism which
> Hawai`i has in a much milder form. The sole hope of the
> dying empires of Western Europe is intensified exploitation
> and continued slavery of African workers through U.S.
> money and munitions. There are strikes in Africa against the
> same kinds of conditions that cause strikes in Hawai`i.
>
> Maybe you think of Africans as black savages, half-
> naked, dancing to the thump-thump of toms-toms in jungle
> clearings, if you think of them at all. You may have gotten
> your impressions through the propaganda of press, radio and
> films, intended to sell the world on the idea that Africans are
> inferior and backward. It comes from the same propaganda
> mill that sells Mainlanders the idea that Japanese and
> Chinese and Filipinos and other people of different cultures
> and colors are also inferior and backward.
>
> (*Honolulu Record* Vol. II, No. 25, 8)

Davis was not afraid to challenge people's comfort zones, prick their
consciences, expand their consciousness, and write fiercely and fervently in
order to expose and to destroy cultural imperialism.

He continued to send, for a small stipend, occasional columns to the
Associated Negro Press which served 200 Negro newspapers in America,
and to write for the non-paying *Honolulu Record*, where he maintained a
column for seven years in which he regularly discussed his observations of
class and race struggles in the islands.

Davis also received some financial support in his paper business and
for his outspoken columns from Oriental businessmen because he defied

"the big *haoles*." He even attacked the House un-American Activities Committee (HUAC) for failing to investigate flagrant abuses of civil rights and democracy such as restricted housing, and for wasting their time to protect the interests of big business. In his "Frank-ly Speaking" column, dated Dec. 28, 1949, he notes:

> The Hawai'i un-American Activities Commission has an excellent chance to break with tradition and win respect for such investigations, by probing the activities and programs of powerful groups that use color, religion or national origin as a basis for denying equality to all.
>
> The matter of restricted housing should be thoroughly aired, and those who perpetrate this evil practice should be forcefully exposed. Naturally, it would hit some of the Territory's most influential persons, many who dominate our economy. Is the commission willing to step on big toes or will it confine its investigations to the weak and powerless?
>
> Restrictive housing covenants hit the majority of the Territory's population, since most are non-haole. In the year that I've been here, I have been blocked by this evil and totally un-American practice. Twice it came up when I sought rental units; last week it was raised again as I contemplated purchase of a home in an area off Kaneohe Bay Drive. It was Castle leasehold property and restricted, I was told. And so the deal was off.   (*Honolulu Record* Vol. II, No. 22, 16)

It is true that Hawai'i and her people allowed Davis his dignity to be a man. However, the FBI denied him freedom of choice, speech, and self-determination to develop his career and talent as a mainstream journalist, the moment it sent Davis's dossier to the local authorities from Washington, DC, effectively barring Davis from all opportunities in the traditional job market, especially since Davis was an intellectual, and not a construction worker. To have a dossier meant that city, state, and federal jobs were off-limits. Plus there was the loyalty oath. Davis says in an interview:

> I had an FBI agent who I learned had been my personal agent until around the early 60's. So this particular fellow one day . . . produced his credentials and said that he was from the FBI and wanted to talk with me . . . accompanied by another

fellow who had a brief case . . . told me that "I know you used to be a Communist, but what made you change your mind. Why did you leave the party?" I said, "Wait a minute, if I say I left the party that would indicate that I had been a member of the Communist Party, and I have never told anybody that."   (Conybeare, 1986a, 6:37)

"And so, in fact, when I came over I am pretty certain that I have every reason to believe that my dossier reached here before I did . . . from the FBI" (Conybeare, 1986a, 5:29-30).

One can only imagine Davis's frustrations at his inability to become a successful journalist and writer in Hawai'i after his promising beginnings in Atlanta and Chicago. He rarely complained, but he must have felt incomplete if not bitter when he found dignity, but not freedom to develop his potential and lead the respected and distinguished life to which he had been accustomed. He writes of his peace and frustration, his losses and gains:

> Not long after arriving in Hawai'i, I began writing a regular weekly column for the *Honolulu Record*, supported mainly by the ILWU membership, and was openly friendly with its leadership. Within a week I had decided to settle here permanently, although I knew it would mean giving up what prestige I had acquired back in Chicago where I was now appearing each year in *Who's Who in the Midwest* and had been told by the editors that in 1949 my biography would be included in *Who's Who in America*. But the peace and dignity of living in Paradise would compensate for finding a way other than as a newspaperman to make a living. *The Record*, of course, was not financially able to add me to its payroll. Koji Ariyoshi and Ed Rohrbough, son of a West Virginia congressman, were its editorial mainstays.
>
> (*Livin'* 323)

But, did the peace and dignity of living in Hawai'i really compensate for Davis's loss of status and profession? Davis's life, the change in his status after he arrived in Honolulu, the arrogant neglect of Davis by Honolulu's business community and intelligentsia, and his decline into the final poverty reveal what happened when this educated, outspoken, experienced African American could not fulfill his creative impulses and dreams to survive with dignity and status as a respected employed member of the local community.

Finally, near the end of his life, Davis was forced to make hard choices just to survive. He resorted to peddling mediocre merchandise of pens, shirts, and miscellaneous small items to small businesspersons in Honolulu for a meager income.

By the 1970's, most African American intellectuals and journalists on the mainland assumed Davis had long since passed on, since they no longer heard his journalistic or poetic voice. The majority of Hawai`i residents under 50 or 60 years old had never even heard of this sleeping giant in their community. He had been long ago blacklisted by those who controlled Hawai`i and he remained forgotten by the next generations until President Barack Obama wrote about Davis's influence on him in *Dreams from My Father*, when he was a young student at Punahou, an elite private school in Honolulu, and visited Davis with his grandfather. He saw the older Davis as a strong, articulate, cultured, Black intellectual and critic who asked important questions and who had been a community activist.

Meanwhile, Davis silently acquiesced to the loss of status and prestige because perhaps he no longer had the strength to fight the system. In one of his last published poems entitled "To a Young Man," he offers this indecisive advice:

> When I was your age/ Fifty years ago/ I knew everything/
> The old man said/ Pointed with his cane/ Of memory;/ When
> I was twenty/ I saw a scarlet sky/ And a blue balloon sun/
> And I had/ An explanation;/ Since then I have drunk/ Half
> a hundred liquid years/ Distilled/ Through rustless coils of
> wisdom/ And if you asked me now/ Do one plus one/ Make
> two or three or four/ I would have to say/ I do not know./ The
> old man turned/ His hammered face/ To the pounding stars/
> Smiled/ Like the ring of a gong/ And walked until/ On the
> slate horizon/ He erased himself.   (*Black World* 48)

The move from optimistic youth to a weakened, indecisive old man is striking, and yet the last line--where the elder is still in control of his destiny in face of the pounding hammer of time and can be the active agent to erase

himself--bespeaks finally of the strength of the man. His condition is yet
another illustration of the American tragedy of racism because his options
were so slim: he and his white wife Helen could stay and live a tortured
life in Chicago on the cutting edge of racial politics, or they could move to
Hawai`i and give up his successful career. Unlike other white Americans,
the doors of success in Hawai`i were closed to him because he publicly
and relentlessly fought the systems of racism, economic exploitation, and
cultural imperialism.

Did the politics of defeat in Hawai`i derail or merely delay Davis's
destination of greatness in his life? Davis has not yet received contemporary
public acclaim for his long writing career, unlike many esteemed African
Americans such as Richard Wright, Margaret Walker, James Baldwin, or
Maya Angelou. Was there any way that Davis, as an African American
professional man in Hawai`i, could remain unconventional, radical, and
defiant in face of strong political, cultural, and economic machines, and
become financially successful? What else could he have done realistically
to channel his abundant energy, and how could he react to a system which
considered him a dangerous and deviant pariah: a militant African American
writer with a radical-seeming political perspective and a white wife? Was
there any way to maintain his political views and aggressive nature and to
prosper with no allegiance to a power base in the community? The answer
is an unequivocal no.

Unfortunately, during Davis's prime years, no significant African
American population and community with a power base existed in Hawai`i to
provide Davis with emotional and moral support, nor an expanded audience
and market for his writing. Also, because he was still concerned with the
issues of freedom, racism, and equality, he lacked widespread multicultural
support. Many islanders felt economic issues were more important, or, they
simply dared not challenge the system again after the year strike. Most
probably felt they should not risk their jobs, security, and well-being, since
most had come to Hawai`i as immigrants and had only recently moved into
a tenuous middle-class status.

Also, the facts that Davis's dossier followed him to Hawai`i and that
an FBI agent kept track of him for ten years after his arrival, branded him

unworthy, immoral, in some sense unpatriotic, and dangerous to the status quo. This subtle form of harassment, denigration, and suspicion may have contributed to other patterns of defeat: his search for alternative modes of power, his wavering faith in the system, and his dropout status after his 1970 divorce from Helen (Davis, *Livin'* 333).

If Davis did not succeed financially, why did he not succeed literarily and gain the status and renown of his expatriot contemporaries like Richard Wright and James Baldwin who continued to publish in exile? Was it merely that France, already aware of the great protest literature of her colonies, was intellectually far ahead of the "sleepy" territory of Hawai`i? Was Davis tired of carrying the race struggle and protest message on his shoulders, or was he a hedonist at heart who preferred pleasure to the tiresome battle of freedom? Did he simply carry his battle to another level? Although certainly not "successful" in the traditional, capitalistic sense of the word, could the life of Davis be said to end in defeat? What constitutes defeat?

It can be argued that Davis escaped defeat like a trickster or a phoenix, playing dead only to arise later and win the race, although the politics of defeat were all around him. If Hawai`i society seemed to defeat him by denying him financial rewards, a successful career in journalism, publication of his poetry, and local status, he continued to write prolifically. He stood by his principles and wrote about them tirelessly. Davis provided a bold and defiant model for writers to hold on to their convictions and articulate them in face of overwhelming odds.

His writings remain. Davis's social criticism and perceptive analysis are just as relevant today when the conditions of exploitation continue to thrive and deprive many people of color, minorities, and those who are poor.

In a militant poem called "Black American" published in *Black World*, Davis distinguishes between the color black and the cultural/historical experience and ideology. He affirms and claims equality and his place as an American. He takes an Afro-centric position of looking back to the histories of great African civilizations, great revolutionary slave leaders, and the many contributions of Africans in the building of America, all while affirming his American-ness. He declares:

The time has come/ to quit barn and kitchen/ And move into

the parlor/ Naturally/ I love my African kin/ But I was not
born there/ My home is America/ And nothing shall drive me
away/ Accept it, Whitey/ And stand aside/ Burn your tired
trash of racism/ Mixed with the moldy manure/ Of unlimited
dollar profits/ Burn your racism/ Or watch our America burn/
I am your equal in every good way/ I will settle for nothing
less/ And if I must die for what I own/ So be it/ Today at last/
I am a proud Black American.   (*Black World* 47)

In his *Honolulu Record* columns, "Frank-ly Speaking," Davis continued
to write and fight with his words for equality and a more just society. One
column dated Jan. 19, 1950 reads:

First of all, let us bring the Bill of Rights back to life in
our Constitution. It has been a casualty of the cold war, yet it
is as important today as it was when it was first framed. For,
to paraphrase Lincoln, we have come to the evil day when
none but the supporters of our bi-partisan foreign policy are
entitled to life, liberty and the pursuit of happiness. That is
not the kind of democracy Washington and Jefferson built in
the young days of our nation; it is a dictatorship of thought,
absolutely repugnant to our national traditions. Let Hawai`i
lead the way back to Americanism.
                            (1949-1952, Vol. II, No. 26, 8.)

He also worked hard to create a union or committee of the various ethnic
groups to fight for equality, often by illustrating how in the United States,
African Americans had worked together with other groups in coalition
politics to accomplish mutual goals.

Since the *Honolulu Record* was created to provide an alternative
perspective to the news and was partially funded by the ILWU, Davis found
it to be the medium through which he could critique the sociopolitical
structure of the Territory of Hawai`i, affirm civil rights, and keep in touch
with the common people. Davis says in an interview:

At that time, there were many places downtown where blacks
were not welcome. And there were efforts made to break this
color barrier. Incidentally . . . I was vice-chairman of the
Chicago Civil Liberties Committee and so the Civil Rights

Congress was in existence when I came over here. And we were, the local civil rights chapter was affiliated with the Civil Rights Congress, which was another thing which did not sit well with the powers that were.

(Conybeare, 1986, 6:34)

In the 1940's, the Civil Rights Congress was considered by the government to be a radical organization as was the NAACP in some quarters.

In his *Honolulu Record* columns, Davis attacked: the HUAC witch hunts, the loyalty oath, fascism, the Smith Act, white supremacy, Jim Crow, the War Machine, imperialism, racism and prejudice, reactionaries, discrimination by Supreme Court appointees, dictatorships, and ultra-conservative wealthy people. He also exposed the mostly unspoken topics of unemployment, land and housing problems, blacklisting, and the exploitation of minority groups. On the other hand, he espoused freedom, radicalism, solidarity, labor unions, due process, peace, affirmative action, civil rights, Negro History week, and true Democracy to fight imperialism, colonialism, and white supremacy. He urged for more coalition politics in the islands between the various ethnic groups. He called for people to investigate the real threats to democracy such as big business interests, repression, censorship, thought-control, the war machine, anti-communist hysteria, reactionaries and fascism, racial segregation. He called upon the ordinary citizen to fight for democracy and revisions in the land and tax laws. He exhorted the people of Hawai`i to wake up from indifference and apathy, to challenge police brutality, to support democratic politics, and to gain economic power from land reform.

In speaking of his writings and influence, McElrath notes in an interview:

. . . he (Davis) wrote some very prescient articles about race relations in Hawai`i and given the fact that Frank, a black married to a white, had come from that kind of situation in Chicago, it's utterly amazing how he was able to size up the race relations here in the . . . Territory of Hawai`i. As a matter of fact in the first article that he wrote, I have the date here, January 13, 1949, he talked about Anglo-Saxon culture being not better, but different from Hawaiian culture,

Japanese culture, Chinese culture, and he talked a little bit
about the typical reaction of the whites to different cultures.
. . started a whole series of articles on race relations. As a
matter of fact, one of his articles ended with this phrase.
"These beautiful islands can still chart their own future."
I'm not sure that Frank would agree that the future which we
have since chartered has been a good one or a bad one.

(Conybeare 1986, 24:3)

Some land reform laws were finally enacted in the 1960's to resolve
some of the problems which Davis had addressed and spoken out about
in the 1940's and 1950's. These have only been finally sanctioned in the
late 1980's, and some economic issues are still controversial such as lease
hold land held mainly by large land owners and the military to fee (private)
conversion, land and water rights, and sovereignty for Hawaiians. One
column in the *Record* dated 19 Jan, 1950 states:

Provision should be made for breaking up the big
estates which control so much of this territory and force
Hawai`i to depend upon a sugar and pineapple economy.
Small independent farmers need to have access to land at a
reasonable fee so that they can engage in diversified farming
and thus make the people less at the mercy of the shipping
industry and importing monopolies for food.

For we have reached a period in our history when not
only political and social rights need to be spelled out, but
economic rights as well.   (1949-1952 Vol. II, No. 26, 8)

In the late 1940's and early 1950's, many who were opposed to the
status quo (economic and political control by a few landed giants) were
considered Communist, but this did not deter Davis from continuing his
path as a social realist, a champion of the common person and Hawaiians,
and a militant voice in a gentle land. He relentlessly focused on the socio-
economic and political problems in the Islands which he observed and could
expertly analyze, due to his 20 years of newspaper experience, labor union
work, familiarity with global politics, and the many years of browsing 35
newspapers a day. Moreover, Davis was used to hostility from the white
community; he had always been an outsider, a *malihini*. He was tough

and not easily thwarted. He was not intimidated by the FBI--although his influence was diluted by their discriminatory practices and harassment-- since he had had previous experience with them in Chicago at the ANP. He had even developed a strategy for giving them misinformation he says in an interview (Conybeare 1986, 5:28).

On a personal level, Davis had many white friends in the islands. His autobiography indicates:

> At the same time, I developed strong friendships with many *haoles* because I am not oriental. I was somebody who came from the same general environment and over-all background. At first it was shocking to hear Caucasians tell me what "we" must do when, on the Mainland, they would likely say "you people." Many whites of considerable residence here are as bitter about racism as any of us and are glad to live in a place where overt prejudice is not customary. I have known *haoles* to go back home for a long visit but return ahead of schedule because they couldn't stand the attitudes of their old friends.   (*Livin'* 317)

Outside of politics, Davis found Hawai'i to be a relaxed and friendly place to live.

In his relationships with women, Davis was conscious of society's fascination with the stereotype of the "black stud", alleged to have an excessive sexual appetite and an extraordinary sex life, and Hawai'i was a vacation spot for fantasies. He reports in his autobiography:

> Goodly numbers of Caucasian females shed their inhibitions in Hawai'i and go on a strong soul kick. At the same time, many haole youths flip over the local dolls of various strains and combinations, for Paradise has some of the most lushly beautiful women on earth. Many local studs are frantic to bed a soul sister who is not a pro; propaganda painting their passion and horizontal ability has fallen on receptive ears. Afro American brothers make out with all kinds of dolls.   (*Livin'* 317-318)

Davis uses Hawai'i's multi-cultural setting as a backdrop for part of his first novel, *Sex Rebel: Black* which he wrote under the aforementioned pseudonym Bob Green. The main character Bob describes how, after his arrival in Honolulu in 1950, Waikīkī became his "happy hunting ground." In love with his wife Charlene, he still sought sexual variety:

> Until I had been seen often enough to win the confidence of local chicks, I found Waikīkī my most happy hunting ground. On Kalakaua Avenue, the main drag, where females of all ages walk the street in skimpy bikinis, and on the beaches virtually kissing the sidewalk where others sunbathed and loafed, and in the bars where many dolls sit eagerly waiting for action, there were always partners available for the male swinger of any color. During summer, Waikīkī swells with coeds from all parts of the Mainland, here ostensibly to attend the University of Hawai`i summer session, but actually out for wild kicks with beach boys and surfing bums. Winter brings an older, wealthier group, usually with husbands who want to learn if it's true what they say about those brown Polynesian maidens. I scored enough with the older babes to satisfy my taste for a supplement filet mignon--especially after I hit upon the idea of going to Kapiolani Park in the middle of the day.   (*Sex Rebel* 264)

One might speculate that Davis's personal and social life was influenced by a variety of sexual relationships and adventures such as Bob engages in, since the Bob character sought empowerment through association. Indeed, Davis was always aware of his own self assumed role as a sex rebel and social gadfly in a society which still did not accept him nor his marriage to a white woman. Indeed, the publication of *Sex Rebel: Black* in 1968 may have strained his 20-year marriage.

Prior to his formal divorce, in June 1969 Davis moved alone to the area of Honolulu then known as "the Waikīkī Jungle." There he had a modest cottage, dwarfed by a rapidly expanding Waikīkī. His cottage was soon to be condemned for a high rise apartment. The porch was only two-or-three feet from the sidewalk, permitting easy conversation with passersby. It soon became a meeting place for a great variety of people, many of whom were neighbors in the "jungle". Some were of the hippie generation that grew out of the 1960's; others were young radicals, non-conformists, university students, runaways, revolutionaries--all a multi-cultural mixed plate comprised of African Americans, Caucasians, a great variety of locals including Asian Americans and Hawaiians, and foreigners from the five continents and the Pacific Islands.

Most were young and many were disillusioned with society. Some were persistent idealists, while others lived the tenuous life of street hustlers, using their hardened wits and even their own bodies to survive. Yet no matter the age, gender, or philosophy, all who entered his cottage seemed to quickly come to respect and revere Davis for his perspicacious wit and practical homespun philosophy of survival that he offered with the sharing of food, including his home-cooked sweet potato pies. He gave them moral support and counseling spiced with his wry observations and shots of sarcasm, always with excellent jazz playing in the background and the television on for the news.

> For the most part they were from California, with a few from as far away as Maine and Florida. In addition there were others from South America, Europe, Asia, Africa, Australia, Canada, the Caribbean, Samoa, Tonga and the other islands of the South Pacific.   (*Livin'* 327)

In the Waikīkī jungle, Davis, living alone, wore the hat of the *désengagé*, the *bohème*. He expanded his nuclear family and his role as patriarch or father to include writers, newcomers, neighbors, and even the homeless. He was often a friend to alienated youth, many scared and naive facing the dangers of city hustles for the first time.

He took pride in his continued role as an intellectual poet and critic of society, occasionally publishing a poem or two in an African American literary publication on the continental United States. He read avidly, consciously shunned the identity of the "super masculine" menial by continuing to earn his modest livelihood in sales with the customers he had established through the years. He occasionally sold items other than paper products such as *dashikis*, the colorful African print shirt popular during the 1960's and 1970's.

Davis's writings of this period reveal his unwavering commitment to the tenets of Democracy. He continued to write poetry about poor and oppressed people, usually choosing specific characters as representatives or metonyms of a theme such as prejudice for example. Davis's subjects were often the weak or handicapped, who, like trickster animals in African and African American folklore, use craft and cunning to arrive at subtle victories over their larger, more powerful foes, and who sometimes receive unconventional rewards.

Of many posthumously published poems written in Hawai`i, three are exceptional--"Tale of Two Dogs," "For Militant Blacks,"and "This is Paradise"--because Davis addresses the class and ethnic problems he discovers in Hawai`i: the exploitation of the indigenous Hawaiians and the immigrant workers by the missionaries and their descendants.

In *Ramrod 8*, he attacks the imperialism of America in a historical poem "Tale of Two Dogs," about the sugar and pineapple industries. He recounts:

> Then the Strangers came;/ They loosed their chained terriers/ Of pineapple and sugar cane;/ Sent them boldly into the yard/ To sniff with eager green noses/ At the sleeping old./ Long since/ Pine and Cane/ Have taken over the front lawn. Snapping impatiently at obstructing ankles; They run between/ The tall still legs of the motionless mountains/ As if they originated here/ And the silent ancients / Were usurpers./ Here in this cultivated place/ Growing the soft brown rose/ of Polynesia/ The dogs have scratched/ Digging for the buried pot of cash returns/ Killing the broken bush/ Under the flying dirt/ of greed and grief./ . . . There is none so patient/ As a tired mountain drowsing in the sun;/ There is no wrath so great/ As that of a mountain outraged/ Destroying the nipping dogs/ Loosed on the front lawn/ By the Strangers.   (4-5)

The accusatory voice, the exposure of the raw power of the usurpers, the poetic description of the destruction of Nature and the original soft place of the inhabitants, wrought by greed and the industries of the Strangers, and the suggestion of revenge by the outraged mountain make this poem very powerful, especially in contrast with the ancient silent power of the motionless mountains.

For over two decades, Davis tried to break the color barrier and prejudice against African Americans in Hawai`i. By the 1970's, the fires and rage of the Civil Rights activists on the mainland had found and flamed Davis's hidden and smoldering embers of bitterness and disillusionment in Hawai`i. In his poem "For Militant Blacks," he once again uses the first person and dialect as in many of his social realism poems to express the anger, rage, and potential violence of the oppressed. Davis speaks of the historical oppression, victimization, nihilism, and dispossession of African Americans, in spite of their contributions to society and their endless appeals and brave protests for freedom.

> When white sees black as white as white/ And black sees white as black as we/ On that day/ I shall be proud of my native land./ . . . And the two-timing politicians/ Who for a hundred years/ Peddled putrid promises/ Of teasing tomorrows/ Grudgingly at last/ Gave us a gift of statutes/ A great garland of lovely laws/ Beautiful on the books/ Nevertheless/ Each day/ Whitey kills another bunch of niggers/ Business goes on as usual./ . . . Yeah, baby, I made the nonviolent scene/ Both South and North/ Marched in Washington, sat in Atlanta/ I been attacked by police dogs/ Stunned by fire hoses/ Kicked, beaten, dragged off to jail/ Seen comrades hurt and slain/ And I found out the hard way/ The only nonviolent cats was us/ This dump where I lives/ Oughta been burned to ashes befo World War II/ But I can't move 'cept to its twin/ We should pay our rent/ To roaches and rats -- / They owns the joint;/ . . . Now I'm tellin you like it is -- / I'm gonna shoot hell outa every honky I sees/ Soon's they pass th word/ An if they kills me, Glory!/ I'd jus as soon be dead/ As livin like I do" . . . We are the poor, despised, the badly schooled/ We are the hungry hordes of the dispossessed/ We are the great black masses/ Proud, yes, of our judges, politicians, athletes/ But vicarious success does not rub off/ Won't put another bean in the pot/. . . .   (1986b, n.p.)

Davis enumerates the historical brutality and violence bestowed upon African Americans by whites, and expands the definition of black from a color to a state of mind, free and confined to a figurative hell.

"Black is not a color/ It is a state of mind/ A vivid pattern of

living. . . . Gladly do we grant asylum to those renouncing
forever/ false gods of white superiority/ by thinking black. .
. ./ Come liberated brother/ Make your home among us. . . ./
But can you take/ Confinement in hell?"   (n.p.)

He also criticizes the US military and calls upon African Americans
to resist fighting foreign enemies and to turn to the enemy within our
country: once again, Davis utilizes dialect to portray a monologue of a
poor, frustrated and angry African American involved in the Civil Rights
movement including the violence which he wants to return to the whites,
preferring death to the life he leads. Although there is a militant call for
revenge against white supremacy, Davis ends the poem with a repetition of
the opening lines "When white sees black as white as white/ When black
sees white as black as we . . . I shall be proud of my native land." In this
poem, written in a style reminiscent of e e cummings and Walt Whiman,
he appeals to others to join with African Americans in their emancipatory
project and struggle. He still believes that America is his home, his native
land. Ironically, never giving up until his death, Davis maintained a hope in
the future of democracy and in a multi-cultural America.

The third poem of note is "This is Paradise", an epic five-section poem.
Davis offers an ironic travelogue in which a superficial tourist from Iowa
might find a quaint, exotic paradise peopled with friendly, peaceful, prismatic
natives contented to serve. In the second section of the poem, he reveals
the "soiled slip" of the real Hawai`i behind the props and stage setting:
"Captain Cook . . . sweeping over the old way/ inundating the ancient gods/
flooding the sacred soil of custom and tradition" (*Black Moods* 199). He
speaks of the missionaries as "magicians, the conjure men of Christianity/
placed the vanishing cloth of Mother Hubbard on the women/ Then whoosh
and presto/ Nudity into nakedness" (*Black Moods* 199). He points to the
irony:

Now that it was uncivilized/ To kill by spear or club/ Guns
became a symbol of progress:/ and at the end of Part II he
writes, "The missionaries came with Bibles/ The heathen
natives had the land/ Now the natives are no longer heathens,/
They have the Bible and Jesus/ and in this equitable trade   /
This oh so reasonable swap/ The missionaries got the

land. . . .   (*Black Moods* 199)

In Part III, Davis begins his critique of the Big Five. "Under the manure of the missionaries/ sprouted the Big Five/ Time was/ When the Big Five had God on their payroll. . . . But that was before the Union/" (*Black Moods* 200-201.). He proceeds to describe the struggle between the ILWU and the Big Five; the Island people finally become freed from fear, but still remain victims of poverty.

In Part IV, Davis speaks lovingly of the ethnic mix of the inhabitants of the island but adds irony. A *haole* tourist from Birmingham states: "Went home after two days of his intended month:/ 'You can take these Goddamned islands,' He told friends in Dixie/ And shove them up your ass/ I don't like Hawai`i/ Too many niggers there'" (*Black Moods* 203). Davis points out the irony of color as a dark Hawaiian speaks to a lemon-light Negro using the expression "boy" in describing his best friend who was African American in the army. Later Davis uses Asians in the poem to ridicule the "funny kind names" of the *haole*. The more subtle problems of miscegenation are addressed when two *haole* parents referring to the Japanese bride of their son say, "It's all right to sleep with 'em/ But for Christ sake/ Why do you have to marry 'em," and where the bride subsequently returns to the islands (*Black Moods* 203-204).

In another ironic passage, the Keakana family goes to the beach on the weekend to fish, "And the tourists from Topeka riding around the island in the prancing buses smile pinkly and murmur: 'How quaint, how carefree the Hawaiians are, not a worry in the world, nothing to do but loaf and fish just like their ancestors'" (204-5). Davis finishes the vignette with the comment that John Keakana weighs his fish to sell in order to eat and "stretch monthly pay within $40 of what the social scientists call necessary for minimum health standards." Davis reveals the low standard of living and poverty which a typical native-Hawaiian family might be confronted with in contrast to the tourist-oriented, technological society in which they find themselves in modern times, and in contrast to their original caring relationship to the land (`aina) in the islands.

In Part V of "This is Paradise," Davis satirizes the myth that there is no race prejudice in Hawai`i, creating imaginary scenes where skin color and ethnic identity are equated with attitudes of superiority and inferiority, largely based on ignorance. He underlines the effective tactics of divide and conquer which the plantation society and later the imported mainland prejudice implanted into the island mentality.

> One week in the country/ And the navy wife phones her landlord:/ "Across the street/ Lives a bunch of dirty Hawaiians;/ Next door on our right/ A family of lousy Japs;/ On the other side/ A house full of slant eyed Chinks;/ And in front of us/ On our very same lot/ A white bitch married to a nigger/ I want our rent money back." (*Black Moods* 207)

In this epic poem, Davis ruthlessly exposes the racism in paradise brought by many White Americans, the hypocrisy, arrogant attitudes, and practices of white supremacy that he witnessed. He did not find a large or sympathetic audience, because typically to this day, people in Hawai'i do not like to acknowledge racism, discrimination, or prejudice.

> Despite propaganda spread by southern whites imported to work for Uncle Sam during World War II and the unofficial attitude of the territorial administration, then headed by Governor Steinback, a native of Tennessee, local people generally were ready to accept Afro Americans at face value. Of course many had strongly warped ideas, drawn from traditional stereotypes perpetuated by press, movies and radio, but in the final analysis they based attitudes on personal relationships. I soon learned many Japanese went through a sizing up period when blacks moved into a predominantly Japanese neighborhood or they came in contact at work, but when they decided to accept you, it was on a permanent basis, not as a fair weather friend. Dark Hawaiians tended to dislike Afro Americans as a group (many lived in mortal fear white tourists would mistake them for Negroes) but developed strong friendships with individuals; Hawaiians are traditionally warm and outgoing.   (*Livin'* 314)

Considering the controversial subject matter of Davis's writing and his edgy critical perspective in a soft welcoming laid back place like Hawai'i, it is little wonder that some whites looked askance at his very presence in the islands.

However, Davis was neither to be intimidated nor silenced, even if it meant not having a conventional, salaried high-status job. He worked quietly, he wrote even when he no longer published his writings, and he talked with those who came to visit him--always seeking to present the truth of his vision, confident that social justice and human dignity would prevail. Indeed, despite his radical rhetoric, Davis remained optimistic that good relations between ethnic groups could and would lead to a better world. His life-long social conscience was reflected in the flavors and tastes of his writings.

Davis was a pioneer to Hawai`i in the sense that he recorded the race and class history of his time, thinking of himself not as a local person, but rather as an ex-patriot who found a community which accepted him and gave him a personal level of human dignity and peace which he treasured. In the articles "Frank Marshall Davis in Hawai`i: Outsider Journalist Looking In" (Takara) and "The Black Diaspora in Hawai`i" (Takara), I have addressed the thorny issues of acceptance and assimilation with respect to the African American experience in Hawai`i:

> Hawai`i does offer a model of racial harmony to the world, but until it includes African Americans and others of African descent in a more equitable way, it is but a fragile myth.
>
> (Takara, *Oral Histories* xxxiii)

CHAPTER 7
The Rise of the Phoenix: The Afterlives of Frank Marshall Davis

I would
not have mourners
only dancers
naked
and no music
a funeral
my fearful people
with no sobbing
no tunes
not even the latest jazz
nor hymns
by all means no hymns

(Davis, *Black Man's* 49-50)

At the end of Frank Marshall Davis's life, he had become a promise of transcendence for me, an example of a phoenix rising again to recognition and respect, a testament to the transformative power of the word. Davis is representative of a renaissance man in a self-conscious role of reflection, a multi-dimensional hero in a national, global, political drama. His writing has been translated and read in several languages. This expanded role is especially apparent in his autobiography, in various interviews granted in the last few years of his life, and in certain posthumously published and unedited poems. Many of the problems of patriarchy, gender, and race which Davis encountered, critiqued, and analyzed in the thirties and forties still simmer and plague the world today: inequality and injustice, poverty and ignorance.

His keen perception and understanding of large issues, popular culture, and politics is evidenced in his life work and in the aggressive and critical tone in his writings. He was a champion of democracy and the working class. Angela Davis, referring to Davis's friend, Paul Robeson, in her essay "Art on the Frontline: Mandate for a People's Culture" articulates the challenges faced by progressive artists and political activists like Frank Marshall Davis. She comments:

How do we collectively acknowledge our popular cultural legacy and communicate it to the masses of our people, most of whom have been denied access to the social spaces reserved for art and culture? In the United States, a rich and vibrant tradition of people's art has emerged from the history of labor militancy and the struggles of Afro-Americans, women, and peace activists. It is essential that we explore that tradition, understand it, reclaim it, and glean from it the cultural nourishment that can assist us in preparing a political and cultural counteroffensive against the regressive institutions and ideas spawned by advanced monopoly capitalism.   (*Women* 199)

Unlike many intellectuals of the academic and art academy, Angela Davis and Frank Marshall Davis seem to both buy into the Marxist interpretation of a role of art as a catalyst and power to ignite the fire of change. Angela Davis writes:

. . . art is a form of social consciousness--a special form of social consciousness that can potentially awaken an urge in those affected by it to creatively transform their oppressive environments. . . . Art is special because of its ability to influence feelings as well as knowledge."

(*Women* 199-200)

Angela Davis exposes the forces of capitalism and oppression at work in society in hopes of informing and inspiring people toward more conscience-driven, conscious, emancipatory projects and strategies, using art to transform their environments and society.

One must not forget that Frank Marshall Davis came of age at a time when people around the world were beginning to consciously define their position between progress and reaction. In his poem "Roosevelt Smith," he captures the frustration of an African American artist, who finally is driven from the literary world to take an ordinary job. Much of Davis's own experience is reflected in this poem:

You ask what happened to Roosevelt Smith/ Well . . . / Conscience and the critics got him/ Roosevelt Smith was the only dusky child born and bred/ in the village of Pine City,

Nebraska/ At college they worshipped the novelty of a black poet and predicted fame/ At twenty-three he published his first book . . . the critics/ said he imitated Carl Sandburg, Edgar Lee Masters/ and Vachel Lindsay . . . they raved about a wealth of/ racial material and the charm of darky dialect/ So for two years Roosevelt worked and observed in Dixie/ At twenty-five a second book . . . Negroes complained/ about plantation scenes and said he dragged Aframerica's good name in the mire for gold . . . "Europe," they said, "honors Dunbar for his `Ships That Pass In The Night' and not for his dialect which they don't/ understand"/ For another two years Roosevelt strove for a different medium of expression/ At twenty-seven a third book . . . the critics said the density/ of Gertrude Stein or T. S. Elliot hardly fitted/ the simple material to which a Negro had access/ For another two years Roosevelt worked/ At twenty-nine his fourth book . . . the critics said a Negro had no business imitating the classic forms of Keats, Browning and Shakespeare. . . "Roosevelt Smith," they announced, has nothing original and is merely a black face white. His African heritage is a rich source should he use it"/ So for another two years Roosevelt went into the interior of Africa/ At thirty-one his fifth book . . . interesting enough, the critics said, but since it followed nothing done by any white poet it was probably just a new kind of prose/ Day after the reviews came out Roosevelt traded conscience and critics for the leather pouch and bunions of a mail carrier and read in the papers until his death how little the American Negro had contributed to his nation's literature. . .

(Black Man's 82)

Davis uses sarcasm, irony, and wit to expose the tragic futility of the efforts of most Black writers, regardless of their literary approach. He critiques the white literary establishment for excluding educated African American artists. He describes society's ambiguity and trivialization of the African American aesthetic. He laments the defeat of the black artist Roosevelt who did everything as a white poet would do, but who was rejected because he was a black man and thus could not be expected to succeed in his art.

Frank Marshall Davis is representative of the African American intellectual of his time. He was a deliberate observer. He was informed by and courageously spoke to the concrete human issues of his immediate ethnic community and of the larger world. He also was concerned with the search for identity and his place as a Black man in the world. His writings have included a significant political discourse similar to the multi-media responses of most African American artists; indeed, historically many great artists have made political statements. In most of Davis's works, he boldly speaks out, challenging the Establishment's exclusion and exploitation of minorities and poor people, and his readers have increasingly been multiethnic, multicultural, and multinational.

In southern parlance, he has been "talking back." bell hooks speaks about the African and African American oral tradition and empowerment through the active voice in her book titled *Talking Back*:

> In the world of the southern black community I grew up in, "back talk" and talking back" meant speaking as an equal to an authority figure. It meant daring to disagree, and sometimes it just meant having an opinion. . . . To make yourself heard if you were a child was to invite punishment. . . . To speak when one was not spoken to was a courageous act, an act of risk and daring. . . .   (5)

Davis's aim, like that of many African American artists, was to talk back, to make himself heard, to risk punishment. His punishment came in the form of censorship and local obscurity, since he was blacklisted by the Big Five media machine in Hawai'i. However, because he continued to write, it is left to those who have followed him to make his voice heard again. He was one of the grandparents of talking back, and as such is an inspiration for writers and activists who can still learn from his fearless example.

Davis was patriotic, although his world view remained leftist in intention and execution. He was anti-bourgeois, anti-capitalist, anti-imperialistic, and *avant-garde*, not only in language, style, and form, but in his presentation of the "isms" in a poetic genre: capitalism, communism, fascism, and sexism. He was a militant protest poet whose work anticipated that of many contemporary young rap singers and jazz musicians. He was *l'homme engagé*.

He did not seek the safety of acceptable topics; he would not be silenced. Even if the public no longer listened to his voice, Davis was still alive and defiantly writing during four decades in his self-imposed exile in Hawai`i. He sought the heart and soul of democracy, its true meaning for all its citizens.

The social criticism implicit in his poems found its object in the unpleasant reality that they often evoked and that he brilliantly described in the individuals forced to endure it. He lived in a time of crisis. He spoke, at times with harsh censure, rage, and visceral indignation, to the unpardonable acts of savagery inherent in Jim Crow and fascism. He understood the significance of a country run by bigots and the industrial/ military complex which he considered a private club that disenfranchised its poor and colored citizens. He reached deep within his subterranean essence to capture and describe his personal anger and pain, and at the same time he reached beyond himself to express those similar emotions of the multitudes. Often his tone was ironic, solemn, and sometimes accusatory. Other times he wrote of horrifying events with melancholic undertones; yet he invited and was open to dialogue as he tried to explain the exclusion of the Black American. James Young comments:

> Unfortunately, Davis's poetry is too frequently marred by his strong social attacks. His truths tend too much to the horrifying and shocking. There is too little attempt to convey truth with controlled artistry. However, his work does contribute to our understanding of the Black American of this era.   (188)

His critics found his poetry didactic, prosaic, and too political, but most agreed that he accurately documented the black urban culture and struggle. Even his harshest critics attested to the value of his work and free-flowing form. On the other hand, his work has been praised as significant by Langston Hughes, George Schuyler, and Alain Locke, and later his work came to the attention of scholars like Stephen Henderson, Maryemma Graham, Kathryn Takara, and John Edgar Tidwell.

In fact, Davis incorporated his sense of beauty, rhythm, sound, and color in much of his poetry as he sought to combine a literary quality with popular appeal.

Unlike Arna Bontemps and Langston Hughes, Davis's view was not a romantic portrayal of black life, called Négritude, a term coined by President, philosopher-poet Leopold Senghor of Sénégal two decades later in the early 1960's. Surprisingly, Davis's preoccupation with African American culture and his condemnation of white hypocrisy and injustices did not often include a direct repudiation of European cultural traditions. Rather, his work was a battle against oppression, privilege, and all that separates human beings. His was an implicit, compassionate critique of life and inequality. He saw the national problem not as African Americans living among whites, but as a group of people who are systematically oppressed by a society that is racist, capitalistic, and imperialistic. He sought political, economic, and spiritual liberation of all oppressed people through education and intellectual development in all he wrote as he documented history in his own unique and courageous way.

Throughout Davis's long life, he remained confident and hopeful, patriotic, and never hateful. He dreamed of the poet's radical utopian vision of change to a more humane world. Thus the thematic scope of Davis's writing is wide. He is especially recognized for his humor, irony, wit, wry sarcasm, cynicism, jazz rhythms, and poems set to music, pulling on a variety of elements which reflect the historical black aesthetic, including communal themes of resistance, empowerment, and struggle. Angela Davis writes:

> Black people were able to create with their music an aesthetic community of resistance, which in turn encouraged and nurtured a political community of active struggle for freedom. This continuum of struggle, which is at once aesthetic and political, has extended from Harriet Tubman's and Nat Turner's spirituals through Bessie Smith's "Poor Man's Blues" and Billie Holiday's "Strange Fruit," through Max Roach's "Freedom Suite," and even to the progressive raps on the popular music scene . . .   (201)

The close connections between music and the word referred to above have historically been a part of the African and African American traditions.

Although Frank Marshall Davis has often been an unsung hero, as an artist and journalist, he enhanced the vision of the global community socially and politically, stressing self-knowledge, self-definition, and self-reliance.

Davis's defiant and assertive attitude is revealed as early as 1935 in his first book, *Black Man's Verse*. The word "black" is the age-old metaphor for all things negative, not understood, and sometimes feared. His dramatic use of it in his title reveals his strength and self-assertion in courageously redefining himself and his people as dignified, cultured, and intelligent. hooks comments on the power of the word and true speaking in the African American community:

> For us (African Americans), true speaking is not solely an expression of creative power; it is an act of resistance, a political gesture that challenges politics of domination that would render us nameless and voiceless. As such it is a courageous act - as such, it represents a threat. To those who wield oppressive power, that which is threatening must necessarily be wiped out, annihilated, silenced.   (8)

Davis not only refuses to be silenced and nameless, but he names himself "black;" he seizes a weapon of negative labeling and thrusts it back at those who would devalue blackness.

Another significant contribution of Davis's work is the building of a modern black aesthetic. Arna Bontemps says in an interview with John O'Brian that the "Renaissance came close to giving America a `new aesthetic'" which he discusses in the following:

> First of all, the white aesthetic eliminates folk sources and sociological topics; it says that these are not legitimate material for art. If you accept that, you really eliminate the black writer's whole range of experience from serious literature, because about a third of all he knows is folk, and about another third is classified--rather arbitrarily--as "sociological," and only one third comes out of the traditions of the English language which he is using. He is so inhibited that he's left out. So, if you could create another literature which employs folk motifs and which doesn't shy away from the problems of urban living and race relations, you would have a new aesthetic.   (*Interviews* 5-6)

Davis's writing falls into the folk/socio-political category of which Arna Bontemps speaks, as do the works of the majority of African American writers, past and present.

As Ishmael Reed says, the traditional Euro-American novel includes a patriarchal epistemology which follows a realistic form in the development of character and subject matter. This world view is primarily Euro-American reflecting those paradigms and values. African Americans, on the other hand, experiment with more forms, have less to risk and more to critique. They combine the world and life, reject socially defined categories, and explore the world of fantasy, dreams, and nightmares, studded with the hard reality of race, class and gender issues (*Mumbo, Jumbo* 171-172). No subject or interpretation is taboo, but the consequences of bold disregard to tradition and an attack on or exposure of blatant white democratic hypocrisy can be a major deterrent to the black writer's acceptance and success in the professional arena. Reed adds, "When a black writer experiments, he gets mugged for it" (174). That seems to be a partial explanation to the mystery of what happened to the voice of Frank Marshall Davis.

Davis recognized and utilized a historical well-spring of "thinly veiled sexual metaphors" existing in the oral and written traditions of African Americans, especially apparent in the blues. Because historically blacks were denied written and political expression, the use of the metaphor and images has been prevalent to create feelings, critique situations, and protest reality (Levine 240-243). To break with idealized American values, it is also not uncommon for many black writers like Davis to include overt and covert sexual references in order to portray another cultural reality of the African American community.

Davis's vision of democracy is optimistic and liberating in terms of the working-class African American experience because he presents the deep feelings and aspirations of African Americans during a racially repressive period of history. Through his writing, he helps to validate the positive aspects of an otherwise invalidated, devalued community. Davis introduces the varied domains of music, emotions, and protest into his journalism, poetry, and characters; he also presents African American heroes and mythologies, generally contrary to the traditional mainstream assumptions and definitions of heroes. For example, he writes about hustlers, prostitutes, martyrs, social rejects, victims, rebels, and those who dare to confront the forces of racism and oppression, to defy the customary avenues of success and prosperity, and who, as anti-heroes due to their alienation from the system, find alternative avenues of creative thought and action. The women characters in the collection of poems called *Horizontal Cameos: 37 Portraits* (of prostitutes) are like the "trickster" figures in old African tales and in much of African American literature where the weak overcome the strong through use of wit and creative solutions.

In one of his poems from *Horizontal Cameos*, entitled "#1 Lani," Davis criticizes the capitalistic mentality that actually encourages or forces women, without access to traditional jobs and other avenues to success, to turn to the secondary economy of prostitution. At the same time, he portrays Lani's intelligence, the irony of her conventional success, and her humanity. He portrays these women full of pathos in unsuccessful situations and renders them human using wit, humor, and irony.

> Lani is at her best/Horizontal/No ponderous perpendicular prelude/Is essential/Unless one insists/Upon romance with love/But that is added expense/For as the slogan speaks/ From the desk of the insurance executive/Time is Money. Lani, age 25, Had distributed a fortune, Before she realized/ There was god in descent from the vertical/Lani, age 30/Has 50 grand salted away/With no change in habits/And has had many husbands/Including two of her own;/But with success has come prejudice/Which never before existed--/Today she will not tolerate/Any man with less than $20/She is a rarity/ Psychologists seldom find--/A woman working/ At her best occupation/Without benefit of [an] aptitude test.
>
> (*Black Moods* 211)

Davis courageously portrays the intelligence, emotion, and compassion of black people often creating a male or female anti-hero, like Richard Wright's Bigger Thomas or Langston Hughes' Simple, thereby introducing new types of characters into American literature, heretofore deemed unworthy subjects of poetry.

Davis offers psychological depth and another level of understanding to African American characters where white and other writers cannot. He includes the practical message of economic survival as well as the urgent message of intercultural communication, using the rhythmic tam tams and musical cadences in his verses, always hoping for a better world. He recognizes the healing power of bold and defiant words, "speechifyin." As bell hooks notes:

> Moving from silence into speech is for the oppressed, the colonized, the exploited, and those who stand and struggle side by side, a gesture of defiance that heals, that makes new life and new growth possible . . . that is the expression of our movement from object to subject - the liberated voice.   (9)

The act of moving from silence into speech attests to Davis's will and courage. And Davis would not be silenced. His was a journey to empowerment as he challenged the privilege of whiteness.

Davis understood the value of imagination, dreams, humor, and irony-- like the blues—that have enabled African Americans to meet and transcend overwhelming sociopolitical and economic odds without the support of a socially sanctioned reality. He used certain under the table buffers when confronted with the horror of reality and recognized that the use of humor for psychological release through innuendo, metaphor, and circumlocution has had a long history in the oral tradition in Africa (Levine 9). The satirical song has always been one avenue of protest which various black artists have transformed into different media, like poetry, drama, and prose. Davis has certainly been an able representative of this rich oral and written multi-genre tradition in his prose poetry, free verse, and musical riffs. He indicates that many of his poems were in fact conceived and written to be performed with percussion, various instruments, and choral voices. Indeed, the African American experience can be seen as a metonym for the "trickster" because as in the old animals' tales, the weaker animal, through native wit and guile rather than power and authority, was able to attain his or her goal.

Davis will also be remembered for his lively multiracial themes and his robust, leftist political stance; social criticism, fierce social consciousness; strong declamatory voice against oppression and privilege; his lyrical realism, and his broad vision to see human frailty and strength. His continuing optimism and belief in American democracy despite its imperfections are due to his social conscience, sense of justice and equality, and his will for the collective survival of Americans with African Americans. Through his lifetime he developed his self-esteem and race pride.

Indeed, Davis was a Race Man and gave a creative voice and perspective to a varied spectrum of African American lives in order to educate the public about self-definition, equality, humanity and the unique, if sometimes distorted, identity of African Americans. He expressed and evoked in the reader a critical consciousness of American democracy. His belief in human rights prevailed. Fanon writes:

> I find myself . . . in the world and I recognize that I have one right alone: that of demanding human behavior from the other. One duty alone: that of not renouncing my freedom through choices. . . . I should constantly remind myself that the real leap consists in introducing invention into existence. In the world through which I travel, I am endlessly creating myself.   (*Black Skin* 229)

Davis's literary efforts and political perspectives illuminate the creative escape mechanisms he chose in order to maintain a sense of dignity. His contribution to the nation and to the world is his unwavering belief in democratic principles, his articulation of the creative gifts, strengths, and sometimes understated spirituality of Black people. It is his vision and courage to speak out and take a stand for freedom and equality for decades on end, in spite of the obstacles and risk of being silenced or worse, that must be seen, understood, appreciated, lauded, and held up for posterity. His contemporary colleague, Alain Locke wrote:

> The position of the Negro in American culture today is strategic and promising; it is his spiritual recompense for generations of long suffering and will, for some generations yet, furnish the basis of his contribution to the spiritual treasure of the nation.   (Chapman 538)

In the 21st century, the United States still struggles to make pluralistic integration a reality for many poor and struggling African Americans and minorities.

There is another part of Davis that has not been mentioned and that is easy to overlook; this is the more sensitive, romantic, and private side of his emotions best expressed in his love poems, his universal questionings, and his sensibility to beauty and Nature. In *Ramrod 8*, writing of the "Moonlight at Kahana Bay," located not far from his home in Hau`ula, Davis wrote:

> Tonight the sea is a lavish lover/ Placing long leis of fragile foam/ About the soft brown throat/ Of the swooning shore;/ Fingers of the wandering waves/ Gently stroke the floating petals/ Fallen from the pikake moon/ In luminous streamers./ Lights from the little houses/ Tinkle but a tiny tune/ Against the strong sonata/ Of moon and sky and singing sea/ And the deep bass beat/ Of the surging hills/ Sounding the scented night/ The flowered friendly night/ Around Kahana Bay.   (3)

This is one of the few gentle, harmonious, romantic poems by Davis with no irony, no appeal, and little movement. It reflects a rare moment of rest, for Davis an uncustomary state of mind, since he usually persisted in both his writings and conversations as the critic and the gadfly, pricking the conscience to wake up. One of Davis's last poems, "Alone," records:

> Limping seconds struggle/ Along string-thin nothing nights/ Clocks shout their tick tocks/ Sleep looks in with frightened eyes/ Then flees silently into the endless dark/ And I lie restlessly alone/ Endlessly counting my collection/ Of worn memories   (*Livin'* 153)

Age, solitude, unfulfilled dreams, the hour glass of time almost empty-- Davis continued to receive guests, comment on the news, and jot down his thoughts and observations up until the end of his life.

Davis is remembered by those who knew him well for his calm demeanor, his rich, raspy voice, his humor, social conscience, and personal generosity. He had a large vision, a sense of relativity, and an optimism which made him open to choose from a variety of methods to effect change and solve various racial, economic, cultural, political, and generational conflicts.

As mentioned earlier, he was the music man, always with the right tune for the time. He had his incredible jazz collection of vinyl which some say exceeded five thousand albums. The great variety of people who were drawn to him will cherish the memory of his open-house policy, compassionate listening, common sense, and practical wisdom, all experienced with a background of jazz.

Finally, Frank Marshall Davis was a leader and a catalyst for authentic change. He was honest, a courageous mover and shaker. He was also a Good Samaritan who especially enjoyed helping others and giving what little money or items he had to anyone truly in need. He freely and generously disseminated knowledge, culture, and history. He lived life fully and sometimes on the edge, sharing women's company, cooking delicious sweet potato pies, and loving his family. He was precise, predictable, and productive as a critic, a writer, and an activist. He boldly challenged the hypocrisy of leaders and citizens who used Christianity as a mask to camouflage their greedy egos, tunnel vision, and corrupt life-styles and who prostituted themselves for personal gain.

At the end of his life, he was still an avid news seeker; he maintained a great sense of relativity and integrity in his steady inquiry. He was able to place things in their proper perspective, including his own aging process and ultimate death. He connected the literary tower with the reality of life's trials. McElrath poignantly stated:

> Here is a man who was not just a poet, set away from the world. But here is a man who was able to make that complete transition between what was generally felt to be a completely literary ivory tower world with what was going on out there where people had to earn a living, where people had to fight prejudice, where people had to go all the way in order to get a measure of equality and I think this is the wedding, for example, of the pure literary person with the activist person which makes really good sense. And I think young people are particularly attracted to that. It isn't either or; it is how do you bring the two together so that your life has a kind of meaning outside of being known as a poet? Goodness knows that's important enough in a world which does not in fact reinforce one's poetic feelings about life, so I think that's very important. . . . He never lost sight of the fact that we live in a world of people, and I think that is the legacy that Frank

Marshall Davis leaves for all of us.   (Conybeare, 24:8-9)

Davis realistically considered the problems, obstacles and dilemmas of the future and wrote down his ideas. He penetrated and renamed the cultures of white supremacy using words such as racism, colonialism, fascism, and imperialism.

He looked upon the youth as the hope for humanity and the warriors of the future facing the prospect of annihilation from what he defined as five sources: 1) nuclear war, 2) bloody revolution, 3) population explosion, 4) pollution and disappearing natural resources, and 5) gas and germ warfare (*Livin'* 328-329). Not surprisingly, near the end of his life in his autobiography, Davis challenged young people of all cultures to unite and fight for the survival of the planet. His became an ideology of sustainability and integrated living.

> And unless the young of all colors can turn back this senseless march to oblivion, we deserve to die. And we ought to halt it before we branch solidly into outer space and pollute another planet. The hope of humanity lies in the young who have not yet become plastic victims of the perpetual brainwashing by the mass media and their skilled shills programming us for acceptance of mass jackassery.
>
> (*Livin'* 329)

For Davis, writing remained fighting the politics of domination until the end of his life. He continued to engage in critical inquiry and reflection in face of the global world crisis, always committed to contributing to a better world by enlarging the conscience and consciousness of any and all who crossed his path. He saw value in reclaiming certain cultural traditions to create more balance and harmony in the world, to affirm a sense of positive identity and respect, and to pass on to the youth values of love and brotherhood for the generations to follow.

> Spiritually I travel with the young. As a black writer I like to think my activities have helped advance Afro America from the say 40 percent black acceptance of my youth to the perhaps 75 percent acceptance of today. However, I will not be satisfied until we reach 100 percent parity with all other Americans while retaining black integrity.   (*Livin'* 330)

Perhaps because he was a self-proclaimed atheist, the aged writer did not seem to fear death. In "Returned," a poem written when he was younger, Davis welcomes death with musical celebration, a sense of cosmic scale and his customary irony:

> Let death come to me at a cabaret while a jazz band prays to its god . . . let the jazz heart miss a beat . . . then let a trumpet cry, a saxophone sob out Handy's hymn of the St Louis Blues. . .
>
> I am but dirt and dreams, matter and sky dust, egotistic owner of nothing . . . a tune frozen into flesh by the infinite . . . borrower among borrowers, . . .
>
> I ask only this: let me quit and check in my time . . . let me go before the Boss comes around and says . . . "Sorry but we can't use you anymore. . ."   (*Black Man's* 40)

Davis's vision has lasted because he was neither imitator, nor eunuch, nor Lazarus. His irreverent humor, vituperative tongue, stark pictures, occasional disillusionment, and distilling interpretations did not hide the optimist he was until the time of his death in July 1987. His broad thoughts and community activism will survive and transcend his reputation as a gruff cynic.

In his death, Davis left a secret for those who remain: rhythm, movement, and creative acts. His belief in the goodness of people and the will to change, his indomitable spirit to communicate and transform, and his choice to live in the Hawaiian Islands all helped to heal the insecurity, anger and bitterness of his past. In a more serious and mature moment, Davis seemed to consider death more like an irreverent marriage between the individual and the universal. In another early poem "Death", he writes of ritual, a passing in Nature, a party without sadness, without religion, without convention. For Davis, death in this poem is a passing to freedom and a new life:

> death
>
> my fearful people
> is an art

which few learn
and yet we
are dead
longer
much longer
than we live

. . .

death brings joy
here is a chance
to think new thoughts
to drink new wines
without even asking

. . .

death

is a wedding
nothing more

the individual
and the universal
become one   (*Black Man's* 49-50)

Davis shunned most conventions throughout his life and was not going to
follow them at the end.

Early July 26, 1987, the day Davis passed away, he called me and asked
if I was coming by to talk, because, he said, he thought I would want a taste
of fresh sweet potato pie. I was unable to accept his invitation because my
daughter was ill. That night, he died of a massive heart attack.

Immediately following his death, in a final testament to Davis during
the filming of the *Rice and Roses* special, some of his friends and followers
said he had helped hundreds if not thousands of unknown people to grow as
human beings, or sometimes just to find consolation or a good meal. He was
a volunteer working with people with drug problems in Waikīkī. McElrath
comments:

> But above and beyond that, Frank always kept his very
> sunny disposition, had a joke about this thing or that thing,
> continued his very sardonic view about life and did very

well with his children. Loved them dearly, went off into "the jungle" and made friends with a lot of the poor people who lived there, the elderly people who lived there which culminated finally in his becoming, very few people know this, a member of the board of directors of the Waikīkī Drug Clinic. I happened to be one of the founders of that clinic, and when all of us had become tired of these duties, Frank volunteered his services, and he was an extremely good member, because he could relate so very well with young people.   (Conybeare 24:6)

The week after his death, Frank Marshall Davis had a simple memorial service in Honolulu provided by his children, Mark Kaleokuaaloha Davis, Jill Moani Ala Spears, Jeanne Moani Hyde, Beth Tiare Konani Charlton, Lynn Makaleka Smith (deceased) and ex-wife Helen Canfield Davis (deceased), in the pine tree park high up on Wilhemina Rise. Richard Hamasaki, a Honolulu poet, said in an elegy for Davis, he "changed channels on all of us" (1987). Davis's close friends were present with his family when his ashes were scattered off the cliffs, and they flew up in the whirl of wind toward the sky, transforming, transcending like a phoenix in flight. He has become the metaphorical embodiment of a transformative life. He has risen from the ashes of disappointment to leave a legacy of courage and conscience.

WORKS CITED

Aptheker, Herbert. *A Documentary History of the Negro People in the United States*. Vol. I. New York: Citadel, edited 1968.

Bardolph, Richard. *The Negro Vanguard*. New York: Vintage, 1959.

Benet, William Rose. Review of *Black Man's Verse*, by Frank Marshall Davis. *The Saturday Review*. 18 Jan. 1936.

---. Review of *I Am the American Negro* by Frank Marshall Davis. *The Saturday Review*. 19 June 1937.

Berry, Faith. *Langston Hughes: Before and Beyond Harlem*. Westport: Lawrence Hill, 1983.

Bigsby, C.W.E. *The Black American Writer*, Vol. I: Fiction, Baltimore: Penguin, 1969a.

Bontemps, Arna. *American Negro Poetry*. New York: Hill & Wang, 1963.

---. *100 years of Negro Freedom*. New York: Dodd, Mead, 1966.

---. *The Harlem Renaissance Remembered*. New York: Dodd, Mead, 1972.

---, and Jack Conroy. *Anyplace But Here*. New York: Hill & Wang, 1966.

Brown, Sterling. Review of *I Am the American Negro*, by Frank Marshall Davis. *Opportunity* July 1936: xiv

Chapman, Abraham, *Black Voices: An Anthology of Afro-American Literature*. New York: Mentor, edited 1968.

Conybeare, Chris, Producer, and Kathryn Takara, Assoc. Producer. Interviews. "Frank Marshall Davis." and associates: Ah Quon McElrath, Henry Epstein, Howard Johnson and Kathryn Takara. *Rice and Roses*. Audiotapes and transcripts prior to edited version [completed in 1987].Honolulu: (KHET) PBS. 1986a.

Cox, Oliver C. *Race Relations: Elements and Social Dynamics*. Detroit: Wayne State UP, 1976.

Davis, Angela. *Women, Culture, and Politics*. New York: Vintage, 1990.

"Davis [F.M.] considers Hawai`i advanced in Democracy". *Honolulu Advertiser.* 14 Dec 1948: 10.

Davis, Frank Marshall. *Black Man's Verse*. Chicago: Black Cat, 1935.

---. *Black Moods: Collected Poems.* Edited by John Edgar Tidwell. Urbana & Chicago: U of Illinois P, 2002.

---. *47th Street: Poems.* Prairie City: Decker, 1948.

---. "Frank-ly Speaking." Editorials. *Honolulu Record.* 1949-52.

---. *Horizontal Cameos.* Excerpts. *Ramrod 7.* Edited by Joseph P. Balaz. Honolulu: Iron Bench P, 1986c.

---. *I Am the American Negro.* Chicago, Black Cat, 1937.

---. Interviews (personal) with Kathryn Waddell Takara. Honolulu 1983-1987.

---. Interviews by Chris Conybeare, producer, and Kathryn Takara, Assoc. Producer. "Frank Marshall Davis" with Davis and associates: Ah Quon McElrath, Henry Epstein, Howard Johnson, and Kathryn Takara. Transcript of *Rice and Roses.* Audiotapes and transcripts prior to edited version [completed in 1987].Honolulu: (KHET) PBS. 1986a.

---. *Livin' the Blues: Memoirs of a Black Journalist and Poet* (memoir/autobiography). Edited by John Edgar Tidwell. Madison: U of Wisconsin P, 1992.

---. Poems. *Black World* [Chicago] "Duke Ellington," "Louis Armstrong," "Billie Holiday." Feb. 1974: 22-25.

---. Poems. *Black World* [Chicago] "To a Young Man" and "Black American." May 1975: 46-48.

---. *Sex Rebel: Black (Memoirs of a Gash Gourmet).* [Bob Greene, pseud.] Introduction by Dale Gordon. San Diego: Greenleaf Classics, 1968.

---. *Through Sepia Eyes.* Chicago: Black Cat, 1938.

--- "Touring the World." *Atlanta World.* Editorial column. [His other columns included "Speakin' bout sports" and "`Jazzin' the news."] 1931-33.

---. "For Militant Blacks" Comp. by Kathryn Waddell Takara. Unpublished ms. 1986b.

---. Poems. *Ramrod 8.* Edited by Joseph P. Balaz. Honolulu: Iron Bench P, 1987.

---. W*ritings of Frank Marshall Davis: A Voice of the Black Press.*

Edited by John Edgar Tidwell. Jackson: UP of Mississippi, 2007.

Diaz Diocaretz, Myriam. *The Transforming Power of Language: The Poetry of Adrienne Rich*. Utrecht: Hes, 1984.

Epstein, Henry. "Davis, F. M.", Interview with Conybeare, et al. 1986a.

"Executive editor of ANP is due tonight." *Honolulu Advertiser* 8 Dec. 1948.

Fanon, Frantz. *Black Skin, White Masks*. New York: Grove, 1967.

---. *PNMB*. Paris: Edition du Seuil, 1952.

Frazier, E. Franklin. *Black Bourgeoisie: The Rise of a New Middle Class*. New York: Free P; London: Collier-Macmillan, 1957.

---. *The Negro in the United States*. New York: Macmillan, 1949.

Fuller, Hoyt. *Contemporary Negro Fiction*. Bigsby 1969a. *The Black American Writer, Vol. I: Fiction*, Baltimore: Penguin, 1969a: 229-243.

Gates, Henry Louis, Jr. Introduction. *To Make a Poet Black*. Redding, Jay Saunders. 1988: vii-xxiv.

Hamasaki, Richard. "Elegy". Davis Interview. Conybeare et al. 1986a, 1987.

Hellman, Lillian. *Scoundrel Time*. Boston: Bantam, 1976.

Hill, Herbert. *Anger and Beyond: The Negro Writer in the United States*. New York: Harper, 1966.

hooks, bell. *Talkin Back: thinking feminist, thinking black*. Boston: South End Press, 1989.

Interviews by Chris Conybeare, producer, and Kathryn Takara, Assoc. Producer "Frank Marshall Davis" with Davis and associates: Ah Quon McElrath, Henry Epstein, Howard Johnson, and Kathryn Takara. *Rice and Roses*. Audiotapes and transcripts prior to edited version [completed in 1987].Honolulu: (KHET) PBS. 1986a.

JanMohamed, Abdul R. *Manichean Aesthetics: The Politics of Literature in Colonial Africa*. Amherst: U of Massachusetts P, 1983.

Katz, William Loren. *Eyewitness: The Negro in American History*. New York: Pitman, 1967.

Lemelle, Anthony J. "Beyond Black Power: The Contradiction between Capital and Liberty." *The Western Journal of Black Studies* 10:2 (1986): 70-76.

Levine, Lawrence W. *Black Culture and Black Consciousness*. New York: Oxford UP, 1977.

Locke, Alain. Review of *I Am the American Negro* by Frank Marshall Davis. [1937]. *Opportunity: Journal of Negro Life*, XVI. 1 Jan: 1938.

---.. "The Legacy of the Ancestral Arts." Excerpt in Peplow and Davis 1975: 234-241.

---. *The New Negro*. Chapman 1968: 512-538.

---. *The New Negro*. Excerpt in Peplow and Davis 1975: 387-399.

McElrath, Ah Quon. Interview with Conybeare et al. 1986a.

Mead, Margaret, and Baldwin, James. *A Rap on Race*. Philadelphia: Lippincott, 1971.

Myrdal, Gunnar. *An American Dilemma. Vol. I and II*. New York: Harper, 1962.

"Negro press editor fails to arrive." *Honolulu Star-Bulletin*. 10 Dec. 1948.

"Negro press executive here." *Honolulu Star-Bulletin*. 14 Dec. 1948.

Peplow, Michael W., and Arthur P. Davis. *The New Negro Renaissance: An Anthology*. New York: Holt, Rinehart and Winston, 1975.

Redding, Jay Saunders. *On Being Negro in America*. New York: Charter Books, Bobbs Merrill, 1951.

---. *The Lonesome Road*. Garden City: Doubleday, 1958.

---. *To Make a Poet Black*. Introduction by Henry Louis Gates, Jr. Ithaca and London: Cornell UP, 1988.

Reed, Ishmael. *Mumbo Jumbo*. Garden City: Doubleday, 1972.

---. Interview with Ishmael Reed. O'Brien 1973: 164-183.

---. *Writin' is Fightin'*. New York: Athenaeum; Toronto: Collier, 1990.

Sartre, Jean Paul. Black Orpheus. *The Black American Writer*. Edited by E.W.E. Bigsby. Florida: Everett/Edwards, 1969.

Schuyler, George. Review of *I Am the American Negro* by Frank Marshall Davis. *Pittsburgh Courier*. 19 Dec. 1935.

Takara, Kathryn Waddell. "Frank Marshall Davis." Interviews with Davis and others. Takara and Conybeare. *Rice and Roses*. Audiotapes and transcripts prior to edited version [completed in 1987]. Honolulu: (KHET) PBS.1986a.--.

---. Interview with F. M. Davis. Honolulu: Jan. 27. 1987.

Tidwell, John Edgar. Edited by. *Livin' the Blues: Memoires of a Black Journalist and Poet*. Madison: U of Wisconsin P, 1992.

---. *Frank Marshall Davis. Black Moods: Collected Poems*. Urbana and Chicago: U of Illinois P, 2002.

---. *Writings of Frank Marshall Davis: A Voice of the Black Press*. Jackson: U of Mississippi P, 2007.

Tuttleton, James W. "The Negro Writer as Spokesman." Bigsby 1969a: 245-258.

West, Cornel. *Prophesy Deliverance!* Philadelphia: Westminster, 1982

White, Joseph L, and Thomas A. Parham. *The Psychology of Blacks: An African-American Perspective*. 2d ed. Englewood Cliffs: Prentice-Hall, 1990.

Williams, John A. *The Literary Ghetto*. O'Brien. 1973: 225-243.

Wilson, William Julius. *Power, Racism and Privilege*. New York: Macmillan, 1973.

Woodson, Carter G., and Wesley, Charles H. *The Negro in Our History*. Washington, D.C.: Associated Publishers, 1966.

Young, James. "Weavers of Jagged Words." *Black Writers of the Thirties*. 1977: 166-202.

SUGGESTED READING

Adams, Romanzo. 1945. "Census Notes on the Negroes in Hawai`i prior to the War." *Social Process*, 1945. 214: 9-10.

Appiah, Anthony. "The Uncompleted Argument: Du Bois and the Illusion of Race." *Critical Inquiry: "Race," Writing and Difference.* 1985. 12 (Autumn): 21-37.

---. [1943] *American Negro Slave Revolts.* New York: International, 1987.

Bergman, Peter M. *The Chronological History of the Negro in America.* New York: Harper & Row, 1969.

Bernal, Martin. *Black Athena: The Afroasiatic Roots of Classical Civilization. Vol. I: The Fabrication of Ancient Greece*, 1785-1985. New Brunswick: Rutgers UP, 1987.

---. *Black Athena: The Afroasiatic Roots of Classical Civilization. Vol. II: The Archeological and Documentary Evidence.* New Brunswick: Rutgers UP, 1991.

Berry, Mary Frances, and John W. Blassingame. *Long Memory: The Black Experience in America.* New York and Oxford: Oxford UP, 1982.

Bigsby, C.W. E. *The Black American Writer, Vol. II: Poetry/Drama.* Deland: Everett/Edwards, 1969b.

Blassingame, John W. *The Slave Community.* New York: Oxford UP, 1979.

Blau, Eleanor. "Richard Wright's Works: This Time Unexpurgated". *New York Times* 28 August 1991: C11.

Brown, Sterling. "A Century of Negro Portraiture in American Literature". Chapman 1968: 564-590.

Brundage, Karla Francesca. 1992. "Desert". *Adam of Ife: Black Women in Praise of Black Men*, Poems, Edited by Naomi Long Madgett. Detroit: Lotus 1992: 93.

Caraway, Nancie. *Segregated Sisterhood: Racism and the Politics of American Feminism.* Knoxville: U of Tennessee P, 1991.

Christian, Barbara. *Black Women Novelists: The Development of a Tradition*, 1892-1976. Westport: Greenwood, 1980.

Cleaver, Eldridge. *Soul on Ice.* New York: Dell 1968.

Cox, Oliver C. *Caste, Class, and Race*. New York: Modern Reader, 1948.

Cox, Thomas C. *Blacks in Topeka, Kansas: 1865-1915, A Social History*.
    Baton Rouge and London: Louisiana State UP, 1982.

Cruse, Harold. *The Crisis of the Negro Intellectual*. New York: Morrow,
    1967.

Cudjoe, Selwyn R. *V.S. Naipaul: A Materialist Reading*. Amherst: U of
    Massachusetts P, 1988.

Davis, Charles T. *Black is the Color of the Cosmos: Essays on African-
    American Literature and Culture, 1942-1981*. New York and
    London: Garland, 1982.

Diop, Cheikk Anta. *Civilization or Barbarism: An Authentic Anthropology*.
    Chicago: Lawrence Hill, 1981.

Du Bois, W.E.B. 1968. *The Souls of Black Folk*. Chapman 1968, 493-511.
    ---. *Darkwater: Voices from Within the Veil*. New York: AMS, 1969.
    ---. 1940. "Dusk of Dawn: An Essay toward an Autobiography of
    a Race Concept". Gates [1985]. 1986, 32.

Fanon, Frantz. *The Wretched of the Earth*. New York: Grove, 1963.

Farrow, John. [1955] *Damien the Leper*. London: Sheed and Ward, 1974.

Foner, Eric. *America's Black Past*. New York: Harper, 1970.

Foner, Phillip S. *Organized Labor and the Black Worker: 1619-1973*. New
    York: International, 1974.

Foner, Phillip S. *Paul Robeson Speaks: Writings, Speeches, Interviews*.
    New York: Brunner/Mazel, 1978.

Gates, Henry Louis, Jr. *Black Literature and Literary Theory*. London and
    New York: Mechuen, 1984.
    ---. 1985. Editor's introduction: Writing "Race" and the Difference
    It Makes. *Critical inquiry* 12:1 (Autumn):1-20.
    ---, Edited by. [1985] *"Race," Writing, and Difference*. Chicago: U
    of Chicago P, 1986.

Gayle, Addison. *The Black Aesthetic*. Garden City: Doubleday, 1972.

Genovese, Eugene D. *Roll Jordan Roll: The World the Slaves Made*. New
    York: Vintage, 1976.
    ---. *The World the Slaveholders Made*. Middletown: Wesleyan UP,
    1988.

Giddings, Paula. *When and Where I Enter: The Impact of Black Women on Race and Sex in America*. New York: Bantam, 1984.

Gilman, Sander L. "Black Bodies, White Bodies: Toward and Iconography of Female Sexuality in Late 19th Century Art, Medicine, and Literature." Gates 1985:204-242.

Gite, Lloyd. "When Boys Are Raped." *Essence*. Nov. 1991.

Gordon, Dale. Introduction. Davis 1968: 3-9.

Greer, R. A. "Blacks in Old Hawai`i". *Honolulu*. Nov 1986.

Gutman, Herbert G. *The Black Family in Slavery and Freedom: 1750-1925*. New York: Vintage, 1977.

Guyon, Rene. *The Ethics of Sexual Acts*. Trans. by J. C. Flugel and Ingeborg Flugel. Garden City: Blue Ribbon: 1934.

Henderson, Stephen. *Understanding the New Black Poetry*. New York: Morrow, 1973.

Hughes, Carl Milton. *The Negro Novelist: 1940-50*. New York: Citadel, 1953.

Hughes, Langston. *The Negro Artist and the Racial Mountain*. Peplow and Davis 1975: 471-475.

    ---, and Arna Bontemps. *The Poetry of the Negro, 1746-1970*. Garden City: Doubleday, 1970.

Johnson, James Weldon. *The Book of American Negro Poetry*. New York: Harcourt, Brace, 1958.

    ---. *Along This Way*. Chapman 1968: 269-287.

Kent, George, and Stephen Henderson. *A Dark and Sudden Beauty: Two Essays in Black American Poetry*. U of Pennsylvania, 1977.

Kessous, Naaman. "Fanon and the Problem of Alienation." *The Western Journal of Black Studies* 11,2 1987: 80-91.

Killens, John O. *Black Man's Burden*. New York: Trident, 1965.

King, Martin Luther, Jr. "Letter from a Birmingham Jail." *Decker's Patterns of Exposition*, 12th Ed. by Randall E. Decker and Robert A. Schwegler. Glenview: Scott, 1990.

Madhubuti, Haki R. *Black Scholar*. San Francisco: 1978: 4-5.

    ---. *Enemies: The Clash of Races*. Chicago: Third World P, 1978.

Mannoni, Dominique O. *Prospero and Caliban: The Psychology of*

Colonization. New York: Praeger, 1964.

Masters, Edgar Lee. *Spoon River Aanthology.* New York, London: Collier/ MacMillan, 1962.

Matthews, Ralph. Review of *Black Man's Verse* by F. M. Davis. *Baltimore Afro-American.*1935.

Missionary Album. Honolulu: Hawaiian Mission Children's Society. 1863.

Morton, Patricia. *Disfigured Images: The Historical Assault on Afro-American Women.* New York: Praeger, 1991.

Nordyke, Eleanor C. "Blacks in Hawai`i: A demographic and Historical Perspective". *The Hawaiian Journal of History,* 22. 1988.

Obrien, John. *Interviews with Black Writers.* New York: Liveright, 1973.

Rampersad, Arnold. *The Life of Langston Hughes. Vol I: 1902-1941. I, too sing America.* New York and Oxford: Oxford UP, 1986.

Record, Wilson. *Race and Radicalism: The NAACP and the Communist Party in Conflict.* Ithaca: Cornell UP, 1964.

Ringer, Benjamin B. *"We the People" and Others: Duality and America's Treatment of its Racial Minorities.* New York and London: Tavistock, 1983.

Said, Edward W. [1985]. "An Ideology of Difference." Gates 1986, 38-58.

Scott, Mark. "Langston Hughes of Kansas." *The Journal of Negro History,* LXVI, (Spring):1981, 1-9.

Scruggs, Marc. "A Black Friend of Hawai`i Missionaries." *Honolulu Star-Bulletin* 12 Jan. 1987. A-10.

---. 1987. "Early Black Businessmen in Hawai`i." *Afro-Hawai`i News.*

Stannard, David. *American Holocaust: Columbus and the Conquest of the New World.* New York: Oxford UP, 1992.

Takara, Kathryn Waddell "Frank Marshall Davis." *Writers of the Black Chicago Renaissance.* Edited by Steven Tracy. Urbana: U of Illinois P, 2011.

---. "Frank Marshall Davis: A Forgotten Voice in the Chicago Black Renaissance." *The Western Journal of Black Studies.* 26:4. Winter 2002: 215-227.

---. "Frank Marshall Davis and the Chicago Black Renaissance."

Humanities in the South. 2002: 46-68.

---. "Frank Marshall Davis and 1930's Black Journalism in Atlanta, Georgia: Journalism as a Healing Trope." *The Black Scholar.* 30: 3 2000: 17-26.

---. "Frank Marshall Davis in Hawai`i: Outsider Journalist Looking In." *Social Process in Hawai`i. The Ethnic Studies Story: Politics and Social Movements in Hawai`i.* Edited by Ibrahim G. *Aoude.* Department of Sociology, University of Hawai`i. Vol. 39, 1999: 126-144.

---. "The African Diaspora in Nineteenth Century Hawai'i." *They Followed the Trade Winds.* Edited by Miles Jackson, Ph.D. U. of Hawai'i P, 2005: 1-22.

---. "Colonialism and Erasure: Blacks in 19th Century Hawai`i". *The Western Journal of Black Studies.* Winter: 2005.

---. "It Happens All the Time--or Does It?" *MULTIAMERICA: Essays on Cultural Wars and Cultural Peace.* Edited by Ishmael Reed. New York: Viking Press, 1996: 54-65.

---. *Montage: An Ethnic History of Women in Hawai`i.* "Who Is the Black Woman in Hawai`i?" [Kay Brundage Takara].Honolulu: General Assistance Center for the Pacific, Honolulu, 1977.

---. *Oral Histories of African Americans.* Honolulu: Center for Oral History, 1990.

---, "The Rage and the Passion in the Poetry of Frank Marshall Davis." *The Black Scholar.* 26:2 1996: 17-26.

Thrum, Thomas G. 1902. *Hawaiian Almanac and Annual for 1902.* Honolulu: 1902: 164.

---. *Hawaiian Almanac and Annual for 1905.* Honolulu. 1905:143.

Toomer, Jean. [1923] *Cane.* New York: Harper, 1969.

Trask, Haunani Kay. *Eros and Power: The Promise of Feminist Theory.* Philadelphia: U of Pennsylvania P, 1986.

Van Sertima, Ivan. *They Came before Columbus.* New York: Random, 1976.

---, edited by. [1983] *Blacks in Science: Ancient and Modern.* New Brunswick: Transaction, 1989.

Wallace, Michele. *Black Macho and the Myth of the Superwoman.* New York: Dial, 1979.

Wright, Richard. *Native Son*. New York: Grosset & Dunlap, 1940.

    ---. [1945] *Black Boy*. New York: Perennial, Harper, 1966.

    ---. *The Color Curtain: A Report on the Bandung Conference*. Cleveland and New York: World, 1956.

    ---. *White Man, Listen!* Garden City: Doubleday, 1957.

About the Author

Kathryn Waddell Takara, PhD, is a 2010 winner of the American Book Award (Before Columbus Foundation). She retired as an Associate Professor from the University of Hawai`i at Mānoa, Interdisciplinary Studies Program. Dr. Takara was also a recipient of the Board of Regents Outstanding Teacher Award at the University of Hawai`i at Mānoa, a two-time Fulbright Fellow, and the recent recipient of a lifetime achievement award for her contributions in education and research on Blacks in Hawai`i.

Takara is a performance poet, lecturer, workshop facilitator, adviser, healer, and consultant whose travels and readings in Africa, Europe, Central America, Tahiti, China, Hawaiian Islands and in cities throughout the USA are reflected in the depth and breadth of her work. She has published three books of poetry: *New and Collected Poems* published by Ishmael Reed Press, *Pacific Raven: Hawai`i Poems*, *Tourmalines: Beyond the Ebony Portal* by Pacific Raven Press and numerous poems and scholarly articles.

Takara has a Ph.D. in Political Science from the University of Hawai`i, an MA in French from UC Berkeley, a BA in French from Tufts U. She taught, advised, and mentored students in Ethnic and Black Studies for 31 years. Takara has also appeared on a variety of television shows, in national and international interviews and documentaries.

Dr. Takara is the daughter of pioneer black veterinarian, author, and world famous Buffalo Soldier, Dr. William H. Waddell, VMD (1908-2007).

CPSIA information can be obtained at www.ICGtesting.com
Printed in the USA
LVOW060313050312

271576LV00003B/3/P